World on My Doorstep

A VENTURE IN INTERNATIONAL LIVING

BY

Harriet Eager Davis

Simon and Schuster, 1947

MANUFACTURED IN THE UNITED STATES OF AMERICA
BY THE HADDON CRAFTSMEN, INC., SCRANTON, PA.

To Billie Eager
Lieutenant, 157th Infantry
Killed January 17, 1945, in France

ᦒᦆᦎ CONTENTS ᦒᦆᦎ

vii

Whoever you be,
Tonight go free
Of the narrow room,
The careful key—
Your garden is infinity,
Whoever you may be . . .

Translation from Rainer Maria Rilke
by H. E. D.

1

Why This Book?

I NEVER wanted to become interested in international affairs. Twenty years ago, like my country, I was completely bored with all foreign politics. They still bore me, temperamentally. I should prefer to pursue the pleasant paths of personal life, untouched by war or the rumors of war, never forcing my fly-away fancies into the harsh, sober channels of masculine thought, and to let "the others" shoulder the social responsibilities of my own fate. But I have come, painfully, to see that this is a childish immaturity, that mothers like myself pay too dearly for our indifference. In this strange era we are entering, the combined efforts of men and women, pulling together, may be barely enough to avert catastrophe. That is why I have written this account of my own slow and halting growth.

The project, in a world full of experts, seems absurd, for I am still so ignorant. Yet, since I started from scratch and thought things out for myself, my experience may encourage others, especially women, who stand appalled before the baffling complexities of the international world. For I have

3

learned that anyone who wishes to can understand the problems that lead to war, and that until we understand, we can do nothing, least of all vote intelligently, to maintain the peace we all now so passionately desire.

But it has taken me as long as it has America to wake up to this simple truth. If I had not married an international specialist, if I had not lived in Geneva and Paris during the tragic years when a wrangling group of national leaders were dragging the League of Nations downhill, if Pearl Harbor had not enlisted my oldest boy in the Navy and killed my brother's first-born soon after the Battle of the Bulge, this book would not have been written. The only excuse for looking back, for letting the heart break because the world's tragedy could have been avoided, is that our future may copy our past. The problem that faced us after the last war—settling disputes without murder—is no different in essence from what faces us today. *Plus ça change, plus c'est la même chose.* Many who once felt hopeful now turn despairingly away from the face of chaos into the illusory security of personal life. To them, and especially to women, I offer this history of three American boys growing up abroad under the shadow of coming tragedy, with a father who saw it coming and a mother who only woke up when it struck. It was like a melody in the treble gradually drowned out by the thunder of the bass, and it began with the gayer notes.

2

The Road to Geneva

Peace, when I was a girl, was decidedly "phony" in America, a sentimental and effeminate preoccupation for visionaries. World War I—"to end all wars," "to make the world safe for democracy"—was over. We were all sick of Europe. Because we hated war, we tried to forget that we had fought one. Yet the tradition persisted that a red-blooded he-man should be ready to fight at the drop of a hat. When I met in New York an interesting and masculine young man named "Jerry" Davis, and we rapidly reached the stage of finding a deep significance in a similar taste for languages, I was secretly disappointed to learn that he edited a struggling international magazine called *Our World*. Its aim was to promote peace by informing Americans about the life, literature and politics of other countries. To me this was a very odd and nebulous undertaking.

"But he's got so much *sense* to be in *that* kind of work!" I wailed to the brother who introduced us. George, a good advertising man, nodded.

"I know," he frowned, adding in the slang of the time, "and he's a peach of a fellow, too!"

My dearest friend, Mrs. William Brown Meloney, also my editor-in-chief on *Delineator*, where I ran a children's page, asked me uneasily what this new man "did." This is a question I have been trying to answer for twenty years about my husband's slightly off-color profession of international specialist. "Missy" Meloney, later the brilliant editor of *This Week*, was deeply patriotic and maternally concerned with everybody's happiness, but she was not at all sure she could entrust my future to a man who, for all his airs of a gentleman, spoke fluently the language of "the Bolsheviki" and who concerned himself with anything so suspect as foreign affairs.

Neither was I, but Malcolm Davis and I became engaged, and *Our World* collapsed almost immediately thereafter, so that I married an internationalist temporarily "resting." Jerry, as everybody called him, was not much taller than I, with that thin, New England look of intense vitality imprisoned in a slight frame. He was the adored only son of a staid old Hartford family. I was lowly sixth-from-the-top among a Baltimore minister's eight children. My parents hailed from Virginia and Mississippi and had carted us all over the map. His had lived in the same house for forty years. Nevertheless, he and I found the same things funny, and some, at least, of the same things serious.

His intense concern with peace, however, I could not share. Like the rest of America, I felt, "The war is over. Now let's be happy!" I began trying, in what I fondly thought were subtle ways, to deflect his interest back to tastes and talents closer to my own. But I might just as well have practiced diplomacy on Plymouth Rock.

"None of the rest makes any sense," he said doggedly, "if

every few years we are going to smash everything up by fighting. Sure, it's because I care so much about books and pictures, and music and the theater that I'm working for peace. It's because war ruins the best in life that I hate war."

I could see this, reluctantly, but I wished he would let "the others" do it. To a woman, the problem loomed so vague and vast and hopeless, and meantime there were more interesting and more lucrative professions close at hand. He had a gift for dramatic writing; he had been industrial editor of the New York *Evening Post* and was all set for a career of labor relations, when that first pistol shot in Serbia redirected his life. As a convinced pacifist, he attempted to form a "White Feather Brigade" of volunteers, offering to do dangerous front-line rescue work for the Red Cross. Then he enrolled in War Prisoners Aid among Allied prisoners and was on his way to Germany when President Wilson broke off diplomatic relations with Germany. Jerry was shifted to the same kind of service in Russia. By the time the United States was in the war, what he had seen of its effects and learned in prison camps had convinced him that there was nothing for decent people to do but smash the menacing evil and then try to build a world safeguarded from war. Registering in Russia, he tried repeatedly to get home for training, but his government thought otherwise—on account of his knowledge of the situation and of his already fluent Russian. So he was sworn instead into the American information service, where, all during the revolution, his gift for the language and his poker face got him past many a guard post. When peace came, he went back to the New York *Evening Post* and became foreign editor. It was after that that he and his chief in Russia, Arthur Bullard, began editing *Our World* together. But the American public was not interested. The magazine failed.

Jerry joined the staff of the Council on Foreign Relations, then, after our first baby was born, he compromised on an out-of-Manhattan job as Editor of the Yale University Press. We were living placidly in New Haven with two babies when the exciting offer came to go to Geneva. He was to be representative and reporter at the League of Nations and the Conference on Disarmament, for the League of Nations Association and the Carnegie Endowment for International Peace. He was also to direct something called "the Geneva Research Center," about whose purpose, though he explained it as publishing studies on League problems, I felt rather vague. I knew nothing of international affairs, but I did know my man. So while Jerry solemnly insisted upon thinking it over, like the minister wrestling in prayer over a call to a larger church, I, like the minister's wife, began packing our trunks.

In mid-August of 1931 I found myself, somewhat dazed by the transition, and escorted by one thin, quiet Davis in an overcoat and two fat, noisy Davises in zipper suits, on the Paris-Geneva Express, pulling into the international peace center of the world. We had sailed in a blistering heat spell and I had not realized that Europe began in mid-ocean. So when the weather shifted overnight to November, the Davises caught frightful colds and arrived, red-nosed and sniffling, to begin the romantic new life "abroad." The trip had been hardly restful, anyway. Jerry and I had barely relaxed from the perspiring scramble of last-minute jobs when Baby Curtis swallowed a key and became the roguish child-star of the entire promenade deck. He beamed jovially until purées, oatmeal and Nature had finally achieved its reappearance, but it took his parents the rest of the voyage to recover.

So nothing could have been further from my thoughts than the League of Nations, as I blew the children's noses and my own and, while Jerry juggled the baggage, peered sleepily out of the *wagon-lit* window at our new home. The train was easing itself in, as dignified as an old Proustian viscount about to grace a salon, but there was nothing Old World about the Gare de Cornavin. It was clean, solid, modern, matter-of-fact, this crossroads of the world, where Briand and Laval, Lord Cecil and Grandi, all those remote headline names came and went about their mysterious international business. Except for *Buffet de la Gare* and *Sortie* signs, posters of narcissus fields and swarms of barking porters, we might have been in dear old Paterson, New Jersey.

Ethan and Curtis turned dazed eyes on me accusingly. "Is *this* Joo-neeva?" they breathed.

To forestall the strangeness, I had been plying them for months with old Swiss post cards. Now, with no Rousseau Island, no swans, no snowy Mont Blanc, not even a lonely mountain goat in evidence, their confusion was complete. Like their mother, they had expected nothing so homelike.

Outside, in a prosaic windy square, we climbed gratefully out of the August cold into a closed omnibus marked "La Résidence." La Résidence, we were told, stood just on the border line between elegant diplomats' hotels and thrifty family boardinghouses. We could not compromise our budding social status by staying in anything lower. Like most advice, this proved entirely useless. I never discovered that where and how we lived affected either my husband's "career" or his prestige among the men, though I imagine it may have affected mine among the women. I say "imagine" because I never knew. An intensely personal yet independent temperament proved ideal for contentment in an international small town; I never managed to learn to which functions and dinner parties my husband's position entitled us, and if we were ever snubbed, I am still happily unaware of it.

But Jerry and I were both very conscious of being babes in the League of Nations woods; we had that absurd humility of Americans befòre European culture, and we were grateful for all advice. La Résidence was charming but stone-cold, for heating began only on the official mid-October date, so we devoured our first Swiss breakfast huddled in winter coats. It looked like heaven, that huge tray of steaming metal pots, with crusty rolls, fresh butter, jam and honey, borne aloft by a ruddy young man in uniform.

"Bon jour, M'sieur, 'dame! Bon jour, les enfants!" he sing-songed in his Genevese French. Ethan piped back cheerfully the only French phrase he knew: *"Mont Blanc!"* while Curtis, paralyzed by intense emotion, only stared hungrily at the honey.

"Mont Blanc" proved to be the perfect greeting in Geneva. Everybody's morning topic was, not the international weather, but the lovely French mountain across our Swiss Lake. It melted out of its cloudy halo for us one rare evening that August, glowing like an icy jewel against the rosy *Alpenglüh*, more exquisite than the dream. And Geneva proved as quaint as any tourist could wish. The Rousseau Island and the swans looked like the post cards; old fountains and lampposts were ringed charmingly with nasturtiums and the route de Florissant lived up to its flowery name. We were immediately plunged into a round of dinners, teas and cocktail parties, and I was relieved to discover that my table partners did not expect me to spout erudite knowledge about politics. The social life of the world's men and women, grouped around the League of Nations, astonished but reassured me, by its smallness, its intimacy, its personal chit-chat and gossip, its tremendous concern with food, good skiing weather and apartments.

Our prospective home, we were told, must include a

fumoir to which the gentlemen could retire for smoking after dinner, and a formal salon where the ladies would gracefully await their return. I did not know how I could combine such correctness with getting two babies to bed and keeping them there, and I felt distinctly awed by the prospect. (Actually, we did our most successful entertaining two years later after we found a simple house of our own, where both European and American visitors used to exclaim: "What a nice American living room!") We would have done better to poke for ourselves about Geneva's cobbled streets and leafy avenues, but our renting agent, a large laconic young man in tweeds, scion of an exclusive old Genevese family, completely intimidated us. We two young liberals from the most powerful democracy in the world apologized each time he opened his car door, praised every apartment—even a gloomy, wainscoted horror crammed with bronze vases and marble busts —never mentioned vulgar price and, once back at La Résidence, thanked him so profusely that he telephoned immediately to a mutual friend to inquire if we were financially sound. Once reassured, he rented us exactly the apartment he wished—his own mother-in-law's.

So we signed a two-year lease for a damp ground-floor with basement kitchen and maids' rooms little better than barred cells. There was an old-fashioned coal range, and no icebox, only a "cold room" useful chiefly for the wines we did not have. But there was that *fumoir*, so hideous in mustard and blue-striped paper and stiff pink furniture that we never took the gentlemen in there, after all! There was a beautiful salon, very impressive after our plain Colonial living-dining room in New Haven, with pale gray wallpaper, baby-blue satin chairs, a delicate Oriental rug, and flowered silk armchairs flanking a marble mantelpiece. A high mirror reflected the inevitable antique clock, under glass. For two years I herded my wistful children, hands up, like criminals, past these fragile treasures of a Genevese aristocrat. We ourselves seemed rather out of place there, like understudies about to enact a French drawing-room comedy in which we did not know our lines. We felt most American in the high glass veranda, which caught warmly what sun broke through the fog of a Lake winter, and gave a glimpse of sky and the dark cedars and holly bushes of our tiny terrace garden.

The "little ones" must not break a twig of this valuable shrubbery, our old landlady warned us. I met her during an exhausting process known as "visiting the inventory." Armed with duplicate lists of everything from the clock to the last broken kitchen spoon, she and I spent a day, in an extraordinary ceremony of mutual distrust which taught me volumes about European life. I learned also the French for a "cracked," a "chipped" and merely a "faded" plate, that a kitchen funnel on its last legs is an *entonnoir—très usé—*and that diaphanous curtains are called, charmingly, *brise-bise*, or wind breakers. Our landlady, although convinced that all American children must be brats, finally set her stamp of approval on us by declaring with relief that I was *comme il faut*—or, in good American, a perfect lady.

My Domestic Problem was settled with an ease which should have warned me of danger ahead. A drab employment office on the Quai sent promptly a sallow, meaching German cook and a sparkling young French *femme de chambre*. Both were willing to start immediately at one hundred Swiss francs, or twenty American dollars, a month apiece! Behind Annie's Teuton correctness I caught a malicious gleam as I stammered, in French, the demands I had been coached to require—three meals a day, marketing, accounts, cleaning of kitchen, dining room and front hall. "And"—I hesitated, ashamed—"your room is in the basement." "Is there a window, Madame?" she inquired, and nodded, satisfied. Pretty Mariette, who could sew and mend and give us table service *très stylé*, I liked immediately. Out of the most casual curiosity I asked how a Parisian maid happened to have landed in Geneva. The girl looked suddenly frightened. Hurriedly, in an altered manner, she murmured that she had friends near by, across the French border. I thought no more of her evasiveness and only remembered it a few months later when the Drama of Mariette and her Young Man began to unfold before our amazed eyes.

So we settled in, happily, on a volcano below stairs and another already smoldering behind the façade of the Peace Palace. My husband began to learn the rolling phrases of diplomatic French. I was ordering oatmeal, buying wool socks and filling prescriptions for nose-drops in what practically amounted to still another language and learning to call the doctor immediately when a Swiss thermometer registered the alarming temperature of thirty-nine point five. We both found ourselves chatting more and more easily to foreign dinner partners whose French was not much better than our own.

Jerry and I began to pick up amusing stories which were chestnuts for old residents, but new to us. There was the Elephant story. Men of various nationalities were asked to prepare a book on "The Elephant." The Englishman returned with a practical manual: *Sportsman's Guide to the Hunting of the Elephant.* The Frenchman brought a charming brochure: *L'Eléphant et ses Amours.* The American produced a glossy booklet on rich paper: *Bigger and Better Elephants.* The German lugged in two huge tomes, full of annexes and cross references: *Introduction to a Preliminary*

Study of the Elephant. The Pole, arriving last, presented a political treatise: *The Elephant and the Polish Question.*

Another story, *"Qu'est-ce-qu'un américan?"* though more amusing in French, bears translation.

> What's an American?
> One American is a millionaire.
> Two Americans are two drunks.
> Three Americans are Prohibition.

> What's a Frenchman?
> One Frenchman is *un blagueur* (a cross between a kidder and a liar).
> Two Frenchmen are a good dinner.
> Three Frenchmen are a public lecture.
> (Another version runs: Three French make a marriage.)

> What's a German?
> One German is a pedant.
> Two Germans are a beer hall.
> Three Germans are war!

> What's an Englishman?
> One Englishman is an imbecile.
> Two Englishmen are a match.
> Three Englishmen are a Great Nation.

> What's a Swiss?
> One Swiss is a hotelkeeper?
> Two Swiss are two hotelkeepers.
> Three Swiss are a Frenchman, an Italian and a German.

It was all very absorbing, this new life, and the League of Nations still seemed to me as remote and impersonal as Mont Blanc.

3

The Dream and the Reality

WHEN we arrived in Geneva, that summer of '31, the League of Nations was over ten years old, but it represented little more to me than a delightful passport out of the academic New Englandism of New Haven into the colorful world of European diplomacy. I hardly know what, in my provincial innocence, I was expecting—pomposity shot with intrigue, I think, salons full of mustachioed diplomats in spats with sloe-eyed mistresses in the offing, a kind of Henry Jamesian world with a political coloring. There were intrigues, of course, and mistresses, too. The most conspicuous, a cultured Englishwoman with a charming, ravaged face, won my heart the first time I met her by falling in love with my Curtis.

· Love affairs, legitimate and illegitimate, went on busily in our gossipy town, but most of the men one chatted with at dinner were worrying about whether to send their sons home to be educated, while their wives talked clothes, servants and children as ardently as any Mrs. Babbitt from Main Street. I soon discovered I could get by, even in a political discussion, by the oldest technique of looking wise and occasionally making appropriate noises indicating interest.

My notions of the League, that pioneer ancestor upon whose courageous failures we have built our United Nations, were so absurd that even now I am almost ashamed to admit them. I believed that America had very good reasons of her own for not joining Wilson's Folly and that Europe was now properly stewing in its own juice. It had been quite a shock to discover soon after my marriage that my husband and most of his friends were Wilson admirers and even "for" that League of Nations. Many of them, like Jerry, had emerged from World War I in such hatred of its brutal stupidity that all their life-plans were deflected into trying to prevent its repetition. This seemed to me a rather dreary purpose, for a very remote possibility, not worth the waste of one's golden youth, especially for a man like my husband, with so many talents. However, I wanted to be a good wife, so before we left for Geneva I got hold of an old *Harper's* article, "What Is the League of Nations?," read it through with difficulty, and promptly forgot every word.

"Harriet," mocked one of my more frivolous friends the day we sailed, "you aren't going to try to be *intelligent* about international affairs, are you?" "Oh," I sighed, wretched before the prospect, but loyal to my serious husband, "I guess I've got to!"

So, more to please him than myself, I broke away from my baby boys to attend my first public session of the League of Nations Assembly that September, feeling as virtuous as a small-town matron at a current events class. I had not even known that there was an Assembly every fall; that each member nation sent its delegate, with equal rights for large and small powers, to vote on whatever international questions were on the agenda; or that these sessions were open to the public.

Of course, as I came to discover, the real work of reconciling diverse points of view was done ahead of time, in committees, just as it is done now in the United Nations. The actual Assembly was usually only the final culmination of behind-the-scenes activities. I felt distinctly awed, as I presented the ticket of admission my husband had secured, and sat down, along with other wives, and representatives of many international organizations, on the long wooden benches in the Visitors' Gallery of the *Salle de la Réformation*, a Geneva hall used by the League. Swiss ushers in resplendent uniform directed us firmly to our places, held doors closed against late arrivals, and quelled whispering or undue demonstration.

They were as adamant as Calvin, those ushers, as I discovered the following May, when England's Prime Minister, Ramsay MacDonald, was addressing the spring Assembly. Tickets were at a premium and I arrived, late and breathless, to find a helpless young woman in a tweed suit arguing with one of these uniformed dragons. She had left her card at home.

"*Je regrette, Mademoiselle,*" he kept repeating doggedly, "*mais il m'est impossible.*"

"*May zhur swee Miss MacDonald!*" she begged with a strong British accent. He shook his head.

I stepped in hastily. "*Mais c'est Mademoiselle MacDonald!*" I explained, with the stress on the last syllable.

"*Ah,*" cried the guard, "*Mademoiselle MacDonald!*" He ushered her in with a flourish and then turned to me indignantly. "But why didn't she say so?"

Privileged guests sat in the Diplomatic Section. Opposite our gallery hung another one of dark wood marked "Press" where the foreign correspondents sat making notes or conferring together in little knots. I slid into my seat and looked down at the large room full of desks and chairs, with a platform and speaker's pulpit at one end. Strange men and a few women were sitting or standing or moving restlessly about everywhere. The room buzzed with many tongues. Then Viscount Cecil, President of the Assembly, unfolded his six feet three of British dignity, rapped his gavel, the human pieces moved slowly into place, and the hall fell silent. I had somehow expected pomp and ceremony, Old World color. This commonplace reality of ordinary men in ordinary suits and white collars, settling down together from the four corners of the earth in the name of peace, hit me suddenly with all the force of an unexpected truth. The League of Nations was just people—fallible men and women bound together by one invisible idea, as by God in church or Justice in a courtroom. I myself sat there, inside the League, and it was alive. A schoolgirl thrill ran up and down my spine, and my eyes stung, absurdly.

But I said nothing to my husband that evening. The world as an international reality was such a part of his bone and brain that my naïve flash of insight might have amused him. Anyway, I felt as abashed as if I had impulsively gone "up front" in one of the old-fashioned Baptist revival meetings that used to color and embarrass my childhood. I did not want to "care" as my husband cared. One idealist in a family, I thought, was quite enough.

∽∾ 4 ∽∾

An Unforgettable Birthday

I soon discovered, to my surprise, that behind the scenes of that fall Assembly official representatives from the United States were in constant session with League committees, especially those on disarmament. Hugh Wilson, American Minister to Switzerland, by this time was practically commuting from Berne, his official residence, and it was not long before he moved over, with his pretty wife and a full staff of advisers and assistants, to an apartment and an office in our town.

Occasionally I improved my French on the *Journal de Genève*, the local Swiss mouthpiece for the League. That fall I read an exultant but surprising editorial—my first inkling of America's importance in Geneva:

"The key to security is in Washington. That is why we greet with peculiar satisfaction the new events that have occurred in the course of this Assembly concerning the attitude of the United States towards the League of Nations, new events full of the best promise for the success of the Disarmament Conference. No, the League is not dead . . . it is more alive than ever because it is more needed than ever. The

difficulties through which the world is passing, far from menacing its existence, only increase its vitality."

This was pleasant news on which one could float serenely,
and like many others in Geneva I preferred it to my husband's
worried skepticism. Of a political situation in the Orient which
was growing daily tighter, I had no inkling. Japan and China,
which I bracketed vaguely together, were little more to me
than a picturesque and backward civilization exporting artistic bowls and embroidered slippers to New York's China-
town; the two were chiefly distinguishable, one by being large
and slow and surrounded by a Wall, and the other by being
small and brisk and broken up into islands. So the "Mukden
incident"—the final flare-up of a long, slow enmity between
two Oriental races which eventually set all our world on fire
—was too far away and too isolated from any actuality I
knew to give me a moment's worry. But I was extremely annoyed that it occurred, ironically enough, on my husband's
birthday, September 18.

It will be obvious to any woman that this coincidence
would fix it forever in my mind. It recently earned for me,
however, an undeserved reputation for accuracy with one of
America's most eminent historians. As editor of a Columbia
University Press book, *Pioneers in World Order,* I chanced
to be in Dr. James T. Shotwell's office at the Carnegie Endowment while he dictated his paper on "Security." After
reviewing the successes and failures of Geneva, he ended
with the words: "In the history of the League of Nations we
may conclude that collective security did not fail, but that it
was never tried." He needed to cite the most important, the
most fatal case, the clash between China and Japan in Manchuria.

Turning to me flatteringly, the well-known scholar demanded: "What was the year of the Mukden incident? I never could remember dates!"

Fourteen ninety-two and Seventeen seventy-six have always been the extent of my repertoire, but I responded glibly: "Nineteen thirty-one," and added, "September eighteenth."

Dr. Shotwell looked at me with respect, and a few weeks later he asked me to work on a complicated manuscript about the Curzon line, the long-disputed Polish boundary.

"But I know nothing about the Curzon Line," I cried, in all honesty. "You don't realize how ignorant I am!"

"Shucks!" Dr. Shotwell nodded genially. "You can teach us pundits a thing or two!"

That September 18, while Geneva cables were sizzling with the news that Japanese soldiers had marched outside their lawful zone in Manchuria, to bombard Mukden, and murder and disarm Chinese troops, my two little boys and I were placidly hunting birthday surprises for Daddy. Annie was preparing partridges (no more costly than roasts, since cold-storage meat is forbidden in Switzerland), beautiful little new potatoes, fresh asparagus with drawn butter, and a handsome pink cake. This proved, on eating, to be, rather like Annie, smooth and sugary outside but damp and indigestible within. Baking is mostly left, in Europe, to the *cordon bleu* or the pastry shop, and Annie, who did wonders with a soufflé or a fish sauce, could never suggest any sweet dessert except stewed apricots!

Ethan and Curtis, clutching one Swiss franc in hot, fat hands, hunted through the shops in vain for a gift really worthy of a man. In our favorite chocolate shop on the rue du Marché they hesitated over a two-foot chocolate Santa Claus and a tarleton bag of chocolate francs in silver paper. But it was on the Quai Wilson, not far from the granite tablet to the President's memory, that my two babies stopped like two hypnotized lion cubs.

"That's what Daddy needs!" breathed Ethan, turning pale with excitement.

"What Daddy needs!" echoed Curtis in a red-faced daze.

Under a flowering lamppost, where a shabby toy-vendor sat winding up his wares, a tiny Mickey Mouse with a painted grin was rattling its feet—"just like the movies!" They could scarcely believe the miracle. They thought they had left Mickey at home in America.

We learned soon enough that Mickey was an international hero. Derso, our brilliant League cartoonist, declared that he symbolized the American spirit, bobbing up again after all vicissitudes, grinning and confident. We found his adventures in French, at Kundig's Bookstore, and my boys pored over "Mee-kee" until their bilingual identity with him became complete. When Curtis saw his first French cartoon, *Mickey dans le Pays des Géants*, and watched his hero borne to the giant's cavernous mouth on a forkful of peas, he leapt from his seat, yelling anxiously: "Look out!" and a second later: "*Attention!*"

So the two francs were exchanged for a little piece of America, and all the way home in the city of peace they fought over who was to carry the box, until the top broke, the sides caved in, and the magic key somehow dropped out on the way. I was quelling the hullabaloo of mutual recrimination when Mariette—looking, in her pert black and white, so exactly like a French maid that it was hard to believe she was real—called Madame to the telephone. It was Monsieur, and he would be late to dinner.

Jerry was regretful but preoccupied. There'd been a serious clash between Japanese and Chinese in Manchuria; they were still waiting for more detailed information, but the

Council had called a special late session. He was phoning between translations and would be home when he could. The cake? Oh, the boys could light the candles tomorrow.

Ruth Sweetser, whose husband had been in the Information Section of the League almost from the beginning, had warned me: "My dear, Geneva is where wives come to be canonized as saints." It had not taken long to find out for myself that the League, humanitarian on one hand, was the great Eater-Up of Husbands on the other. One sent a man forth in the morning, never knowing at what ungodly hour he might return that night. Distinguished guests might drift in to a dinner party at nine o'clock, or never turn up at all. When I went, a little intimidated, to my first Geneva tea, I found all the women, from Lady Drummond, wife of the Secretary-General, down, indignantly comparing notes on the hour at which husbands or men guests had finally sat down to table the evening before, and what the cook said about her entrée being ruined. To one fresh from America, a cook, at five dollars a week, who would serve anything at nine-thirty in the evening seemed hardly a ground for complaint. My sympathy, that birthday evening, was not with China but with Annie and her overdone partridges. I felt distinctly annoyed. The League might have chosen another day for its "incidents."

Curtis soon fell placidly asleep, philosophical even at three, but Ethan demanded explanation. Where was Daddy? I could see Mickey's grin from the black marble mantelpiece, where he stood, a contrast in centuries and cultures, as I tried to translate my feeble knowledge into baby talk. You know that big office on the Lake where Daddy and Alan Sweetser's daddy and Colette Streit's daddy and lots of other daddies from all over the world come and talk about how to keep

people from fighting? Well, some people called the Japanese
got mad with some people called the Chinese, and instead of
telling the men here in Geneva about it, so they could help
to settle the trouble, the Japanese broke their promise and
went and killed a whole lot of Chinese with guns.

"Killed?" Ethan was incredulous. "But those are bad
people."

"So the men in Geneva are meeting to decide what to do."

"Ho! Daddy will tell them."

"Well, no, Daddy can only watch, because he's an American."

Ethan flushed indignantly. "But why? Why, Mummie?"

Fortunately I did not have to invent lame excuses for America's foreign policy. We heard the familiar rattle of a huge
foreign key in the front door, Ethan, a whirling dervish,
threw himself into the hall, yelling: "Daddy, Daddy!" and
Curtis woke, cross and pink, demanding the Mickey Mouse.
I left the ensuing rumpus to our internationalist and went to
tell Annie she could serve dinner.

When Jerry joined me at table and unfolded his enormous
French napkin he was chuckling to himself.

"What on earth," he demanded, "have you been telling
Ethan about Manchuria? He's all excited."

I explained, rather sheepishly. To my surprise Jerry looked
at me with respect.

"Well, I don't know why that isn't a perfectly good explanation of unwarranted aggression," he said. "Anyway, Ethan
knows the way to stop the Japs. He says if everybody will
take all their Christmas-tree ornaments up in the air and drop
them, with a big pop, then 'all those bad people will get
scared and run away'!"

We laughed, in our superior adult way. But the memory

was not so funny when we trimmed our first Christmas tree
without Ethan. He was seventeen and in the United States
Navy, and we had not yet dropped the atomic bomb on Hiroshima.

~ 5 ~

Briand Handles a Crisis

ETHAN's four-year-old interest in Manchuria having been aroused, I had to share his indignation and find excuses for those men on the Lake, who had not yet chased out the bad people. I had to show him Manchuria on the map, where we learned together that it was a part of China, opposite the islands of Japan. Daddy told us it was full of soybeans, coal and metals, so the Japanese were trying to grab it, "the way you grab Curtis's cookies when you've eaten yours." What was harder to explain to a fresh mind was why action moved so slowly. My son thought Mickey Mouse could have done a better job.

So, although Ethan usually sulked when I left the house in the afternoon, he allowed me to attend my first meeting of the League Council, because I promised, rather rashly, that today something would surely be done and I would tell him all about it.

The League Council was made up of fourteen members, elected by the Assembly, of which it was really an executive committee. The Council handled special problems, upon which it reported to the large body. It had great prestige in Geneva, and its public meetings were always more exciting than the Assembly. But the Council had no autonomous authority for quick action such as the United Nations Charter —profiting by that costly Sino-Japanese mistake—has now delegated to our Security Council. Nor was our Council always "sitting," on watch for the danger signs in the world, like the United Nations Council. One can only hope that the new Council will live up to its most solemn duty of impatience.

But impatience, in those Geneva days, was not admired. All the old routines of formal diplomacy still had their stranglehold on the League—the face-saving, the constant play of governments for power and prestige in the name of "sovereignty." It was a long time before I stopped being awed and baffled and began instead to trust some of my own simple American "hunches." There was something neurotic about a set of international habits so strong that they obscured the real danger. Perhaps my memory is colored by my own ignorance, but I seem to recall that the Orient felt very far from the Quai Wilson. The familiar enmity between France and Germany, and a vague distrust of the unknown Soviet Union, loomed far larger at our dinner-table discussions than the Sino-Japanese dispute. So I attended my first Council meeting—a momentous one, as it turned out—merely from curiosity. My friends were going and I wanted to be able to talk about it afterwards. I had not as yet made the slightest connection between the "Mukden incident" and my two little boys yelling good-by from behind the railed protection of our little terrace garden.

In the famous Glass Room of the League building near the Lake, several wars had already been averted by prompt action, but with no resulting fanfare. Peace is so much duller than war. Aristide Briand, President of the Council, was presiding that day. Although Laval soon succeeded—I almost wrote supplanted—Briand as French Minister of Foreign Affairs, and was constantly in and out of Geneva, I cannot, for the life of me, remember the face of the butcher's son. But Briand, whom I saw twice, fifteen years ago, I have never forgotten, nor the tired, mellow yet sardonic tones of his voice.

He was greatly loved in his own country. The plain Frenchman knows a good man when he has one. It is the quarreling intellectuals and the grabbing politicians who are always obscuring the French political scene; the people have common sense and simple morality. Later, not long before the second World War began, I met one of Briand's admirers on a bench in the Tuileries Gardens. A French peasant with close-cropped head, he sat "minding" his frail granddaughter as I "minded" my round, pink-cheeked boys. Not long before, Jerry and I had lunched charmingly in the London home of Viscount Cecil, that old aristocrat of peace. Cecil was no more gracious and dignified than my new friend. It was one of those moving encounters, like a moment from infinity, when two strangers are immediately in touch. The old peasant asked me, eagerly, as people often did in European parks, what I fed my boys, and didn't I believe that milk and fresh vegetables and *le grand air* would benefit his little granddaughter. He told me the secret of all human happiness— "*C'est la famille, Madame!*" The mention of Geneva, where my youngest had been born, brought unashamed tears to his eyes.

"Ah, Madame! What a loss for France, for the whole world, when Briand died. Our great man of peace! This Laval—frankly, Madame, I am worried. People say to me: 'What do you care? You have no sons to lose, only a daughter.' But I cannot look at all these fresh young men without weeping. They are all my sons."

When the sunset breeze stirred the horse-chestnut leaves and set the colored pinwheels whirring in the toy-booth, I bought one for each of the children, mine and his. The old man looked about, helpless and embarrassed, then he plunged his gnarled hand into a creased paper lunch-bag.

"Tiens, Madame, tiens!" he cried, dropping on my lap a huge bunch of purple country grapes. When I hesitated he added, with dignity: "Permit me to thank your entire country, in your person, for coming to the rescue of France in 1918."

It was another Frenchman, the masseur who came that first Geneva winter to recondition my broken leg, who explained to me the difference between Briand and Laval.

"And do you understand, Madame," he panted, the perspiration rolling down his forehead as he tortured my knee muscles under huge fingers, "the difference between a politician and a statesman? The politician works for himself; the statesman for his country. *Tiens,* I will give you an example. Laval is *homme de politique.* Briand is *homme d'état.*"

Briand sat in the Glass Room, that day, among his colleagues at the broad, shining old oak table, his massive head hunched over weary shoulders, his face wrinkled and brown with illness, but his eyes as bright as any stubborn, dying old lion's. Now and then he would stroke his drooping mandarin mustache, absently and affectionately. As the sun moved slowly around the high, glass walls and a uniformed usher tiptoed squeakingly over to adjust another shade, Briand's sad eyes shifted automatically to follow, as though any interruption were a relief from handling a bloody tragedy with kid gloves and fine words.

This was the first time that the Chinese and the Japanese delegates had faced each other across the peace table. Passes to the Visitors Section were prized that day, and though most of us completely missed the fatal implications of a situation which led directly to Pearl Harbor, the human drama held us all fascinated.

Doctor Sze—calm, broad-faced, thoughtful—I trusted before he spoke. The Japanese diplomat looked as alien to my Western eye as an old gray idol from a heathen temple. One could feel the room taking sides, like an audience in a theater, and Yoshizawa was everybody's choice for villain. We all knew, as well as Ethan, who was right and who was wrong. Every statesman at that table knew. But the complicated habits of old prides and old fears, the great chasm between isolated Geneva and the indifferent plain people all over the world, who would pay the price, befuddled a very simple issue.

Sze, stating China's case, requested that the League send an impartial commission to ascertain the facts in Manchuria. His broad, Oriental face was emotionless, but his voice carried the deep, tragic undertones of China, helpless before its small but determined adversary. Briand called for the translation, the room broke into a buzz and half the men dashed out into the corridors to compare notes or to telegraph the story. Then one of those bilingual geniuses known humbly as "translators" rose to read the French version of the Chinese statement. With a few notes in hand these men could deliver a fluent, almost verbatim replica of any speech into either of the two official languages, French or English.

People drifted back from the corridors, the room fell quiet again under Briand's gavel, and Yoshizawa began his reply. For at least ten minutes, I took the mumbled nasal jargon for Japanese until an occasional familiar word revealed that it was French. Some Geneva wit said that Esperanto was not necessary as an international language, since the League had already invented its own—bad French. Bad English was

equally official and one often waited for the clear, fluent translation to seize the finer points of a speech.

Now we heard Japan's claim. Japan had acted in "self-
defense," had no territorial ambitions, sought only the safety
of her own citizens in Manchuria. (I was reminded of my
wily Ethan, who always found such good reasons why he
"had to" hit Curtis.) Japan refused intervention by the
League. She was not at war; her military actions were merely
"punitive." She would negotiate directly with China herself.

Even I could see that this was "hooey." Yet, crazy as it now
seems, the United States backed Japan on the technical point
that as the commission had been requested by China and not
by a neutral country, it could not be impartial! I learned long
ago in Geneva that, between nations, where there's a will
there's a way. If President Hoover and Secretary Stimson
had been far-sighted, some other equally convenient tech-
nicality could have been dug up to halt a tiny war before it
became world-wide. Politicians can always hide the truth
behind legalities.

Like most women, my first impatient reaction to parliamentary procedure was: "Oh, why can't they say what they mean
and be done with it?" My strongest impression of that first
Council meeting, besides a vivid mood of tension, was baffled
admiration for masculine patience, that endless, long-term, intricate and maddening patience of political maneuvering. Perhaps men have been forced to invent it to discipline their own
capacity for violence. Without rules, without face-saving, it
would be all too easy for any debate to end in a fist fight. Ask
any mother of sons! The tank, the bomber, the machine gun,
even the atomic bomb, are only extensions of that primitive
fist. As I went on living near the League of Nations, I came
to see that all the boring and intricate technicalities of pacific
settlement were indispensable. But when men become too

absorbed in merely beating each other in the complicated chess game, they need us simpler creatures to pull at their coat-tails and protest: "But your pawn is my baby!"

All that afternoon, as the debate dragged on, with its issues as plain as day, I heard "my honorable colleague" this, "my worthy opponent" that, from the lips of men who must have been raging to tear each other's eyes out. Briand gave courteous ear to both Orientals; no voice was raised; everyone walked, politely, gingerly, on eggs. It made one want to yell or throw a book—anything to break the carefully woven spell.

"Heavens!" I cried to my husband that evening, "I don't see how these men stand it. I should think they'd all go home and raise hob with their families tonight."

For a Geneva wife, I had learned a valuable lesson. When my internationalist came home from chairing a wrangling group of peace workers, looking as if he had been pulled through a knothole and refusing all food but soup, I remembered—sometimes—not to complain about the latest German-French crisis between Annie and Mariette below stairs.

But I did not have much to report to Ethan that night, after all.

❦ 6 ❦

First American at the Peace Table

GENEVA was astonishingly full of Americans—the place was running over with them. There was Clarence Streit, for the New York *Times*, with whose youngest daughter, age five, Ethan promptly fell in love. Clarence was a tall Westerner who seemed always, even then, serenely idealistic. The Derso-Kelen cartoon, which probably still hangs in the Bavaria Café, showed a smiling young giant with his feet in the clouds and a flower in his buttonhole. There was John Whitaker, for Associated Press, a handsome, liquid-eyed Southern boy always hunting, eagerly and honestly, for the truths behind the events he had to cable home so objectively. There was Arthur Sweetser, an old friend of Jerry's, with whom he had started out as a cub reporter at six dollars a week on the old Springfield *Republican*. Arthur too had seen World War I at first hand. From war correspondent and Air Service captain, he had moved to the Press Bureau of the Versailles Peace Conference. He was a big, good-looking ex-football player with a deep hatred of war that made some of his easy-going friends in the State Department smile: "Arthur is too emotional about the League." He was in the Information Section of the Secretariat.

I had always thought of the League of Nations as a political body which met now and then to engage in parliamentary disputes. I was astonished to find a vast, busy, all-year-round staff from every country of the world, conferring and working together in such diverse fields as child health, the drug traffic and the standardization of statistics. Many of these internationalists, both in the Secretariat and out, were Americans.

A leading member of the Health Organization, Dr. Frank Boudreau, was an American. The Vice-President of the Permanent Opium Board, Herbert May, was an American. Arthur Sweetser's associate in the Information Section, Benjamin Gerig, was an American. One of the judges of the World Court, who appeared regularly in Geneva, Manley Hudson, was an American. Of course there was a whole staff grouped around our Consul, Prentiss Gilbert. Soon, as the Oriental situation grew worse and the Disarmament Conference began, the American Minister moved over from Berne. It began to be borne in on me, first with surprise and then with humiliation, that when important issues were at stake America managed to be there, but when co-operative responsibility was asked she backed off in alarm. After any important League meeting, when everyone congregated in the corridors to talk, my husband was besieged by Europeans.

"What do you think America will do now? What will your position be on this?" they asked eagerly.

For the first time I began to see why a country needs to formulate its foreign policy and why the absence of such a tremendous power as the United States would leave any international organization out of balance. My country's so-called "isolationism" looked rather absurd, when we kept going all around Robin Hood's barn to be in Geneva but never of it. I had never cared whether or not America joined Wilson's idealistic project. But now I wondered if it would not be more dignified and efficient to appear, properly, at the front door instead of always devising ways to wriggle cleverly up through the cellar. I saw why patriotic men like Jerry and Arthur Sweetser were almost ashamed of our lame pretexts, so unworthy of a great country. I had taken my native land very much for granted; Europe was older, more colorful, the mature parent of a younger civilization. But I began to see that this child was regarded, over there, with anxious and worried respect. If America was still unaware of what a tremendous weight she pulled in the world, Europe knew. This new sense of our importance stirred my first national pride. With patriotism dawned also a vague, uncomfortable sense of responsibility. But it was still very vague, and still not too uncomfortable.

The day the first American sat down, officially, in an open meeting of the League Council, Geneva was all agog; the Europeans more excited than the Americans. As we gathered again in the Glass Room our foreign friends moved about with beaming faces to shake our hands in congratulation. Prentiss Gilbert, our Consul General, was to read aloud a communication from the State Department, as evidence that we backed up League action in the Manchurian dispute.

Prentiss was already, in that rapid Geneva way, a personal friend. He had quickly unbent from his rather pompous official manner when he discovered, at an International Club luncheon, that I knew his two best Rochester chums. Diplomatic correctness was alien to Prentiss's real temperament. He loved practical jokes and sometimes tortured his wife by suddenly walking on his knees and talking squeakily up at her on the street just as some Geneva dignitary was approaching. When she had granted his most absurd request, Prentiss would rise to his handsome height in time to salute the dignitary, who had usually noticed nothing.

You could have heard an invisible hairpin drop that October day in Geneva, as Prentiss took his place, along with Briand, Lord Reading, Viscount Cecil and Grandi, at the symbolic table. We heard speeches in beautiful Parisian French, in broken Japanese French, in British English and in Chinese American. Then Briand called upon the representative of the United States. I saw Charlotte Gilbert, very pale under her frame of blond hair, nervously knotting her gloves as her husband cleared his throat and began to read. The familiar cadences of upper New York State broke the silence like a letter from home. Suddenly all America was there in that polyglot room. Surprised by my own thrill of excitement, I looked around, to find fellow countrymen hiding a similar emotion under poker faces. The Europeans hung breathlessly on every word.

But the text disappointed me. I was still politically childish enough to expect, for such a historic occasion, something simple and meaty. All I heard was a carefully worded reiteration of the Briand-Kellogg Pact as a justification for America's participating in the Council's debates. There was nothing to explain to people like me the truths behind the speech—that the United States had such urgent national and business concerns in the Far East that we had to find an excuse for appearing in Geneva and for urging the League to pull our chestnuts out of the fire. I thought we had kept out of the League because we did not want Europe "using" us to settle their squabbles. But here we were, using the League to further our own interests.

"But why," I asked my amused husband, "aren't these

things ever told, if all the government leaders know them anyhow?" He said that was diplomatic convention, and that
Geneva newspapermen did try to explain what was happening. So did the monthly report of his Geneva Research Center, which sent back to America an objective monthly survey
of League doings.

"But that's for people who already know," I protested.
"Even the correspondents don't write for women like me;
they always assume you've read what they wrote the day before, and maybe you've missed it."

Jerry laughed.

"Well, there's a job for you," he challenged, and I retorted
that men always got so personal.

For I was busy and life was interesting, and I most certainly did not want to be bothered to help educate the American public. Two lively sons to raise were enough. I preferred
being a spectator at this distant drama to taking any responsible part.

The Manchurian affair dragged on. Sometimes Minister
Wilson and sometimes Consul Gilbert consulted for the
United States with both the Council and the Assembly. America sent protesting notes to both Oriental governments, and
meantime the battle areas in Manchuria were slowly spreading, like an ink-blot. The war, never finally declared, was always termed "punitive action" by the aggressors. The "fero-
cious buffoonery," as Léon Blum called it, was soon to give
Hitler and Mussolini their encouragement to do likewise. But
meantime the League Covenant was technically intact, Japanese honor still unsullied. The United States, as paralyzed as
Europe by its own musty traditions, had let the chance for a
strong stand slip by.

The Council held its final meeting on *my* birthday, a beautiful October 24. The vote was to be taken about requesting

Japan to evacuate the territory seized in Manchuria, so that peace negotiations could properly begin. Briand presided for his last time. Across the polished table Doctor Sze, morose but composed, again faced the Japanese delegate. Of Yoshizawa I could only glimpse a little bony back in a conventional dark Western suit. The deadlock was all quite familiar by this time, and my eyelids drooped under the drone of the long phrases, and their translation, in that stuffy room. But we woke up when Briand put the question.

Up to that moment—for I had never read the League Covenant—it had not occurred to me that the two parties to the dispute would be allowed to vote. It was obvious that an aggressor would vote against his own condemnation as surely as the party with a grievance would vote for it. Yet— as Jerry again explained to me afterwards—except in special cases under the League Covenant, all Council members voted on Council action, and what was more, such action became ineffective unless the vote was unanimous! My common sense balked, bewildered, before such strange lack of practical realism about human nature, but I felt too humble to sit in judgment on the great of the earth. So for the moment I merely added this oddity to the other vast international questions beyond my comprehension. I remembered it, however, years later, when the debate about the "veto" raged in San Francisco. Unfortunately, the politicians, the national leaders who put "sovereignty" above peace, and would rather win the chess game than save the lives of real boys, won out. Any one of the Big Five on the United Nations Security Council may nullify military action in a dispute in which it is itself involved or interested, exactly as Japan checkmated the old League Council from even requesting it to withdraw its troops from unlawfully won ground. Of course none of the Big Five today expects to play the villain. But the principle remains the same. If you're big enough, you leave a loophole before you agree to submit your quarrels to arbitration. Recalling the rightness of my untutored instinct of years ago, which is confirmed now by the most thoughtful experts I know, I wonder if average people, once they understand, might not be sounder in their judgments than the leaders they elect.

Briand called for "ayes" on the proposal to request Japan to evacuate Manchuria. Promptly around the table, thirteen masculine hands rose high—including Great Britain, France, Spain, Italy, Germany, and naturally China. Then, while the room held its breath, the old Frenchman called for "nays." Dead silence—then slowly, hesitantly, one brown hand crept a few inches upward. The white cuff fell back to reveal a lean Oriental forearm.

For weeks afterwards I could see that ominous hand. Many spectators shared my premonition. Lange, the beautiful old white-haired Norwegian delegate to the Disarmament Conference, whose blond grandson was already one of Curtis's playmates, said to my husband:

"We are moving closer and closer to the brink of disaster. I think I already hear the roaring of the falls."

Lange died, peacefully, in Norway before his prophecy came true. At the time I dismissed it, rather irritably, as typical Scandinavian gloom. I wished that Jerry would take more pleasure in the red-and-golden charms of a Geneva October, reminiscent of the America for which we were already a little homesick.

7

Social Advantages of a Broken Leg

B UT meantime my real life centered around the boys, home, new friends—and Jerry, when I got a chance at him, for he was growing more and more absorbed in the Geneva scene. Well-meaning friends had advised us to cushion the shock of a strange land by packing a few familiar toys, but Ethan's battered bear and Curtis's cotton doll were immediately tossed aside, while my healthy pair found daily adventure in the new life. They were entranced with our landlady's blue-flowered china toilet, so majestic in its isolated cubbyhole that it invested even life's daily duties with glamour. Within a month, four-year-old Ethan had become cosmopolitan. With loud American, a few French words, and many gestures, he was getting cookies out of the maids and swapping horse chestnuts with Swiss boys in the near-by park. Curtis, baby intellectual with a musical ear, held his tongue for six months and then suddenly began speaking almost perfect French. But they would have no truck with my using the new sounds.

Only once, I made this mistake. Ethan's eyes popped in horror.

"MUMMIE!" he yelled, in a long wail of anguish, as though I had changed before his eyes into a complete stranger.

I switched hastily back to English, and the pink returned to his cheeks.

"Never, never talk to me like that again!" he commanded passionately, and I never did. Anyway, within the year I was having to insist upon English at home, or they would have forgotten their own tongue or spoken it with an accent.

Geneva, for its size, has more parks and playgrounds than any American town I know. The boys' favorite was Les Bastions, where all one side of the old ramparts was covered by the famous Reformation Monument. They sailed boats and floated twigs happily in the peaceful fountain under the carved giants of Calvin and Knox, towering like stone ghosts of the past above the yellow American heads. Many a woman sidled up to feel the brown suede cloth of their zipper suits. *"Qu'ils sont braves, les petits!"* they smiled. "And how practically they are dressed."

For my part, I was equally awed by the exquisite hand-knit suits worn by the poorest babies. I think every female creature with a pair of healthy hands knitted in Geneva. You saw their needles clicking on park benches, on streetcars, in doctors' waiting rooms, even in the small Lake craft called *mouettes* (sea gulls) which ferried picturesquely from one side of the city to the other.

Jerry and I had assumed that anything so modern as a nursery school was left behind in America. We had not reckoned with the lasting influence of Madame Montessori on European education. Off the route de Florissant, near the Clarence Streits' villa, we found a quaint brown chalet in a grove, presided over by a gentle and humorous lady whose father had been one of the Swiss pioneer educators in the

Montessori method. Mademoiselle Ferrière prepared infants for the International School, where many of the League families sent their children. I know nothing of Mademoiselle Ferrière's qualifications by American standards, but she understood children. My two young rowdies responded to her, like flowers to the sun, and could hardly wait to get there each morning. A shy beauty with blond curls, who used to slip over each morning from the Streits' house, soon became an added attraction for Ethan.

A warm, wide, natural affection for childhood permeated that little chalet like a stove in a cold Swiss winter. There was less insistence on the purely practical skills, with which we Americans falsify democracy (as if a bricklayer is *per se* more democratic than a poet), and more awareness of the mental hunger of even small children. One noon, when I called for Ethan and Curtis, I found my merry baby, whose boredom with shoestrings, buttons and jungle gyms had branded him as "babyish and backward" in an American nursery school, sitting alone at a diminutive blue table. He was singing lustily: "It was Friday morn when we set sail," while his fat hands performed miracles of speed and logic, fitting complicated shapes into their corresponding holes.

"A mental type," Mademoiselle boasted, adding, with European enjoyment of individuality: *"C'est un numéro—il n'y a pas à dire!"*

Ethan, muscular, practical, high-strung, was always trying, along with other young fellow countrymen, to explore the mysteries of the neighboring gardens. American children, his teacher told me humorously, always seemed to need more space than others. They were never content, like a European baby, to play quietly "inside a frame."

The Swiss take child care seriously: I know of no other institution like Geneva's *pouponière—poupon* being an affectionate name for a small child. Here ordinary girls, many of them fresh-cheeked peasants from German Switzerland, are scrupulously trained. They study Montessori and Froebel methods, the symptoms and nursing of children's diseases, with experience in local hospitals; and they cannot graduate until they have knitted an entire baby outfit from cap to booties. These cheerful girls never seemed to feel degraded by taking care of other women's children. Like Swiss trained nurses, who feel dedicated to a cause, they appeared content to express rather simple womanly affection.

We hired a *pouponière* from time to time, but I could not relinquish my American ways. Despite growing social demands, I still took care of my own babies. With domestic cares so competently handled, trailing around luxuriant parks in the afternoons felt like a perpetual holiday. When it rained we took the belt-line trolley, sitting through several rounds of the city, while a correct and puzzled conductor collected our triple and quadruple fares, frowning over American wastefulness.

Perhaps I should have paid more calls, or played bridge with the wives of notables, as some of my more experienced Geneva friends advised reproachfully. They said it was essential to my husband's career. But he seems to have managed nicely without my well-meaning hindrance, and I learned more about Europe by talking to women on park benches, chatting with workmen on the street, whose excavations so fascinated the boys, or listening to the political views of the merry young barber who "cut ze haar" for my wriggling children while I sat deciphering foreign joke-papers. Soon after Christmas I furthered my international education by breaking my leg. By taking a skiing tumble in the Bernese Oberland I learned that Americans hang together in trouble like a band of pioneers in a wilderness.

It had been only too easy to fall into the condescending Geneva habit of complaining about the dull Swiss and quoting the French wit who said: "Switzerland is a bonbon box filled with potatoes." Meanwhile we were enjoying their traditional neutrality, their solid virtues and their excellent cheeses, and the cosy resorts perched on the edge of grandeur where everybody took winter vacations. Everybody skied— Clarence Streit was one of our most skilled American addicts —and week ends marked a general exodus. There was something for every purse, from the swankiest hotels at the highest altitude, to crude wooden ski shelters at humbler heights, crowded with ruddy young Swiss drinking white wine. One might find one's own maid here on her day off. Winter sports, in democratic Switzerland, were not the prerogative of the wealthy.

Shortly after Christmas, Mariette, the boys and I preceded my husband by a few days to Gstaad to join the Arthur Sweetsers in their favorite *pension de famille*. Four hours by third class involved changing to three different local trains, lugging our leaden bags, but there was always some kindly workman to lift them out for us. I had begun to discover that no stigma is attached in Europe to thrift. Financial limitations are taken for granted, and self-respect depends upon how cleverly one manages one's income in order to squeeze out the last bit of good. "Only fools and Americans" traveled first class.

The everyday world fell away as we stepped from the hot and rattly little train into the cold, delicious silence of a mountain village in winter. Early night had fallen, and there was only starlit sky and a world of snow, frozen into stiff ruts on the road, piled neatly on rooftops, brooding white on all the hills. We stood awestruck, and even Ethan was silenced.

Sleigh bells jingled everywhere; red-faced sportsmen were plodding home to dinner, and a horse-drawn sleigh awaited our little party. With our bells tinkling romantically and horses' hoofs flicking up clouds of snow, we glided off into a quiet country road. This valley village of Gstaad, with its orderly *Gemütlichkeit*, its mottoed chalets, and its guttural speech, looked German to an American eye. Actually, we were in the very heart of democratic Switzerland, with its sturdy William Tell traditions. Nowhere was Hitler more hated than in its German-speaking cantons. Long before the war started, a foreigner in Switzerland whose German smacked too strongly of Berlin drew black looks or worse.

In our big, comfortable *pension* with its bustling proprietress and the sturdy girls who did our spotless rooms in self-contained silence, it was only too easy to forget the problems of the sick world beyond our mountain. Ethan soon discovered that the sounds which facilitated chestnut-swapping in Geneva's parks were of no use to him here, and he began to imitate the warning *Achtung* of the red-cheeked boys and girls on the hilltops. It came out a lusty American "Ox-tongue!" but with excellent effect, and he always managed to be part of a gang. Curtis, on his dignity even at three, observed everything in silence. When a *pension* guest, not sure of his nationality, asked what language he spoke, he retorted: "American, Fwench, *Italien* and German," and waddled away before he could be put to the test.

I found a skiing "Professor" with honest blue eyes set in a weather-beaten face who took his art very seriously. So when I managed to turn a double somersault on a twisted leg, it was not only my bones that broke. I was, my landlady told me reproachfully, the Professor's first accident. The day I was borne off, in a plaster cast, for Geneva, I saw him standing, shy and desolate, on a snowy corner, staring after us with tears in his wintry eyes.

In my foolish American way I had put on such a show of fortitude that at first nobody, even the cool, pink-faced old surgeon, thought it more than a twisted ankle. A lady, in Europe, if she is hurt, is expected to cry, and then somebody does something about it. I spent a feverish night alone, changing my own compresses and cursing the Spartan code acquired from four American brothers. The next day, when I toppled trying to obey the doctor's orders, he discovered two bones broken. Still, the old Bernois spoke no word of sympathy. The Sweetsers sent their car for me and I was carried on a chair to the front door. As I saw a few feet yawning like an abyss between me and the waiting car, suddenly all my false courage ebbed away and I wanted to bawl like a baby. I don't know how the doctor knew, but his steely old arms picked me up as if I were a featherweight and set me, in one skillful swoop, on the car seat. Then he turned to my husband.

"She is ver-ry br-rave," he nodded, and this time I cried like a real lady.

Back in French Switzerland again, my Geneva surgeon, thin, elegant, and sympathetic, asked what sedative the Gstaad doctor had prescribed.

"Why—none," I confessed, feeling rather silly. "I've hardly slept since the accident."

Doctor Reverdin shook his head, exasperated both with me and with his colleague. Then he began to chuckle.

"Madame," he boasted, with native pride, "he was a Bernois!"

News of the accident traveled fast in the American colony. After New Haven's academic reserve we had been astonished by the warmth of our American welcome overseas. Now misfortune only seemed to accelerate my social progress. Lying on the chaise longue of our veranda, I made more friends in a few months than in as many years at home. For the boys, Mummie's leg spiced life with one thrill after another: the constant ringing of the doorbell, the house full of flowers—a potted plant, to their delight, from "Mrs. Fox" of the Y.W.C.A., gorgeous roses from "Mr. De Wolfe" of the State Department. The donors, however, when they appeared in person, proved a bitter disappointment, not being Disney animals.

Mariette tended the boys and me devotedly, but Annie, robbing me right and left and treating all her friends in the basement kitchen, disapproved of Madame's cheerfulness. She was full of morbid German *Schadenfreude* and warned me daily that when massage began—"Ah, then Madame will suffer much!" After a tea party, when all the guests had scribbled sentiments or sketches on the plaster leg, I showed it to Annie. She eyed the frivolous sight grimly.

"Ah yes," she sighed. "Americans will make fun of anything!"

The moment Monsier Bain, *masseur diplomé*, arrived on the scene, Annie hated him for being French. In Germany, she said, pursing her lips, he could not work in shirt sleeves but must change to a correct white coat—it was the law. She probably eavesdropped on our lively conversations about politics, hoping to regale her young protégées below stairs with a juicy morsel of scandal. Annie told me meat was high in Geneva because all the butchers kept half a dozen mistresses; she hunted hungrily everywhere for lascivious implications, and I was a great disappointment to her. I should never have dared tell her my best story. Ethan, playing doorman one afternoon, ushered in Geneva's primmest bachelor with the cheerful shout: "Oh, Mummie—here's a nice man to see you, but not the one who comes to rub your leg!"

Authority suddenly transferred to a neurotic German and a temperamental French peasant, who both used the boys for their own private warfare, changed Ethan and Curtis into imps of Satan. Annie began praising German education. In Germany they raised boys like little soldiers. When her brother spoke, his children jumped! Lying helpless on my chaise longue, I began to doubt my few simple principles, but I was too American to doubt them for long. It was the beginning of many arguments and a long struggle to bring our boys home, broadened by Europe, but fitted to be American men in an American environment.

In any event, it was American humor which solved the problem of discipline. One chilly afternoon, when the two boys lay cuddled contentedly under the throw of my chaise longue, both carefully on the side away from the bad leg, I invented two guardian angels. Pim and Pow were a pair of flies living invisibly on our ceiling, buzzing sadness or approval over the actions of their protégés below. My poor innocents vied with each other to please their imaginary censors, and all went well until one afternoon Ethan spied a hardy Genevese insect on the veranda glass. He and Curtis nearly came to blows as to whether this were Pim or Pow. I settled it—it was just a Swiss playmate come for fly goûter—and the two angels retired again into the spiritual sphere, where they were useful for a long time.

∽ 8 ∽

My Country—Right or Wrong?

"I NTERNATIONALIST," I had begun to suspect, was by no means synonymous with "expatriate." Geneva attracted its full quota of cynical career diplomats, politicians with an eye to the main chance, and little men hanging on to a safe job in the Secretariat. But the finer types, from whatever country, seemed to be expressing, in their concern for world peace, an even more passionate preoccupation with the welfare of their own nations. I heard more anxiety about America's future, more anguish lest its sons have to fight again, among the American men in Geneva than at home. My husband's patriotism had always astonished me, and now I met other fellow countrymen to whom America was a great reality.

My own national sense was growing stronger by the minute. As for my children, within a few months they were ardent hundred-percenters from a dream country which could do no wrong. Ethan nailed an American flag to his Swiss scooter. Curtis, when refused cold lobster by an amused waiter at Thanksgiving dinner in the Hôtel les Bergues, "becoss it giffs little boys ze stomach-ache," retorted calmly: "Ho, but not me, because I'm an American!"

The turkey of that annual American colony dinner meant more to us than turkey. European cooking was a treat, but one's palate felt lonely for home tastes. All the little nagging lacks—clear, sweet coffee and cream instead of a rusty chicory mixture with hot milk; crunchy cereals, peanut butter—oh, how my soul ached for peanut butter!—these became the symbols of home, remembered whenever Americans got together.

Our faults, our isolationism, the blindness of our State Department, were under constant fire—when Europeans were not around. But American living was in our bones, and though we all made good friends from other countries, there was something comfortable about a group of just Americans, free to criticize the foreign policy of the United States.

While I lay recovering on my chaise longue, events had moved on in the League of Nations. Japan promised to behave. China withdrew her request for an impartial commission. The Council made a report of progress to the Assembly. Suddenly Geneva was all a-buzz again with fresh alarm. Tokyo, thumbing its nose at the world, had sent more "punitive" armies to destroy Chinese towns. Arranged riots broke out in Shanghai. An American consul was attacked by a Japanese soldier. The United States sent protesting notes to both aggressor and victim. Japan expressed diplomatic "regret" for the attack. Yoshizawa of the ominous hand went home to become Minister of Foreign Affairs, and another wizened little man, Matsuoka, brought his top hat and his filibustering tactics to the peace table.

At last I could tell Ethan, who clung stubbornly to his sympathy for "those poor people in that place," that the League had appointed a Commission of Inquiry to Manchuria to make an objective report to Geneva. Headed by an Englishman, Lord Lytton, its members were a Frenchman, a German, an Italian, and—an American, General Frank McCoy, another compatriot with a long military record who did not believe in war.

Jerry was always bringing home serious articles and pamphlets to my veranda in the forlorn hope that they would interest me as they did him. I struggled loyally to get through them, but they were not written for me. Despite all the foreign correspondents, the delegates from international societies, the experts making objective reports, the hard-working League of Nations Association, there still yawned an unbridged gap between those who understood and those who needed to understand. While Washington was using the League to defend our national interests, our State Department at home never took time off to inform American citizens of danger ahead.

Fourteen years too late, in 1945, just a month before the atomic bomb proved all prophets wrong about everything, I found a full-page ad in the New York *Times*. Some whisky manufacturer had wrapped his product coyly in the flag, jumped on the band wagon of deeply aroused national sentiment and printed this warning:

"Take a look at just one Japanese hide-away—Manchuria. The Japs grabbed it from China in 1931. It's more than twice as big as Germany, about sixty times as big as Massachusetts. It has one of the richest soils in the world . . . wheat, corn, soy beans, rice . . . coal, magnesite, metals . . . great areas of trees. The Japs have been hustling . . . have made Manchuria a mighty arsenal. And this is just one Japanese hide-away. Can Japan fight a long war? Well—we leave it to you."

Back in 1932, our brilliant advertising profession might

have been very useful to me and to Ethan and to other Americans. I was trying to digest paragraphs like this from my husband's publication, *Geneva—a Monthly Review of International Affairs.*

"The conflict between China and Japan, serious enough in itself, is a test of the efficacy of world peace insurance. Public opinion the world over views the strife in Manchuria not only as a major diplomatic issue, with control of one of the world's crossroads at stake, but also as a means of measuring how far international relations have actually been changed since the World War. In nearly all countries, disarmament depends on the degree of security felt for the national life. If the organized peace forces of the world can succeed in settling by conciliation perhaps the gravest controversy since 1914, then the argument for disarmament will be strong; if they cannot, then the feeling that each nation's safety lies in its own strength will greatly increase."

I could read such paragraphs over two or three times, only to find my mind wandering to the thumps and laughter in the boys' room, or to my latest visitor. By being "talented" in artistic and literary ways, I had managed to escape good teaching in economics or history. I had carried over into adult life a mental block about the reality of government, and a foolish humility before the vast complexities of "politics." I was baffled by the convention of bracketing each country into an entity: "Great Britain says . . ." "France contends . . ." "Germany claims . . ." as if the map heaved up into geographical monsters who parleyed together in booming phrases. Nor had a Southern upbringing among men who perpetuate their need to feel superior under the name of "chivalry" helped me to intellectual maturity.

But I had not married a Southern man. He wanted companionship in his life-work, so I began to try to understand. The contradictions were very bewildering. While Lord Lytton and his new Commission began "preliminary discussions" of the investigating job to be done in Manchuria, preparations were under way for the long-delayed Disarmament Conference. A whole flock of newcomers drifted into town—delegates, advisers, experts, interpreters, secretaries, from every country, even Russia. There were more Americans than ever: Ambassador Hugh Gibson, Norman Davis, Senator Swanson, Miss Mary Woolley of Holyoke, all delegates to the Disarmament Conference. Crazily enough, there were more Japanese than ever, too, for Japan was still a member of the League and of the Disarmament Conference.

For some time, on the quiet rue des Pâquis, Swiss workmen had been constructing a special disarmament building, smelling of new wood and fresh paint. It looked, against the old gray Geneva houses, oddly improvised and temporary. But everyone had high hopes of permanent good from the Disarmament Conference to be housed there. At last the people of the world might be relieved of the terrific burdens of defense taxation. Reduce armaments and the standard of living in all countries would surely rise.

Lowering taxes made sense to me, but for all the countries of the world to meet together to discuss with what weapons they would kill each other, in case they quarreled, seemed crazy. If they ever reached the point of actual shooting, would anybody abide by mere agreements? Across the Pacific, in plain sight, soldiers of two of the conferring nations were murdering with the very weapons under discussion. I could not fit these two pieces of the picture puzzle together. What bothered me most was the elaborate glossing over of everybody's open secret: Japan was the aggressor and therefore the culprit. I was accustomed to curbing daily in my boys the

natural human impulse to grab. Why all this elaborate pre-
tense? Why not admit, openly, every country's selfish motives
and so clear the way to mutual concessions for the sake of the
common welfare?

The irony was not entirely in my own imagination. Jerry
came home the evening of February 2 to report that the opening session of the Disarmament Conference had been post-
poned for one hour, because the League Council had hastily
called an emergency meeting. The Sino-Japanese "dispute"
was getting completely out of hand. It was already too late.
The next day Matsuoka had found new technicalities to block
diplomatic discussion. By the time the Lytton Commission had
investigated, and returned to report that Japan was in the
wrong, the Japanese were firmly entrenched in Manchuria,
hustling, as our belated advertiser warned, to make it into an
arsenal. By that time no nation in the world was willing to send
out an army against them. The League had no international
force, no authority to summon one. Not a government leader
dared brave the ignorant public opinion of his country.

With so much time on my hands and such strange contradictions in this world at my door, I began for the first time to
think about peace. What was it, anyway? In the scant attention I had ever paid the subject, I had thought of it as a lack
of war; peace was normal, war was abnormal. Peace was what
left women like me undisturbed to carry on their personal
lives. World War I had passed completely over my head—
my chief emotion had been a youthful resentment of any
interruption of my own plans. But war kept cropping up,
growing steadily worse, like some horrible disease. The irritating truth seemed to be that peace, like health, had to be
worked for to stay alive. Otherwise it would die, anemically,
under somebody's vital impulse to grab. Maybe Wilson had
something in his League of Nations idea. Maybe Jerry and

his friends were right. And maybe the United States was very, very wrong.

With the dawn of my first patriotism came my first criticism of my country. I still felt rather foolish to have any ideas at all on politics, but I could not help seeing that America was trying to eat its cake and have it too. If we wanted peace, if we believed in general disarmament, then we had to take responsibility. We must co-operate, ahead of time, with the countries in whose disputes we kept getting involved. We must state plainly and clearly our policy and our principles, and then stick to them.

When I had reached this simple conclusion, I discovered to my surprise that I was expressing the mature convictions of Geneva's best internationalists.

Among the friends Jerry sometimes brought home for dinner that first winter was Paul Mowrer, Paris correspondent for the Chicago *Daily News*. Paul's younger brother Edgar held a similar post in Berlin, and the two used to keep each other posted almost daily by long-distance telephone. Edgar sometimes came to Geneva too. He was thin, nervous, aquiline, warm-hearted, and if he lives to be a hundred he will always keep some of the ardor of young manhood. Paul, only fortyish, looked rather like some Oriental philosopher, with his calm, light-colored eyes, his quizzical smile, his fine, bald forehead, stroked absently by a hand surprisingly small and fine-boned. Paul had a poet's heart and wrote lovely classical verse which he sometimes read aloud to privileged friends, but his mind was cold as steel and never took sides except the side of enlightenment. His emotion about peace seemed less intense than my husband's, and his concern, though no more objective, was more detached. Some of my happiest hours were spent while these two similar and dissimilar friends exchanged opinions in that offhand manner which men assume when they are most serious. One evening, as we sipped coffee on the veranda, I remarked: "Well, I don't know anything about politics, but these few months in Geneva have shown me one thing. It's less important for America to join the League than to formulate some definite foreign policy these people over here can count on."

Paul Mowrer leaned over to pat my shoulder with unusual enthusiasm.

"Good girl!" he cried, and my husband laughed.

Afterwards Jerry told me: "Paul was very pleased with you. You see, that's been his own political position for years."

I felt as abashed as *le Bourgeois Gentilhomme* when he discovered he had been speaking prose all his life. Was it possible that plain common sense—and a woman's, at that —could apply to international affairs?

ew 9 ew

The Tragicomedy of Mariette

Later that spring I enjoyed a triumph of a different sort with Paul Mowrer. For half an hour this veteran journalist-philosopher and Pulitzer prize-winner sat spellbound as I related what had been happening to my *femme de chambre* while I lay on the chaise longue. Still in the cane-and-hobble stage, I was dining with Paul and Jerry in one of those Lake restaurants tucked away behind foliage and vines, where sweet rock gardens run down to the water, shining and neat as a child's toy.

When I had finished my story, Paul, reporting on the Manchurian dispute and the Disarmament Conference for the Chicago *Daily News*, gave an envious sigh.

"Shuh!" he said. "Here we've all been feeling so sorry for you because you were laid up with a broken leg. Why, you've got the best story in Geneva!"

My first inkling of the drama came one morning soon after our return from Gstaad. I was lying in bed in my plaster cast when Mariette, in her old felt house slippers, carrying her invariable feather duster, came to *faire la chambre à Madame.*

That bunch of gray feathers on a stick, together with her trim figure, her mop of dark hair and her brilliant eyes, made her look stagier than ever. The duster became indelibly engraved on my memory. Once Mariette had begun to talk, she stood holding it idle in mid-air for two hours, while she wept and poured out her heart.

Madame would remember that Madame had asked her why she came to Geneva and she had told Madame she had friends near by. Well, she had lied to Madame. And certainly now—this was where the tears began—she was not being treated like a friend by her young man's family. They kept a hardware store at Gex, just over the French border. She and René had met at a dance in Paris, where she was a chambermaid, and instantly, it was *le coup de foudre*. Naturally—eyes and feather duster dropped shamefacedly, but not for long—with the lightning striking them both like that, things came to pass which should never have come to pass. Madame could understand because, she hinted delicately, Madame knew what it was to *bien aimer quelqu'un*. "And then, Madame"—the duster waved cheerfully upward—"one day, I learned that I was to have a little baby. I was happy. Madame has seen how I love Monsieur Ethan and Monsieur Curtis. Of course René had to tell his parents. His father was kind to me, but his mother! Oh! She taunted me with being older. It is true, Madame, I lied to René about my age, but only by two years. I am only twenty-eight—that is not so old, is it? Ah, what a fool I was to believe that woman! His mother promised, if I would have an operation, she would consent to the marriage. I suffered, Madame—how I suffered! I wanted our baby. Oh, *le bon Dieu* has punished me for my crime! I remember nothing of the operation. I was unconscious. But I should never have let them put me to sleep. I should have kept my eye on that woman!"

Mariette wiped her eyes with the back of her large, work-worn hand.

"Why, but what did she do?" My imagination was baffled.

The black eyes flashed, then tears softened them and her shoulders drooped.

"Oh, Madame! That woman had something done to me so I can have no more children. Somehow, between them, they fixed it so I can never become pregnant again!"

She turned away and sobbed, still clutching the duster.

"But, Mariette," I reassured her, "no doctor would do that without your consent. Besides, you didn't have a surgical incision, did you?"

But mere logic had no effect.

"You don't know that woman, Madame! She could arrange anything!" Mariette shook her head wretchedly. "René and I, we have been together since then. Madame understands, when one is full of temperament . . . And nothing has happened, nothing!"

She cried again, and for a moment, while I tried to think what to say next, she poked futilely with the duster at the carvings on the old Brittany wardrobe. Then she turned, her eyes flashing fire.

"Now, they won't let me marry him! Oh, they find excuses: Their business is not going well; we must wait; he is young; I have no dowry. That is true. But I have my economies put by. Why, of all the generous wages that Madame gives me, I save everything except a few francs to get my hair done before I go to Gex. Yes, Madame, that is where I always go, on my bicycle, on my Sunday afternoons off."

"And René," I asked, "does he still want to marry you?"

She shrugged her shoulders, almost as if his wishes were of no importance. The bitter fight was with his mother.

"He treats me more coldly because she influences him. He says I have changed, that I cry and make scenes."

Out of all the wisdom I could muster, I ventured in my still inadequate French to offer some advice.

"Mariette," I said, "you won't get anywhere just fighting his mother, especially if he's an only son and under her in-fluence. You've got to be the way you were when he first fell in love with you. Men hate hysterics—it makes them uncom-fortable. Remember the kind of person you were before all this happened and try to be like that again. Then maybe he'll begin to feel the old way, too."

She dried her eyes and gave me a very watery smile of gratitude. Still carrying the feathers and apparently under the illusion that her presence in the room for nearly two hours had automatically dusted it, she begged Madame's pardon and hurried off to bring the children home from the Montessori chalet.

One mid-week afternoon she burst into my veranda, in a curious state of high-pitched excitement. It was absolutely imperative that she go to Gex. I consented, for she had not been too distracted to find and pay a substitute, a soft little dove of a German girl with dark Madonna eyes, named Leni. But as Mariette's states of excitement culminating in depar-ture for Gex became the rule rather than the exception, so that Leni was serving us almost as often as Mariette, I realized, a little late, that I was just a sympathetic American damn-fool.

Besides, it rather cut my pride to discover that I was by no means her only confidante. The coiffeuse, who arrived at the house with her paraphernalia one morning, learned all about Mariette's sorrows too. The concierge of our apartment house, a small, bitter-faced woman who had once been our land-lady's maid and looked dourly upon us interlopers, thawed out long enough one day to speak to me of Mariette. How cruelly that woman had treated her, what agonies the child was suffering! Even Annie, emerging now and then like a bat from her basement, to bring me her padded account books and to ask brazenly for more cash, actually expressed a begrudging sympathy. Oh, yes, she knew—and did Madame think they had really performed that operation?

One Monday morning Annie instead of Mariette came upstairs with the morning coffee. She said in a frightened voice that Mariette's door was locked and she did not answer. The girl had come in very late the night before, disheveled and without her belt. She claimed she had tried to hang herself near René's home. Now there was no sound from her room.

Sick with apprehension, I woke my poor husband, and he struggled into bathrobe and slippers and followed Annie down the basement stairs. My coffee stuck halfway down and I felt nauseated and frozen. At last Jerry's slippers shuffled back down the hall. He was smiling.

"She's all right. But I don't think she'll be much good to you today."

It was not till afternoon that Mariette appeared, red-eyed and washed-out. Yes, she had tried to hang herself to soften René's hard heart. Two of the Gex villagers had seen her hanging to the tree and had cut her down, saying: "*Tiens*, aren't you René's fiancée?" His mother was furious and had warned her never to come back. Oh, she was through! She would never darken their doors again. All she wanted was to go home to her Papa's farm and see her *Maman*. She was homesick for the country, the fields, the animals, even the smell of the manure. As soon as her month was up, she would leave and Madame could take Leni.

But before the month was up, one Sunday evening the doorbell rang, and to save Annie the climb from the base-

ment I went to answer. In the broad entrance hall of the
apartment house stood a shamefaced man with gray hair and
a stocky little woman with a red face. Mariette, her drawn
skin as yellow as an Oriental's, a silly smile on her face, was
wandering around aimlessly over the tiled floor, now and then
pushing out her hands in strange, idiotic gestures.

"She fell ill. We brought her straight home in our car to
her good *patrons*," cried the man, eagerly, his frightened eyes
on my face.

"One good night's sleep and she will be herself again!"
nodded his wife brazenly.

I thumped over to the girl on my crutches.

"Mariette," I said, with a firmness I was far from feeling.
"It's Madame. Come in—you're home."

Her dulled eyes looked straight through me.

"*Maman, maman!*" she murmured, in a weak baby voice.

I took her hand, clammy and inhuman, and she giggled,
with an odd little sound like dried leaves rustling, and resumed her wandering. Jerry waited behind me, like a watch-
dog, and we four stood eying each other in silent distrust while
the idiot who had been Mariette whispered to herself.

The concierge, meantime, had dashed out with a shawl
over her head (the telephone apparently being too slow) to
fetch the nearest doctor, and she now returned, panting, with
a quiet young Swiss in tow. He gave us all the same long,
cold look, took Mariette's arm and, with Jerry's help, forced
her into our nearest room, the *fumoir*. He asked for cold
water and a cloth, ordered Jerry to stay, and closed the *fumoir*
door firmly. While the French couple huddled together in
the vestibule, I swung, shivering, around the blue satin salon
on my crutches. At last Jerry came for me.

"She's answering the doctor's questions now. She wants to
see you."

I hobbled in weakly to find Mariette on the couch, very pale, but recognizable. The room reeked with aromatic spirits of ammonia. I could have done with a little of it myself. The French couple hurried away, and Annie, for once actually kind-hearted, got Mariette to bed. The doctor explained to me. It had been a case of extreme hysteria apparently brought on by fright. The girl was unstable, but her self-styled "rescuers" had done something to bring this on. Perhaps I could find out what. I seemed to represent for her at the moment a symbol of goodness and justice. We had already been so kind. Would I agree to invite these people back to my home, together with himself and Mariette's priest, and let her have the whole conflict out with this woman, before me? It might be just the emotional release she needed.

I agreed. Next morning I did discover what had frightened her. It was as incredible as everything else. When Mariette had arrived at Gex that Sunday on her bicycle—yes, yes, it was true she had said she was never going back, but she had to see René once more—his mother had slammed the door in her face. She knocked and begged, she called René, then she sat down on the curb near the house and waited. The whole village strolled by on its Sunday afternoon walk and said: "*Tiens,* isn't that René's fiancée?" A crowd began to collect and his mother was furious. Stepping out on the front doorstep, she cried: "Well, if she won't go back to Geneva, I know where we can take her!" and she made some Gallic gesture symbolizing the insane asylum. From that moment on, Mariette remembered nothing until she woke up in our mustard-and-blue striped *fumoir* and saw Monsieur's familiar face.

"Oh, Madame cannot imagine how beautiful the *fumoir* and Monsieur both looked to me!"

When Monsieur Bain, the masseur, heard the dramatic

events which were everybody's secret by now, he nodded his head solemnly.

"One thing alone," he proclaimed with a portentousness of which only a Latin man is capable, "will quiet a hysterical woman. *C'est l'homme, Madame!*"

Monsieur Bain was probably right. I was encountering for the first time the Latin attitude towards what we call "sex" and they call "*l'amour*"—simple, unashamed and deeply emotional. Hysterical, too, of course, but it contrasted favorably with the frightened, childish prurience mixed with romanticism of my own American youth. Excess and abnormality exist in France as everywhere, only more openly. But my sons, who, after Geneva, lived in Paris, heard no dirty stories from other boys until they returned to their own country.

You would never have found Mariette devouring lurid love-story magazines. When she was not embroidering for her hope chest, she read a much-thumbed school edition of Victor Hugo's poetry. Novels, she said, were so untrue to life, but poetry was real—did not Madame agree?

Mariette did not only want her man; she wanted his children, and she was cheerfully ready to scrimp and scrape to put by the bit of dowry which might make her eligible for the honor of marriage. I found this admirable. With all her Latin fireworks, she had her carpet-slippered feet firmly grounded on reality.

She went about for several days, subdued, but still polishing brass door-handles with patient vigor and calling punctually for the children. In Europe work is more important than love. Europe's upper crust is perhaps more idle than ours, more coldly hedonistic, but the people take pride in well-done tasks and count labor as a natural element in existence. They are not haunted by the American dream that anybody can be a millionaire, that somewhere they may find the mechanical push-button to the Perfect Life. With all her griefs and her limitations, Mariette was richly alive.

On the appointed afternoon the doctor and the priest arrived. Mariette's father-confessor looked exactly as he should —stout, round-bellied and kind, with a great, ruddy face pleasantly wrinkled. Mariette waited below stairs while Annie scurried importantly to answer the doorbell and usher the two worried French *bourgeois* into our blue satin salon. She reported that René, whom I had not yet met, was waiting for Mariette in the *fumoir*.

I had promised to talk with him first, so I limped down the hall to the smoking room. I had just discarded crutches for a cane, which lent me, I felt, some much-needed dignity. Having lost ten pounds on the chaise longue, I did not feel very impressive.

Not expecting much—for who can understand another's love affairs?—I opened the door upon the object af Mariette's devotion. Even so, René was a distinct shock. I saw a gangling, milky youth, with a pale face and bulbous, watery eyes, who bore all the earmarks of alternate babying and henpecking by his indomitable mother.

"Mon Dieu!" cried the coiffeuse later. "All those tears for *that?* With his air of *grand bébé* and his poached-egg eyes?"

René's moist glance kept shying away from mine. He had always wanted to marry Mariette, he murmured mildly, but she had changed. He had first loved her for her amiable disposition but now she quarreled and made scenes which embarrassed his parents.

"If you'd only stand up for her with your mother," I suggested, "you'd get your old sweetheart back again," but René only looked frightened and asked if he might see Mariette alone. I hobbled over to open the door—and nearly knocked over Mariette and Annie, both glued to the keyhole!

They sprinted noiselessly back down the hall and Annie yelled loudly down to an empty basement: "Mariette! Come quickly! Madame wants you." After a credible interval, a rap came on the door and Mariette slipped in, dramatically quiet. Looking straight at me, she said icily: *"Bon jour, Monsieur!"* The father of her child, helpless as a puppy, addressed the window. *"Bon jour, Mademoiselle!"* There was a dead silence.

America, of course, stepped into the breach. As soon as I had spoken, they burst into fiery accusations. Both paced the room like tigers, passing each other coldly midway. The contrast between their fine French phrases and their shabby persons was almost more than my American risibilities could stand. The *fumoir* had never looked so pretentious or so ugly. Suddenly I saw that Mariette's feet looked very large and flat. She was still wearing her battered old carpet-slippers. Murmuring something, I escaped to the hallway, and leaning against the wall, with my cane, I laughed until my ribs ached. It gave me courage. We still had to beard the lioness in the salon.

Followed by Jerry, the doctor and the priest, I opened the paneled door. René's father, big, gentle and respectable, sat slumped in a flowered armchair, the picture of misery. His wife, only four feet high, but made of sterner stuff, perched bolt upright on the edge of the stiffest chair. Her face was purple with fury and fear; I thought she would burst before our very eyes.

We all greeted one another with that politeness which is routine in all European encounters, and then the old priest took the floor. Jerry and I, feeling as if we must be dreaming it all, did not dare to meet each other's eyes.

"And now, Monsieur and Madame," the father-confessor finished, after reviewing the story, "we must reassure this girl that she may still know the holy privilege of motherhood. I ask you both to tell me the truth about this operation."

Silence, then the mother snapped: "We know nothing of an operation."

"Nothing," lied her wretched husband, squirming in his silken chair.

"No baby and no operation!" cried the woman, growing bolder, and looking at her husband for support, but he sat silent, pulling at his gray mustache.

"Strange, strange," murmured the priest.

"But then why," I asked, grasping my cane for moral support, "would Mariette have invented such a story?"

René's mother all but spat.

"Bah! That girl would lie about anything. Didn't she lie to René about her age?"

The lovers were called in from the *fumoir*. Mariette's eyes were sparkling and René looked almost like a man. Left alone, if they had not made up, they had certainly kissed. The priest called upon the young man, before God, to speak the truth. Under his mother's glare, the boy repeated the family denial.

Mariette now burst into a loud theatrical laugh. Ha-ha-ha —what a farce! What lies! She described the abortion details zestfully, while the mother crouched, like a cat against a wall, and father and son cringed. But nothing broke down the family defense. In a burst of impatience, I cut through diplomacy.

"Well, Madame and Monsieur," I said, rising to my feet in what might under less wobbly circumstances have been dignity, "there is nothing more to be gained by talking. Mariette no longer wishes to marry your son, so perhaps we had better part."

The priest followed the trio out of the house, trying to

wring a confession, but returned to me, shaking his old head. *"Ah, la nature humaine,"* he sighed. *"C'est bien étrange!"*

Mariette, bright with triumph, packed her bags, thanked us devotedly, hugged the boys with tears and went off, lugging her two suitcases. She actually seemed less exhausted by the strange drama than I.

Gentle Leni slipped into the household as if she had always been there. We had a touching letter of gratitude from Papa's farm, where Mariette was happy to be with her dear parents again. The coiffeuse and I still laughed over the "poached-egg eyes." Summer passed, then towards the approach of winter, who should emerge from the basement one day but Mariette! Yes, she was back in Geneva and had an excellent place not so munificently paid as at Madame's, but still very good— eighty francs a month. The only objection was that she could get to Gex only every other week.

"To Gex?" I repeated in astonishment.

Oh, yes! René regretted everything and they were soon to be married. But not in a bridal veil. No—she had always said that she would wear white only if she deserved it. Mariette gave the boys a striped cornucopia of sticky candy, left her respects for Monsieur, and tripped happily away.

The next we heard was a letter from Gex. Madame and Monsieur would be content to know that she and René were now man and wife. She kept house and cooked while her mother-in-law helped her husband and son run the hardware store. The only cloud on their horizon was that she and René were as yet childless but they were hoping.

It was nearly two years before we had another communication in her spidery French hand on cheap, blue-lined paper. Madame would rejoice to know that she and her dear René were blessed with a little one—not so robust as Madame's boys but still a beautiful son. She would never forget that she owed her great happiness to Madame and Monsieur.

I got together some baby clothes and mailed them to Gex. With the old priest, I decided that human nature, especially the French, is very strange.

10

New Technique for Peace Workers

AFTER that, whenever I read that the French Cabinet had "fallen" again after violent debates, catcalls, and insults, and then re-formed under a new Premier, with the same ministers shifted about into different posts, I thought of Mariette and her in-laws. There was the same apparent instability, the same fireworks and drama, and yet somehow afterwards, on a solid basis of reality, different from our own but very vital, French life went on again. Besides, I reflected, didn't we Americans pass through similar political crises, only less often? I had always taken this for granted. Of course we fought like fiends every four years, each side passionately claiming that the rival candidate would send the country to the dogs. Of course business stood practically at a standstill. But once November's elections were past, we settled peacefully down together for Thanksgiving and Christmas. We called this a triumph of the democratic process. To foreigners, however, it looked like a crazy enigma. Perhaps the French too, in their own way, were demonstrating their brand of liberty and free speech. A Premier who steps down because he has lost the vote of confidence of his Chamber merely expresses a national temperament and history. Perhaps in a crisis, quick changes may prove no worse than an immovable object.

In the involuntary role I had played in Mariette's affairs, I saw an interesting parallel to America's role in European disputes. If my country could not always live up to the "goodness" so hopefully expected of us, we could, merely from our more detached position, symbolize justice. Geneva had already made it clear to me that at our best we offered a welcome objectiveness on deep-rooted quarrels and tangled passions. Our remoteness created our value. We could, if we would, play an important part in keeping the peace.

It was no mere accident nor even his fine personal qualities alone which kept my husband in such constant demand as a chairman for international groups abroad. If a European committee needed an impartial convener, it usually looked about for the right kind of American. He must genuinely represent his country's sentiments and concerns, and he must be at the same time a sympathetic observer of European affairs. An able Englishman not given to compliments once told me, "Your husband is the type we need over here—an international-minded American who cares so much about your own interests that he helps us to understand them. These expatriates of yours who prefer Europe do us no good."

It was in this capacity of American mediator that Jerry had made one of his first and best moves among the unofficial peace groups which cluster around any international organization. As soon as the United Nations settles into its new home, similar bands of citizens from every nation will come to live under its shadow. They will exert a powerful influence on people at home. My husband worked out a plan to get together for regular informal consultation representatives of the various national groups concerned with peace and disarmament. Around a table they thrashed out freely their viewpoints and then conveyed that agreement, however small, to their waiting organizations at home. It was called, heavily but inevitably, "The International Consultative Group."

One of the handicaps of trying to stir an indifferent public to interest in world affairs is the clumsiness of organization titles. The mystic initials of Washington in wartime were nothing compared to Geneva's peacetime alphabet. I stopped trying to keep track of my husband's memberships. The first time I picked up a fat, heavy, paper-backed volume of nearly five hundred pages from the League Publications Division, *Handbook of International Organizations,* I groaned aloud. Such names, such strange purposes, such wasteful duplication! All my popular-magazine training revolted. Actually, it was a highly useful reference volume which will have to be duplicated again by the United Nations. Here were recorded with the greatest possible brevity the essential facts—seat, foundation date, object, members, governing body, historical facts, official publications—about all the international associations, bureaus, and committees of the entire globe! Besides six official bureaus and three institutes directly under the League, there flourished about seven hundred unofficial groups. The sixteen subject divisions ran the gamut of human experience—from pacifism to medicine, religion to feminism, trade to sports and tourism. They included: International Seed-Testing Association, International Commission on Large Dams, International Cyclists Union, International League Against Rheumatism, International Commission on the Teaching of Mathematics, International Union of Food and Drink Workers, International Committee for the Campaign Against Charlatanism, International and World Federation of Cremation Societies, International Bobsleighing and Tobogganing

Federation. The International Wine Office stated as its object: "to collect, study and publish information demonstrating the beneficent effects of wine"—and its seat, naturally, was in Paris! Two organizations of ex-servicemen from the first World War, one founded in Paris and one in Rome, and a widespread interlinking association of "Mutilés de Guerre et Anciens Combattants," were dedicated to "the improvement of international relations and the maintenance of world peace." In all, Americans were members or officers. Twenty-five of the societies listed in the handbook had their seats in the United States.

The more I looked at that dull book, the more revealing it grew. Here in these overlapping international societies was a plea for unity more eloquent than emotional appeals for a better world. Patiently compiled by a League committee for practical use, the handbook represented an unconscious admission by private citizens everywhere that the affairs of this world are inextricably entangled. Isolationism had actually been nonexistent for years. Whatever governments might decide, ordinary people had known for a long time that in the sprawling hit-and-miss preoccupations of peacetime, as in the sharper exigencies of war, men and women of one country simply had to get together with men and women of other countries. So roller-skaters, authors, jewelers, department-store heads, painters, farm women, journalists, suffragists, lawyers, trade-unionists—from A—Austria to U—Uruguay, from Alcohol Abolitionists to Zionists—had all devised ways to meet together for common purposes. They had not come to blows. What was the matter, then, with political representatives in high places that they could not reach the same results?

I was beginning to grasp, because Jerry kept telling me so, over and over, that most men play politics, not for the common welfare which they publicly claim, but for the joy of power. Some of my own sex too have this drive, but the motive is alien to the average woman, who prefers her power in more intimate and more emotional spheres. But I did not need to stir from my own nursery for proof of this strange urgency in the male breast. Having no daughter, I could only remember my own childhood for comparison, and I seemed to recall that my deepest desire was to be loved and understood and to be allowed to play unmolested with my dolls, my friends, my water colors, my roller-skates and my scribblings, while my brothers were out with their comrades throwing things at the rival "Potato Gang" a few blocks away. To me a fist fight over a mere taunt never seemed worth the bloody nose with which the victor returned so proudly. I preferred to yell back another insult, stick out my tongue and go comfortably home. Yet now my two male babies, the closest of comrades, could half kill each other for a piece of rusty iron pipe hidden under the dried leaves of the little garden, and then, when the battle was won, or called to a halt by Mummie, leave its material cause unheeded and look proudly about for more worlds to conquer.

It was rather late in life to wake up to such a simple fact about the drive behind politics, but it began to answer many puzzling questions as to "what makes them do it." The trouble seemed to be that there were too many politicians working for themselves, too few statesmen working for their country, and almost no world statesmen with the genius to grasp the whole complicated globe in their gaze. The kind of men— and one meets them from all nations—wise and disinterested enough to understand the long-term international cause and effect are not the type to desire political power or to win votes if they run for office. This seemed sad but inescapable. So perhaps the only hope lay, as I had already begun to surmise, in educating the people to understand their own interests. If men could curb their belligerence and their false pride and women could rouse from their childish, self-centered indifference, and together bring pressure upon those they elect to office, who want to continue in power positions, then peace might get somewhere.

It is hard to remember just when one arrived at these gradual conclusions, but meantime, right under my nose, the International Consultative Group was, in its quiet and unobtrusive way, doing exactly that. Its method was novel and, as it proved, sound. Instead of becoming a pressure group, banding together in Geneva as spokesmen for a wide international public, it cleverly reversed the process. After finally reaching agreement around the table on the policies best for governments to follow, for the general good of all countries, they made no move to influence the important figures in Geneva's political scene. Instead, they informed the folks back home just what their mutual agreement was, and then left it to the national groups to exert their own pressure on their own governments and their delegates to the League. The Consultative Group never requested that its conclusions be adopted. Yet in practically every case, the home groups confirmed the resolutions and followed this up with action. From the first modest snowball, the Group rolled up considerable power. When it held its first public meeting in 1933, to take a stand on policies for the Disarmament Conference, telegrams of support came from Prime Ministers, Presidents and even from Molotov himself, then Foreign Commissar of the Soviet Union. (Russia was not yet a member of the League.)

But what a price that hard-working handful paid for their power! I was not the only wife who hated the Consultative Group meetings that brought husbands home late for dinner and white around the gills. Occasionally I attended a meeting, but I still knew so little that peace and disarmament seemed very remote from home and I was frankly bored. I sat sleepily through my first session, hearing little Inagaki of the Japanese League of Nations Association argue vigorously but bewilderingly for fifteen minutes about "bottled sheeps" before it dawned on me that he was discussing battleships! When Jerry asked hopefully afterwards what had struck me most, I answered honestly that it was his own remarkable talent for understanding the Japanese member!

Every important country, except Russia, came to that informal table (including Great Britain, Spain, Germany, France, the Netherlands, Japan, the United States, China). Every major peace movement had a spokesman. Many world organizations, like the Y.M.C.A., the Y.W.C.A., the Universal Christian Council, the Friends International Service, which had combined to appoint special disarmament committees, sent delegates to the International Consultative Group.

All these individuals were moved by the same impulse to do away with war. But human nature being so diverse, a common purpose by no means implies common agreement on method. With the best will in the world, peace groups can wrangle as stubbornly over a word or a procedure as any two warring nations, each convinced that it holds the key to salvation, the only road to the Temple. Those discussions held weekly while the League was in session were full of good-tempered or irritated bickering. This was where my husband's American brand of diplomacy came into its most successful play. It was partly inherited from an educator father, "wily as the snake and harmless as the dove," who successfully managed the politicians of a New England school board for years. Jerry kept his eye on the ball—common agreement—with that long-term masculine patience which still filled me with exasperated admiration. Eventually, agreement was always reached and transmitted to the people at home. Policies were advocated on the Sino-Japanese dispute, disarmament, the Italian-Ethiopian affair, Hitler and the Rhineland. When we left Geneva in 1935 an English Friend, Bertram Pickard, one of the Group's most useful members, became Chairman.

All those hours and headaches may look now like a complete waste, yet the method is more important than ever. It stands ready for use again in our immediate future. In our New York apartment dining room a shining Swiss clock, inscribed "From the International Consultative Group to its first convener, Malcolm W. Davis," still ticks accurately away—a lasting symbol of one American effort in international understanding.

᭰᭰ *11* ᭰᭰

Disarmament—When Is a Battleship Not a Battleship?

I HAD forgotten how American Americans look until our Disarmament delegates began to arrive, hallmarked "Made in U.S.A." We Geneva residents had already begun to take on some of the protective coloration of foreigners far from home: French phrases dotted our daily vocabulary; we drank wine with our meals and peeled fresh fruit at table; our children's clothes wore out and were replaced by Swiss woolens and clumpy Swiss shoes. From constant association with Europeans of limited English, Jerry and I were using fewer colloquialisms and articulating our words very distinctly. Of this we only became aware on a visit home a few years later when we were told with a touch of irritation that we had acquired an "accent." As one of my young nephews reproached: "You know, Aunt Harriet, you've learned so many foreign languages you don't speak ours right any more. Why, you talk English the way our teacher says we ought to!"

If I did, it was entirely unintentional. Indeed, nothing annoyed me more than to find myself, with a group of Britishers, imitating their clipped consonants and their broad A's. Once to a pleasant Geneva acquaintance from across the Channel I was analyzing our irrational American dislike of the English accent when she interrupted me politely:

"But, my deah, of course there's no such thing as an *English* accent. There is the English language and the American accent!"

She could not understand my amusement nor believe that Britishers sound to most of us like affected snobs. As I went on to attribute other prejudices, on both sides, to a hang-over of issues from the American Revolution, she interrupted again.

"What do you mean," she puzzled, "by the American Revolution? Are you referring to the Secession of the Colonies?"

This was my first inkling of the reason an international organization needs an educational council like UNESCO, or of the task that still remains to be done in co-ordinating the textbooks of the world, without national bias. For a moment I stepped into a British skin and saw how my own country appeared to an inhabitant of the British Isles. To our exasperated parent of centuries ago, we were still the rebellious child who had run away from home, refusing to conform to the superior habits of his elders. That the prodigal son had grown strong, rich and proud was only an additional cause for annoyance.

One soon developed a technique for giving as good as one got and felt oneself rise immediately several notches in British esteem. One observed too how roughly they treated each other, hurling personal insults into an argument, with no feelings hurt, and with an underlying assumption that everyone stood up for himself and all hands remained good friends in the end. Americans, I discovered to my surprise, while less conventionally polite, are more thin-skinned than our British cousins, who rather enjoy a good knock-down argument.

One Englishman, my partner at a huge dinner party, surveyed me down a long thin nose, above a choking high collar, and remarked with what he meant for geniality: "I suppose all Americans think that the British Court is a gay, wicked, immoral sort of place as it was in the days of George the Third?"

"Oh, no," said I impulsively. "We've seen too many photographs of Queen Mary in a hat."

My remark, more honest than witty, was a blow in the solar plexus. I almost heard him grunt. For a whole minute he sat silent, then he sighed and smiled.

"The dear old Queen," he said. "She *is* rather a frump, isn't she?"

There were no broad A's about Senator Swanson and Ambassador-at-large Norman Davis and their wives. They moved placidly and spoke softly with a Southern twang that made me homesick for the Virginia summers of my childhood and the awe-inspiring grandfather who read us Uncle Remus stories on the hot front porch.

Grandfather Board had been an all-round citizen, close to the pioneer traditions—doctor, dentist, lawyer, mayor, school-board member, notary public, library director. It was always an accolade to an unimportant little girl in a lawn dress to be smiled at on the old wooden boardwalks of Bedford City as "Doctor Boh'd's granddaughter." So my pleasure may be imagined, the first time the Swansons dined in our carved-oak dining room, when I discovered that the Senator from Virginia had known him. Jerry looked down from his end of the table in amusement to see his wife and the honor guest shaking hands vigorously over the soup.

Thereafter, Swanson always addressed me jovially and loudly as "Neighbor," somewhat to the mystification of Europeans. It was not their only mystification. Neither Claude Swanson nor Norman Davis acted like a European's idea of a diplomat. Their offhand ways, their more casual clothes, their homely similes in the Lincoln tradition, baffled Geneva. When the Disarmament Conference reached one of its many deadlocks that spring, Swanson said, "We-ell, we're tryin' to run an American train on European tracks and we got to go slow." Davis told Nadolny, head of the German disarmament delegation, "You fellows are big enough to get yourselves *into* trouble. I don't know if you're big enough to get yourselves out!"

Nadolny was furious, but not long after that the Germans made their disastrous break with the League.

Such homely directness looks impudent and childish to Europeans, shaped for centuries in the frock-coat and high-hat school of diplomacy. When this simplicity combines with innocence of moral intention, it is misread as naïveté. Few Europeans saw through Norman Davis' bland smile to the shrewdness in his blue eyes. Even for Edmond Kapp, a sensitive and brilliant artist from London, doing a series of Geneva lithograph portraits for the British Museum, our Ambassador-at-large remained an enigma. When "Peter," as we called him, had finished Norman Davis's portrait, he brought it to Jerry and me in apologetic depression.

"That's the way I see him—a businessman trying to look like a statesman."

Peter accepted our protests, but he never saw the face we saw. He struggled for days over a portrait of Jerry, throwing away sketch after sketch. The spirit, being old England, eluded him. Even I, a quite transparent American type, puzzled him.

"You're completely modern," he once exclaimed, "and yet you *look* so old-fashioned!"

With each of these friendly misunderstandings one learned not to trust one's own snap judgments of foreigners. We all have a tendency to prefer the familiar faces of our own conditioning. None of us can escape the instinct; we can only give it conscious correction.

It was a Spanish friend, more discerning than most, who reported to us with chuckles the gossip of the corridors about our new Ambassador-at-large. Alfonso Albeniz, son of the composer, was an aviation specialist, Spanish delegate to the Disarmament Conference, and member of my husband's Consultative Group. A handsome, affectionate man with the mingled sophistication and childlikeness of the Spaniard, he was lonely in Geneva without his wife and children, and he dined frequently in our home. It had not occurred to me that we were doing anything out of the way for Alfonso until one evening, as he kissed my hand in Latin farewell, he said, with moist eyes: "I am so touched that you invite me, intimately, *en famille*."

In the United States the more honor we wish to show a guest, the more formal the occasion must be. In Europe formal meals are social duty, and home life remains almost barred to the outsider. The Europeans do not have our pioneer tradition of hospitality to a passing stranger.

The other disarmament delegates, Alfonso told us, were saying of Norman Davis: "This man is a child, an innocent pretending to be a diplomat!" Actually, no ambassador ever had a more delicate situation to negotiate. Davis faced the almost insuperable task of finding a way for America to co-operate with the League on the Far Eastern war which would please both Washington and Geneva. Our position must remain legally within the limits of the international agreements we *had* signed and at the same time not violate any of the League principles. It was hardly a child's task.

Davis was a far-sighted diplomat. I heard him say that the real problem confronting the League and the Disarmament

Conference was how to prevent any nation from trying to alter existing circumstances by force, and at the same time to begin working out an orderly readjustment of the grievances which might incite them to aggression. The two horns of the same dilemma now confront the United Nations.

Early that spring France startled Geneva into a buzz of talk by proposing what was then a brand-new innovation: a system of "collective security," placing internationalized air forces at the service of the League. That made sense to me, but I soon decided I must be all wrong, for on every side one heard amused jeers: "Isn't that just like the French? Drawing up a nice, logical plan on paper that looks good but would never work." It was rapidly turned down by the nations' delegates on disarmament. Thirteen years later a sobered world, still deep in blood, met in San Francisco and placed authority over national air forces at the service of the new Security Council of the new United Nations.

At the time, however, we were all, including the United States, exacting concessions of others before making any ourselves. The belief that armed strength instead of co-operative action brings protection persisted as blindly as it does in many people's minds today. To one who watched this illusion slowly culminating in war, there is tragedy in a *New Yorker* cartoon of the lady asking, "How much more will we have to re-arm before we can be at peace with the whole world?" Very soon now, the United Nations will face the dilemma of mutual agreements on disarmament, as the League of Nations faced it with utter failure—fourteen years ago. All the same old problems, weary ghosts in new clothes, will haunt the new table.

"As soon as the people of the world realize," said Norman Davis that spring, "that the World War is the chief cause of this unprecedented depression, when they understand that we cannot get relief without reducing the burden and the menace of armament, I believe that public opinion will help do the necessary work. But will this realization come in time? The only two alternatives are disarmament or disaster."

This statement of our "innocent pretending to be a diplomat" sounds startlingly modern today.

Norman Davis was not the only important American in Geneva trying to wangle our way through an ambiguous position. Stimson, Secretary of State, caused a flurry in our international town by appearing in person. Time had been when the United States would not even answer correspondence from the League. Now one of President Hoover's Cabinet members was calling on the Secretary-General, conferring with large and small powers, inspiring confidence in America's promises to the Disarmament Conference. While I still lay on my chaise longue, pouring tea for some of the new American observers from home groups, Ambassador Hugh Gibson, head of our Disarmament Delegation, was clarifying confusion in a more vital sphere. Geneva's attention was distracted between the reality in Manchuria and the still unresolved theories of disarmament. The six commissions of the Conference got immediately into a Corticelli-kitten snarl between defining general principles and getting down to technical discussion about which arms should be eliminated. It was like deciding whether to design your house first or to start shopping for the furniture. Gibson cleared the air by submitting a resolution to reach agreement on certain principles first, so that the commissions could then proceed to details.

Those early weeks, trying to get sixty-one nations to agree merely on how to proceed to try to agree, qualified under the Department of Utter Confusion. A Preparatory Commission had been for six years drawing up what was currently referred to as the "Draft Convention." (Before the United Nations is much older, a dictionary of international jargon should be compiled by someone—not a specialist, however, for like the Cabots, they speak only to other specialists and God.) It took me awhile to discover that in international parlance a "Convention" is not the whooping theatricals of an American Presidential election, nor is a "Draft Convention," as one's frivolous mind might imagine, a Republican rally with windows open to the fresh air. A "Draft Convention" is merely a tentative outline of an agreement offered for further debate. If accord is reached it is then legally ratified. But despite this Draft Disarmament Convention so painstakingly prepared, the deadlock of the opening sessions made clear an old political dilemma. Which came first—the chicken or the egg, the French demand for security or the German insistence on equality?

At this point an Easter recess was declared, and the world's tired delegates scattered gratefully to the tonic air of the mountains or the lazy spring sunshine of Southern France and Italy. The Sweetsers were giving a big Easter party and the Davises were all invited. Thereby hangs the tale of how Curtis and I furthered Swanson's political career. Grandfather Board would have relished the story.

✦ *12* ✦

The Easter Egg and the Senator

Ruth Sweetser and I had already begun an informal exchange of our children on Thursdays, the European school holiday. One week her Alan, a slender, blond angel, came for lunch and a romp in our pocket handkerchief of a garden. The next Thursday Ethan and Curtis rode off in the Sweetsers' car for a happy day at Mérimont, a lovely, rambling country estate overlooking the majestic stretch of the Jura. From their first visit my babies returned dirty and blissful to report a wonderful lunch—crabs and strawberry jam!

"You mean the big people ate crabs and you ate jam?"

They shook their blond heads. No, Curtis had eaten four crabs and Ethan had eaten six, all full of strawberry jam, and why didn't Annie cook some too? My stomach crawled.

"But you don't like fish at home."

"Fish?" Ethan cocked his head in affectionate scorn. "Mummie! It was *crabs*. That's what the Sweetsers call their pancakes!"

So *crêpes*, huge, crisp and rolled over jam, became our Thursday luncheon dish too. Quite an international crew had begun to collect in our home on school holidays. Little Colette Streit brought her blond curls and her perfect French. There was Norwegian Eric, Lange's grandson. There was a Belgian "Pierre" from the International School who was, Ethan explained patiently to me beforehand, not a stone but a boy. There was young David Hsia, whose father was head of the Chinese legation and is now chief Chinese delegate to the United Nations. Sometimes, to his mother's astonishment and Annie's disapproval, there was our concierge's little Daniel. He wore a tiny black apron and high red felt slippers, and it was months before I could convince my overalled young Americans that he was not a girl. Daniel was a sad, rambunctious baby, always playing alone in the barred cement areaway outside their basement apartment. Now and then he was yanked in for a meal or a spanking from his unhappy mother or curses from his father. It was from this three-year-old Swiss that we innocent Americans learned the worst insult in the French language.

Descending peacefully at our corner from the Ceinture trolley, I saw a respectable woman shaking her finger angrily up at our terrace garden, where Curtis lolled cheerily in his red knitted suit, grinning down on her, six feet below. From the other direction, a Swiss gentleman with a cane was approaching. Suddenly, Curtis shouted: "*Salaud!*" It was a shot in the arm. The Genevese looked up sharply, and Curtis, who had been painstakingly gathering his ammunition, spat accurately down upon the upturned forehead. His victim raised the elegant cane, and my son trotted hurriedly back into the protecting darkness of those valuable bushes. Torn between a longing to grab my offspring or to turn tail and run, I compromised by a dignified advance, trying to look like a refined maiden lady who had never given birth to a disreputable baby, and whose connection with 4 avenue de Champel was wholly coincidental.

Curtis listened, abashed but astonished, to my reproaches. The spitting, yes, he grinned sheepishly, but the word? Why, Daniel and his Papa said it all the time!

A similar phase in "bad" English words had been successfully skirted back in New Haven by paying no attention. But this international situation was complicated. We represented America abroad. We might be asked to leave our correct apartment house. Jerry's position might be jeopardized. Suppose Curtis spat on an ambassador!

Curtis listened, amused, to my explanations that you don't use words that hurt people's feelings, and if he couldn't remember, I would have to—well, I'd wash out his mouth with soap. I felt ashamed of my old-fashioned impulse, but nothing else came to mind. Eventually, after several sessions at the wash basin with my poor baby bawling through the suds like a portly dwarf with hydrophobia, it worked. Grandmother's remedy probably prevented an international incident.

At Mérimont that Easter noon the little Davises found a motley Babel of playmates such as only Ruth would have the courage to collect. She managed to combine harried mothers tagged by all their offspring with bachelors to whom a child was at best an amusing domestic animal, celebrities with nonentities, and fun out-of-doors for small fry with conversation over sherry for their elders. All those years when the United States clung to its ambiguous isolationism, the Arthur Sweetsers filled an important gap by serving indefatigably as unofficial American hosts to the world. It was not only the "big shots" they entertained. A quiet professor arriving in Geneva to study the League, a group of summer students, a newly appointed young consul, sooner or later almost every American was invited to a tea or a luncheon at Mérimont.

Hunting Easter eggs around "Brick House"—a play home built by the Sweetser children—was a family tradition. My two babies, looking very small against the gorgeous backdrop of majestic snowy mountains, trotted solemnly off, each clasping a bright-colored basket. Their "best" suits of brown jersey had not yet lost the tailored smartness of a good New York department store. A young girl spoke to me shyly, with tears in her eyes:

"Oh, they make me so homesick! They look just like my little brother."

As we grownups from the four corners of the earth stood enviously watching, Senator Swanson strolled out from the house, where some of the men, who could not drop Disarmament even for an Easter recess, had been holding him captive. He was standing benignly surveying the clusters of children when Curtis, clutching his purple basket full of gaudy hard-boiled eggs, wandered over to our group. Bearing straight for Senator Swanson, he thrust his treasure into the lean brown fingers.

"Here, Man," he ordered. "Hold this for me!" and as Swanson nearly dropped his cigar in surprise, my son trailed off to the farthest end of the garden. Everyone laughed. When Ruth appeared presently to call us in for lunch, Swanson shook his head, proudly:

"No! That boy trusted me! I'm going to wait here until he gets back."

The rest of us drifted into the dining room, where a long flower-laden table was set for sixteen. Children were chattering like bright-eyed monkeys around another groaning board, flanked by smiling nurses and maids in white aprons. The last I saw of Swanson, he was finishing the stub of his Virginia cigar and peering down the garden, while the icy spring wind from the Jura ruffled his white hair but not his composure.

Later, he joined us in the dining room, minus the basket, and took his place as honor guest at Ruth's right.

Of course the story was too good to keep. Knowing how the folks back home love to hear of encounters with "important" people, I wrote the episode to a sister in Swanson's native state and then forgot the incident.

The Disarmament Conference resumed its sessions and Jerry again began to come home late to dinner. Since the United States, through Gibson, had offered the plan of procedure, we had to make the first move. Even in the smallest club, if one proposes an idea, one pays the penalty by becoming chairman of the new committee! But for all its august aura of officialdom, America's new proposition struck me as tomfoolery and nonsense. Of course I said nothing, but the remembrance is now a pleasant little sop to my ego, and an encouragement to other women who bring only common sense and no special knowledge to the world's affairs. Believe it or not, our revered State Department proposed this guiding principle in disarmament: Decide which weapons should be abolished by making a distinction between "aggressive" and "defensive" arms. The idea was that by abolishing tanks, heavy guns and gases ("aggressive"), a nation could still protect itself with battleships and airplanes ("defensive"). These elaborate discussions seemed to me to make about as much sense as the medieval argument about how many angels could stand on the point of a pin. Looking back, I can only concur even more heartily with myself of fifteen years ago. They *were* nonsense and tomfoolery.

But England, through Sir John Simon (labeled by the incorrigible newspaper crowd "Sir John Slime-on"), backed up the United States. Beautiful Grandi, making the hearts of the ladies in the gallery go pit-a-pat, agreed for Italy. He proposed to abolish also bombing airplanes, capital ships, submarines

and aircraft carriers as "offensive." Now, however, Tardieu
spoke up for France. Weapons were, after all, aggressive
or defensive according to how they were used. He proposed
instead placing the most dangerous arms at the service of an
international commission.

Again I found myself in secret sympathy with the realistic
French. They were no better, when it came to assuming international responsibilities, than the rest of us, but at least they
made fewer highfalutin' assumptions of nobility. Once a war
started, I reflected, how could anyone distinguish between
offensive and defensive arms? If, even in peacetime, governments twisted technicalities about for their own immediate
purposes, in war every nation would use any weapon to win.
Take the "offensive" hammer away from an angry child and
he could still throw the "defensive" scissors. Then, while
your back was turned, he would grab up the hammer again.
Oh, no—I had settled too many scraps in the Champel garden.
Yet I felt uneasy not to be agreeing with my own country's
position. My mind struggled, like a Puritan with his conscience, to accept the edicts of the mighty. In the Conference
the two viewpoints clashed. Result: deadlock. The question
was placed on the agenda for further discussion and eventually a highly unsatisfactory compromise was reached.

One agreement was achieved, however: to disarm gradually.
That suited every nation. Then the various commissions proceeded to discuss "practical" details. America and Great Britain condemned submarines as "aggressive" while safeguarding
their own navies by labeling battleships and airplane carriers
"defensive." Italy declared that only ships of over ten thousand
tons were "aggressive." ("Creatures over ten feet high should
leave the courtroom.") Japan claimed that no naval arms were
"aggressive" except airplane carriers. Again the French protested: navies are aggressive or defensive according to how

they are used. Flame-throwers, along with gas and bacteriological warfare, were unanimously ostracized.

My conscience and I were still struggling with a simple maternal horror at legalized murder in any form, at the stupidity of discussing what to kill boys with instead of how to prevent killing at all, when something happened that temporarily eclipsed for me the entire Disarmament Conference.

Jerry came home, poker-faced, from his office one evening and laid at my dinner plate a long clipping from some Virginia newspaper passed on by the Information Section of the League. There, to my horror, I read my entire letter about Swanson and the Easter basket, including my description of our disarmament delegate as "a typical shrewd, humorous old Southern politician." Remembering even more indiscreet communications, I cabled frantically home: "PRINT NO MORE LETTERS."

But already the story in my sister's home-town paper had been picked up and copied in other states. Curtis and I seemed to have started something.

For days I went dodging about Geneva, trying to avoid the Swansons until Arthur good-naturedly offered to act as mediator. He telephoned me, chuckling.

"Why, the old chap's tickled to death! He wants to see you."

So, when I could gather my courage, I put on my best hat and went to the Hotel des Bergues to interrupt Swanson's preoccupations with naval parity.

"Howdy, Neighbor!" he hailed me, more jovial than ever. He laughed at my apologies.

"Why, little lady, you couldn't have done anything better for me, politically! Do you realize that story has traveled all over the United States? Editorials have been written about it —'the man who kept faith with a little child'!"

And with twinkling eyes Swanson launched into his glorified version of the story until his own eloquence began to hypnotize the Senator himself and he forgot, as he gestured largely, that his audience of one was too far from home to vote and not a Virginia resident anyway.

That summer Swanson was called home, the Disarmament Conference bogged down completely, and the Senator became Franklin Delano Roosevelt's First Secretary of the Navy, with a new armament building slogan: "A Navy Second to None." I used to wonder sometimes, as we paid our increased income tax, if Curtis and I had not helped to turn a disarmament delegate into a Cabinet member.

ᑫᔭᔭ 13 ᑫᔭᔭ

Home—The Great Illusion

LOOKING back to those cosy days in Geneva, I marvel at my own stupidity in the face of the gathering storm. If war is "the Great Illusion" for men, home with its deceptive air of security is an even greater illusion for women, especially for the contented mother of small children. It all felt so safe, that blue-satined nest perched on the edge of nothingness.

It never occurred to me, even living at the very heart of the slowly accumulating tragedy, that I was merely repeating my mother's pattern. I can see her now, looking up with amused exasperation from her mending when Father groaned aloud over the latest European situation reported in the Baltimore "Sun-paper."

"Seems to me they're always 'situating' over there," she would retort with her wry smile. "There's nothing you can do about it. Anyway, everything goes on just the same."

But everything did not go on just the same in America. All four of the boys whose socks she was so devotedly darning grew up to be drafted in World War I, and my oldest brother's business, on which part of the family income depended, was wrecked by it. World War II is over, and a whole crop of new "situations" stemming from the old ones confronts our country and our world. Mother and Father lie peacefully beyond all worry now, but their grandchildren fought the second conflict and their great-grandchildren may die in a third one. Or perhaps the pattern is broken now. Perhaps young Americans today are not wrapping themselves in the cotton wool of first love and early parenthood. Perhaps these girls know with their hearts as well as their heads that almost overnight treble voices deepen to bass, fat legs in socks grow lanky enough for uniform, and the baby you protected with your life must march away to die for you, grown suddenly middle-aged and helpless. Perhaps they know this now. I hope so.

For if women ever banded together to extend their protective urge beyond their own front doors, they could split something more powerful than the atom. If they could somehow get behind the men of vision, together they might bring some realism into the concept of patriotism. A nation might be seen for what it is—a piece of geography filled with human beings who share the same historical memories but who would rather live for a real future than die for an exploded myth. All those fancy names—"patriotism," "sovereignty," "national honor," even (save the mark) "national security"—for which a mother is expected to murder her sons and be proud of it, are masculine concepts, a shadowy extension of the power craving. By our indifference, by our failure to keep that urge from running amok, we women share equally the bloodguilt of war. But if we ever grow up enough to harness our instinct for saving life to political action, a country might become part of a larger world, and something to live for, not to die for.

Myself I can offer only as the bad example. Even in Geneva, even with a husband so intensely concerned, it was a long time before I saw beyond my nose. My mind, of course, was beginning to grasp some of the problems, but my heart, that mainspring of a woman's action, lived cheerfully untouched. A sniffle and a flushed cheek, a cough in the night, a banged knee, could throw me into a panic of protectiveness. But the slow disintegration of the Disarmament Conference, the spreading blot of war in the Far East, the inconsistent advance and retreat in the policy of the Washington leaders to whom Americans had confided their destiny, remained quite unreal. I never saw—because I did not want to—that all these dull and complicated meetings were deciding the life or death of the amusing little boys and girls who yelled and scuffled about our garden. Conscientiously I was trying to train my boys towards a self-controlled freedom as good American men in a prosperous democracy, but the possibility of war I left completely out of account. As for most of my fellow countrymen, it was so easy for me to believe that the future must automatically be better than the past. I never dreamed that it could be worse, or that Ethan and Curtis would someday have to bend their inquiring minds to the blind, sterile, military discipline I abhorred.

Nowadays a mother who is not also a thoughtful citizen is not a good mother, and I did not even have the excuse of most American women of being overwhelmed with domestic chores. One insignificant wife on Lake Geneva could hardly have altered destiny by neglecting her job and taking to the soapbox, but I might have begun earlier trying to explain to other women what I had learned.

Perhaps it was to stifle my own conscience that I used to argue with Jerry that it was all so hopeless and one person could do nothing, anyway. These discussions usually occurred after he had been overworking, typing until midnight and then dashing out into the cold to catch the boat-mail with his private reports to Dr. Nicholas Murray Butler and the Carnegie Endowment trustees, or accepting another committee chairmanship or holding up dinner because he had been clarifying the American viewpoint to a Russian.

Where my cheerfulness was immediate, my husband was often overharassed by the present. Yet his philosophical optimism took a far longer range than mine. His urge, of course, was as masculine in its way as the more usual power drive, just as my need to be happy now was a normal woman's impulse. So it annoyed me to watch him plugging away so doggedly at his unseen objective, half killing himself for an ideal that could never be achieved in his lifetime.

"But some of us have got to keep working at this thing," he used to answer me. "Sure—*I* can only do what *I* can do. But I *can* do that."

"But it may be all for nothing!"

"It may. Perhaps we can't get rid of war. Perhaps the human race is too stupid to learn that even when we win, we lose. We may have another world war and even a third, and if so the United States is bound to get involved. But even so, afterwards some of us will have to keep on working at this thing of getting all nations to settle their disputes by arbitration."

"Oh well," I said, "we're all just a lot of ants on a chip, being carried downstream in a whirlpool. It's too big for us."

"Even so," Jerry persisted obstinately, "I still believe that if all the ants would get together on one end of the chip, they might shift the direction and get safe to shore."

I laughed, for he was an experienced sailor.

"And they might all get drowned."

"They might. But don't you think it's worth trying, for the sake of the boys?"

And Jerry pulled over his face that expression which one of his most admiring secretaries used to call his "dead-cat look,"

New England's mask over emotion. For the possible war which remained an unpleasant theory to me was for him an ever-present and horrible reality. When it actually occurred, he was far less upset than I.

I had been relieved, however, to discover that my internationalist was by no means a pacifist and that he believed in teaching the boys to defend themselves. Jerry had been leader of his gang in the old Hartford days, and his baby sons never tired of hearing about the day he climbed the fence and socked a member of the rival bunch smack in the face with a tomato so beautifully ripe it was quivering. Though not large, nor tall, he had been strong for his age, and very quick, so he was often chosen to settle affairs of honor with a candidate from the other side. He usually won these fist fights but he told me, reminiscing, that he never enjoyed them. Even as a kid, he said, the whole thing seemed both boring and stupid, and he only acted out of loyalty to the gang.

Like all the best of the internationalists, both American and European, whose concern for peace brought them to Geneva, he gave the same troubled loyalty to his country. It was because they knew that once war started, they would have to see the thing through to its hideous bloody finish that they worked so desperately to avert a start of trouble. Some held positions directly in the Secretariat, some reported current problems for home newspapers, some went back to lecture or write for an often indifferent public, some tried to induce politicians in power to understand the long-term repercussions of short-sighted national policies.

Except for the Quakers, whose courage one deeply respects, one met few out-and-out pacifists in Geneva. The sweetness-and-light sentimentalists were usually women of the type whose hearts weigh heavier than their heads. These came mostly from the romantic Northern, not the earthy Southern, countries and they were very well-meaning and very irritating. I used to wonder how the men ever put up with them. Of course many remarkable women took part in the work for peace, but there were always plenty of chicken-brained ladies pestering people with questions they did not really want answered. Time and again one heard them ask earnestly:

"Oh, Mr. So-and-So, do tell me what you think about this-and-that?" but before the expert had opened his mouth they added eagerly: "Now *I* think . . ." and proceeded to unload upon his weary ears a string of untenable theories in the best stream-of-consciousness style.

They were so severe with the League, too. "But why doesn't the League *do* something?" they fumed. "If the League would just take a strong moral stand . . ."—as if an international organization were a sovereign body able to act independently of the governments which had signed its limited charter. Obviously they had never read the Covenant of the League of Nations. They felt injured to be reminded that the most high-minded and far-seeing delegate is helpless against a stubborn home administration.

One Disarmament Conference session was rendered completely inaudible for me by an ample American in a picture hat loaded with pink roses, who sat in the Visitors Gallery buzzing personal chitchat in my ear, like Alice's annoying gnat. Finally she rose with a discouraged sigh. Frowning down upon the tired delegates from many countries, she leaned over to press her large bosom against my shoulder and whispered loudly: "Oh, wouldn't it be *wonderful* if they'd all have a change of heart and decide to Turn Unselfish?"

These silly sisters led Herbert May of the Opium Board to remark that all the charming American women stayed in America because of personal lives, all the clever and intelligent ones because of jobs—but all the rest came to Geneva!

I encountered the same sort of sentimental idealism in some women educators, especially towards the question of letting boys fight or learn the use of weapons. One teacher told me with the utmost conviction that if you removed all toy weapons from children for a generation, you could stop war, forever. I reminded her that even without the pistol there was a stick, and without the stick there was the fist. I argued that a mother of sons can only guide, she cannot falsify their masculine nature. I quoted Madame Montessori, who said that adults do not make war because they once played with toy guns; children play with toy guns because they see adults making war. But of course neither of us ever convinced the other.

On the very eve of the Disarmament Conference, Ethan and Curtis came bursting into my veranda like two rosy elves, proudly popping their first weapons. I had sent them out for a walk with Mariette, and they had promptly exchanged their fifty centimes from Daddy's salary from an Endowment for International Peace for two very shiny, very noisy cap pistols. Like an armaments manufacturer in wartime, some canny Swiss shopkeeper had seen golden opportunity in the current Geneva topic. Mariette, who came from a country so often invaded that to her a man with a gun was second nature, explained that she had tried to persuade them to buy a box of beautiful officers on horseback, but they didn't seem to understand what they were for. Annie was charmed and called them proudly "her little soldiers." I said nothing, so between bath and supper, and supper and bedtime, the brothers happily "killed" each other—bang, bang, bang!—all over the veranda rug, their blue eyes bright with the new sense of power. At last, dead tired from their many deaths, they climbed into bed, firmly tucking the pistols under their pillows "to show Daddy."

I was not sure how Daddy would take it, but to my relief he

agreed with me. The weapon was of no importance. Forbidding it might only whet their appetite. A home where he feels loved and secure will eventually dispose of primitive belligerence in any child.

At our children's first American summer camp in Maine we found an unexpected ally. When Ethan and Curtis had lived abroad five years, I began to worry about their eventual adaptation to their own country. The British, who send boys from home very young, solve this by boarding schools in England, but I was American enough to believe that a child's place is in the home. Besides, it seemed a pity not to give our sons the benefit of the European education, usually possible only for the sons of the rich. Happily, we hit on the plan of sending them back to the United States for two months in one of our best national institutions, the summer camp. So we found Camp Kawanhee in Maine, where Ethan and Curtis spent many happy summers. Our theory justified itself and was one of the wisest moves we ever made, for the boys had little difficulty, as some foreign-raised children do, in adjusting to American boy life.

All the way over on the steamer the chief goal of their excited anticipation had been a New York ten-cent store. Like that February day in Geneva, they bought lavishly of toy machine guns, tanks, bombers, Buck Rogers Disintegrating Pistols—every weapon, aggressive or defensive, in Mr. Woolworth's arsenal. The whole collection traveled to Maine in their camp trunks, to be unwrapped from its protecting handkerchiefs and socks by a wise young counselor. Shaking his head, he put every treasure aside to be returned at the end of the season.

"At Kawanhee," he smiled, "we never let our boys play at killing each other with toys. We have a rifle range under expert supervision. Every camper learns to handle a real rifle. That way he realizes how dangerous it is."

Ethan and Curtis and my Geneva-born baby Malcolm, when he reached the camp age, all learned to shoot on that range, winning their diplomas as marksmen, first and second class, sharpshooters, and so on. Not one of them has ever expressed the slightest interest in personally owning a weapon.

Ethan, when the time came, accepted along with other American boys of seventeen the necessity of beating the Germans and the Japs. When he enlisted in the Navy, he found the marksmanship training child's play. But on his first leave home he said to me soberly: "I suppose when you're in battle you can do anything. But so far, I don't see how I could really *kill* another man."

I remembered how conscientiously his parents and his educators both abroad and at home had all worked to foster this decent and manly respect for human beings. From the State Department down to his own mother, I felt, America had handed Ethan and his generation a pretty raw deal.

∽ 14 ∽

Red Rosettes in the Old Square

GENEVA, like any town, had its own intensely absorbing local affairs, and on these my plump coiffeuse on the rue du Glacis became my authority. As for most Genevese, the League was for her little more than a rather boring visiting convention which raised living costs for the real residents. This brisk and sturdy woman and I chatted endlessly about everything. She confided how her husband wanted her to have a baby but she was afraid. Was it so terrible? She and her husband were excellent friends, but she was not like her French sister-in-law, always pestering him for *l'amour*. It was fatiguing for a man—wasn't it?—after the day's work. Still, what was a ménage without a child? Evidently I calmed her fears, for a year later she gave birth to a daughter and turned her shop over to her assistant.

America, she informed me, was a wonderful country. Her man worked for an American company. Americans were very *chic* to their employees, always showering them with bonuses and prizes. It was the "Kawl-Gaht" Company. I said I had never heard of it, and she protested—why, it was one of the biggest. Suddenly it dawned on me—Colgate! Later I learned from a member of the firm that her diligent husband not only outsold annually every salesman in Switzerland but practically every Colgate employee in all Europe. In any event I basked in his reflected glory, and his wife could always shift appointments for her American client.

It was the coiffeuse who told me about Nicole and the Social Democrat party, which was trying to win control of Geneva's City Council. The First Families felt the world was coming to an end, but my coiffeuse, though no radical, just a comfortable bourgeoise, declared that *les aristos* had brought Socialism on themselves.

"First families—pah! With their fine airs and their intermarriage! They treat us working people like untouchables. Hah—if they only knew how we despise them, what we say behind their backs!"

The morning after the *émeute*, a local tragedy about which Geneva talked for months, she was quivering with indignation. Jerry and I were sitting placidly on our veranda one November evening of 1932 when a sudden, sharp rattle made us jump. We were not hardened in those days to quick, wholesale, mechanical death. I had never in my quiet life heard machine-gun fire, but, like the warning of a rattlesnake, I knew. Nor was I deceived when Jerry remarked with careful casualness that it was probably a car backfiring.

Nicole and his Social Democrats were holding a political meeting in a hall fronting on the wide square of the Plainpalais. The conservative government still in power had posted soldiers to keep order and, according to my coiffeuse, had deliberately called in raw recruits from the canton de Vaud, traditionally at odds with the canton of Geneva. These unseasoned boys were ordered, in case of trouble, to fire machine guns into the air. Shoved about by a quarreling crowd of rival Genevese, they lost their heads and fired at random. A dozen innocent citizens were killed or wounded. The Swiss papers were full of the tragedy, and the war in the Orient, never of much local interest, was relegated to an inside page. I remember touching accounts of a beloved and honest butcher, whose hearse was followed by weeping neighbors and customers. He had been merely sitting in a near-by café, sipping a drink after the day's work.

The coiffeuse and I shivered together over this imminence of violent death from political disagreement. Why, it might have been she, or I with my children, strolling across the fatal square! And then, the way women do, we switched to the serious problem of a permanent for fine hair like mine, and she entertained me roguishly with a story of an amorous salesman who accused her of being exactly like her country, a volcano buried under ice.

My first impressions of Geneva had been correct. We might just as well have been in dear old Paterson, New Jersey.

One year later Nicole and his Socialists won out. They polled a majority for the City Assembly, and their leader became the chief executive of the City Council. I was less interested in these November elections than in a party the Davises were planning to throw on the twelfth of December. The *Fête de l'Escalade* was Geneva's big day, a kind of patriotic Mardi Gras. Every shop window displayed big and little soup kettles, of wood, of copper, of brass, of peanut brittle, of chocolate, all overflowing with candy vegetables. Over each presided a woman puppet with gray hair brandishing a wooden spoon as long as herself, while toy soldiers in helmets hung on a cardboard rampart below. The puppet was Mère Royaume, legendary heroine of Geneva's victory over the Duke of Savoy in 1602. The soldiers were the Savoyard troops sent by the treacherous Duke late one December night to scale the walls around the Protestant Cathedral of Saint-Pierre and capture the city. An old woman stirring her vegetable soup in her kitchen near the ramparts caught sight of the dark figures and dumped her boiling pot over their heads. This gave the good Protestants time to yank on their clothes hit and miss, rush out and save Calvin's city.

So every December 12 thereafter the Genevese donned hit-and-miss carnival costumes and flocked out into the cold streets with a hilarity of which Calvin would hardly have approved. Voltaire, who loved the city too, from Verney near by across the French border, must have turned chuckling in his grave.

The Davises had already reacted from the correctness of diplomatic occasions by seizing every excuse for an informal party. The *Fête de l'Escalade* seemed almost as good as our Halloween. So we invited in a gay crowd of Americans with a few British, and shortly after midnight, bundled in wools and furs and all wearing false noses, we braved the freezing night to mingle with all Geneva on the streets. Stars shone frosty in a blue-black sky, the bitter air caught at our lungs and sent tears trickling down around the edges of our papier-mâché noses. Laughing boys and girls, arms around each other, whole families of Genevese working people, were crowding upwards to the medieval square of Saint-Pierre Cathedral. One grinning youth, his teeth shining in a blackened face, seized our prettiest American girl and shook her fondly:

"*Eh, la petite!*" he cried. "*Tu es trop jolie!* That nose, it doesn't do you justice!"

I even bumped into the coiffeuse, who hailed me with a raucous shout considerably stimulated by good white wine. We followed the crowd up the steep *Degrés de Poules*—the Hen Steps—to the Cathedral Square. That cobbled court on the hill, with its dim and gentle air of protection, was always worth the breathless climb. Here, for a moment, one breathed a soothing peace from a past that seemed still potent and still alive. The great cathedrals—Milan, Rheims, Chartres—are timeless in their beauty. But plain Saint-Pierre, flanked by worn stone houses with graceful windows so close to the chimes, always brought the Middle Ages alive with uncanny vividness. One could feel Calvin here, too, casting his long, cold, righteous shadow over his beloved town.

Tonight the Square, though dark with huddled figures, still belonged to the past. Then, around the corner came the Midnight Procession. Flaming torches borne aloft, a man on a white horse carrying the original scroll which had pro- claimed victory, the descendants of the original defenders in costumes from Geneva's Historical Museum—they all pre- served the medieval illusion. At their head marched a few men in ugly modern overcoats, felt hats in hand. The spell was broken. We were back in the present. I noticed bright red rosettes in their lapels and mistook them for a carnival note.

"Striking, aren't they?" whispered Jerry, to whom I was huddling very close to keep warm. "Those Socialist emblems in the old square?"

"Oh, so that's what the rosettes are for!"

"Of course. That's Nicole and his Cabinet. I'm told the old families kicked up quite a row at being led to the Cathedral by Socialists."

We did not know it then, but we had seen, that night, one of the first Leftist chinks in the social structure of Europe.

ᴄᴀᴍ 15 ᴄᴀᴍ

Lost: One Marriage Certificate

Our third son chose a fine moment in world affairs to make his appearance. On the very New Year's Day, 1933, when Japan launched her fresh attack on China, dangerously near the Great Wall and the Northern provinces, another Davis arrived howling in Geneva. He had reason to howl, this new American.

An absurd Austrian nobody with a lock of hair had been "elected" Chancellor in Berlin. Germany, having once quit the Disarmament Conference in a huff and then sulkily returned, now pushed more boldly for "equality." The French stiffened their demand for gradual disarmament in proportion to security—basically sound international common sense. Just before Christmas, Japan had claimed its right to a navy almost the size of America's and Great Britain's. With Japanese armies firmly installed in Manchuria, now brazenly labeled "the new state of Manchukuo," Tokyo's intentions, naval or otherwise, could hardly be trusted. So disarmament was at a new deadlock.

Meantime, in another part of the Geneva consciousness,

the League Assembly had been trying to persuade Matsuoka to accept the Lytton report. Though admitting that China needed to set her house in order, it placed blame squarely on his country as aggressor. Naturally, he clung stubbornly to his plea of "self-defense." The Assembly adjourned on deadlock, for Christmas, leaving the Tokyo war government the season of peace and good will for reflection. Japan, having already gotten away with murder, now hit China again. They chose the first day of January, just as the Davis baby was tipping the Swiss scales at four kilos plus, or nine pounds.

To add to the joys of international life, Sir Eric Drummond, the League's Secretary-General, had resigned and maneuverings were under way for his successor. Like the similar post in our United Nations, this appointment carried great national and personal prestige, and it must now be held by another nation, probably France. Across the Atlantic, America hung suspended between Hoover's depression and an unknown Presidential quantity waiting to take his oath of office. Franklin Roosevelt, we heard, was called "Featherweight" in college. He did look, in his Paris *Herald* photographs, almost too handsome to be real.

Friends began writing us how "lucky" we were, living in probable luxury abroad, beyond the reach of the American depression. I grew a little tired of those letters, with their backhand slap. The Davises too had lost hard-pinched savings in that first Wall Street crash of 1929 but had nevertheless left a safe post in New Haven for an uncertain tenure in Geneva. International economics were still for me a boring mystery. I realized as little as my friends at home that the depression was world-wide, that the unpayable costs of the first World War, the accelerated armaments race and consequent taxes, the high tariffs preventing free flow of world trade, had at last caught up with us all. I never gave a thought to the economic fact that a crisis in one country eventually reacts on others and then boomerangs back again to the first, like ripples in a pool. But already Geneva prices were rising, and soon I woke up to the news that overnight two-fifths of our income had vanished. Roosevelt's depreciated dollar now gave us only three Swiss francs instead of five.

A World Economic Conference to get some of the mess straightened out was planned in London for the coming spring. All governments, including the United States, hoped to reach agreement on lowering tariffs against one another's goods. This would solve world depression and unemployment by stimulating international trade, and even moderate some of the economic drives towards war. But with political agreements going so badly, and that ink-blot in the Orient slowly spreading, gloom hung over Geneva, as heavy as its winter fogs.

In the midst of this our most beautiful baby was born. Since Ethan had been a Valentine and Curtis came on Flag Day, it was charming of Malcolm to choose New Year's, the day of gifts in Switzerland and France.

"That woman has talent!" Paul Mowrer exclaimed, when he heard.

Malcolm Eager Davis was pink and plump, with Santa Claus cheeks. Above those familiar "ah-wahs" in the delivery room, I heard a Swiss nurse cry excitedly: *"Mais il est superbe!"* Lying unheeded under my blanket, I felt gloriously important to be doing my country proud at even such a personal moment.

It had been a happy time anyhow. To breakfast luxuriously in bed those first queasy months, to be pampered by the American colony because I was presenting them with a new citizen, and most of all, to be treated by Europeans high and low with a respect quite different from the self-conscious aversions of my own country—it was a revelation. Where American children had snickered or stared, here youngsters hardly noticed me on the streets. Where most men in America, on the few social occasions when I had dared appear, had left me stiffly alone, European men went affably out of their way to show me small attentions.

This was the moment which Alfonso Albeniz chose to repay our hospitality with a restaurant invitation. In one of Geneva's best dining spots he reserved a table for three, planning a special menu, ordering vintage wine and even providing the flowers, with a corsage for me. Nobody at the other tables seemed to find me odd, with my two cavaliers, and the waiter hovered over my wishes with a special air of protection.

In America, where we worship Mother, deify the child and fantasy endlessly about love, our famous respect for women takes time off, for nine shamefaced months. Puritan sensibilities cannot stand the earthy look of pregnancy. It is by no means only the men who force this retirement. Four months before Ethan was born in New York, a supposedly sophisticated woman invited us to dinner and Jerry innocently accepted. On a hunch I telephoned her the news of my social ostracism. Her embarrassment, though silent, came eloquently across the wire. She hemmed and she hawed, until finally, with my help, she had retracted the invitation. It wasn't—huh, huh—"that kind of a party."

But in Geneva all parties seemed to be "that kind"—teas, cocktails, dinners, either public or private. On Christmas Day we joined a huge group of families around the Sweetsers' gay table, where a fairy tree turning slowly on a tinkling music box kept Curtis too fascinated to eat. Ethan saw and ate everything in sight. No one seemed to think I was corrupting their children's morals by my presence. It was only one American man who fastened on me the hypnotized stare of a small boy spying his first dirty word on the back fence.

"For me," Alfonso had said, with that floweriness any woman eats up, especially at such a time, "woman is next to God, because she creates." It felt very pleasant to be next to God instead of next to the back fence. One might almost have wished to have all one's babies in Europe—except that one knew, of course, that American doctors beat the world. I discovered however that every other nation feels the same way—about their own doctors!

Young Mrs. Albeniz, who joined Alfonso later that year, urged me to go to Madrid to her wonderful Spanish physician, so that they could feel quite happy about me. I could hardly admit that, to an American imagination, my childbed would have been full of fleas, and blood poisoning through dirty instruments a foregone conclusion. Ethel Bullard, who had been educated in England, begged generously to pay my airplane fare to a London hospital or at least to bring over an incomparable English nanny.

But through Ruth Sweetser, whose brood of five made her an authority, we were already committed to Doctor Koenig, one of the best obstetrical surgeons in Europe. I chose him also because he spoke excellent English. Somehow, fluent as my French was becoming, for this highly intimate occasion I preferred my native tongue. Dr. Koenig, a cool, pink-faced old dictator, constantly reminded me that this was the healthiest event in any woman's life and displayed none of that American concern with everything from my emotional state to my blood pressure and weight. The latter were checked every couple of months without fuss. He offered no promises of rectal ether, gas or any other new-fangled alleviation; and obviously, as later events proved, he found my case too normal to be worthy of an expert, accustomed to sudden, skillful operations in emergencies. But despite his austerity, the old doctor had a precise gentleness which inspired confidence, so Jerry and I moved serenely forward until early December, when we had a shock.

Casually, Doctor Koenig announced that he would be out of town at the expected time. Oh yes, he always went skiing at this season. But his young assistant would take over, and in case of an interesting emergency the master could be reached within a few hours. Knowing the habits of seasoned skiers, who pack a lunch and vanish to the sunny, high peaks for a day at a time, my heart sank. We protested feebly, but Koenig went off on his winter vacation, leaving his cloak to fall on a youthful Swiss who spoke no word of English.

We had already discovered that when the Swiss get obstinate, the blood of William Tell runs strong in their veins. Early in October, flanked respectably by my two little boys, I had gone to engage my room in the pleasant private hospital recommended by my doctor: Le Bois Gentil. I was always forgetting that indispensable European identification, my passport, but this time I had remembered, and I handed it proudly to the starched young woman at the desk. She studied it carefully and then demanded my marriage certificate. I burst out laughing.

"Why, but I don't even know what ever became of it," I cried. "Americans don't travel with such things."

Highly displeased, she handed back the red folder stamped with the American eagle, pointing out firmly that although my photograph and the children's were there, my husband's was not. For convenience, since the boys never traveled without me, but their father often had to go alone, we had divided up the family. Jerry and I laughed together that night. The last we had seen of our license was in my pastor-father's hands, the hot June day he married us. But legal red tape is no joke in Europe. The public hospital, whose clientele made it more tolerant of illegitimacy, began to look like our only refuge.

Jerry burst into the American Consulate demanding of Gilson Blake: "Well, Gilson, am I a married man or am I living in sin? The Swiss want to know." Gilson heard the story with twinkling eyes and then drew up a handsome, red-sealed document, declaring in solemn State Department phrases that, it being presumed that the United States Government issued passports only to properly married couples, Malcolm and Harriet Davis were legally man and wife. The starched young woman was impressed, and our new American citizen entered Geneva under the most respectable auspices of Calvin's home town. The Blakes always claimed that they were his real godparents.

The whole community had already had a finger in this pie. There was something about sharing a common concern with international peace which drew people together in Geneva, despite the irritations, the political quarrels, the intrigues and the gossip. Gifts showered in on us. Mary Gerig, whose husband was now an associate of Jerry's on the Geneva Research Center, brought me a pile of her Johnny's outgrown infant clothes, and relined for us the bassinet which had been going the rounds of the younger Americans, ever since Ruth Sweetser bought it for her Alan, now one of our garden playmates. Clarence Streit's French wife, a vivacious small woman who loved to dance but possessed all the thrifty common sense a crusader needs in his home, crocheted a charming pink jacket. David Hsia's mother began a sweater for the new baby which she later mailed me from London. The correct Englishwoman who had made the remark about the Secession of the Colonies brought, with a roguish air, one pink and one blue pair of booties, just "in case." German Leni worked overtime to cut the kind of practical dresses I wanted from a Butterick pattern. Ethel Bullard sent one of those exquisite sheer frocks full of tiny tucks and midget buttons which gladden a foolish mother's heart. But Ruth Sweetser added the crowning glory. Discovering that I had been haunting the shops for weeks for American "bird's eye," she sent me an enormous supply of the only diapers available—a wiry gauze cut in triangular pattern, with a soft inside piece easily removed and washed. They worked quite as well as ours, once you got the hang of them.

Someone told me that Janet Comert knew a clever dressmaker on the Grand Quai who made what the French so delicately call a "dress of circumstance." Madame Pierre Comert, American wife of the Director of the League's Information Section, was later a German prisoner at a notorious concentration camp, from which she emerged thin and white-haired but still dauntless. In those Geneva days she was a friendly and gay-hearted woman full of domestic wisdom. I scarcely knew her, but when I telephoned her home she greeted me with gratifying cordiality. A dressmaker? Why, yes. She mentioned two of the swankiest Paris houses in Geneva.

"But," I demurred, "you see, this is rather a special dress. We're expecting an addition to the family!"

Her gasp was very audible.

"You don't mean—a *robe de circonstance?* Why, but—who *is* this speaking?"

I told her and she laughed merrily.

"Oh!" she cried. "I thought you were Mrs. Norman Davis!"

The wife of our Ambassador-at-large had been eight times a mother and many times a grandmother. When I saw Mrs. Davis again at a reception, looking like a Southern miniature, with her frame of white hair and her heirloom lace on black velvet, I told her the story. She smiled sweetly.

"Only your third?" she murmured in her offhand drawl. "Why, I always say you can't really begin enjoyin' 'em until along about your fifth."

I repeated this to a German newspaperman, and his eyes glistened.

"Mrs. Norman Davis said that? Oh, how Hitler would love to hear it! There's the answer to the foreign criticism of Hitler's attitude towards women. Mrs. Norman Davis!" And I caught a calculating look on his face, as if he were figuring how to further his prestige with the party by channeling this important bit of diplomatic gossip back to the Führer.

Long before the twenty-fifth, the children's packages and even their stocking gifts were wrapped, be-ribboned and hidden away. Curtis, who was in the phase of adoring a toy animal, demanded a wardrobe for Pooh-bear, so, being neither a knitter nor a dressmaker, I betook myself one early December day to the infant counter of the *Uni-Prix*. From the neat piles of machine-made sweaters, caps, leggings and booties in tiny sizes, I collected a bright blue Swiss outfit and held out my francs to the salesgirl.

"We have many more very useful articles, Madame," she coaxed, in her sweet-voiced Geneva singsong. "Bibs, teething rings, nipples, safety pins." I shook my head impatiently, for my single-track mind had not yet made the connection. Suddenly, as she insisted, it dawned on me.

"Oh," I exclaimed, with my American accent, "but these aren't for a *baby*! They're for a little bear!"

She gave one alarmed look into my apparently sane face, murmured, *"Mais oui, Madame!"* and handed me my package and change without another word. I laughed to myself all the way home on the jangling belt-line trolley.

Even at six, Ethan had a tender heart and a strong love of family, and that fall afternoon, when we were turned away from Le Bois Gentil, he looked at me with frightened eyes. "But, Mummie, what are we going to do now? Can't we have Our Baby?" While I gave him rash reassurance, Curtis went on scuffing his small, fat feet dreamily among the dried leaves of the winding path through the grove, his head apparently in the moon. But suddenly his face flushed red. "I don't like that Mademoiselle," he said, kicking a pebble. "She's dumb."

For naturally, both the boys "knew" and they spent many moments lying on their stomachs in the veranda, studying the charts of a little American book, of which I could have found no equivalent in French: *How Babies Are Born.* Leni, whose sweetness and integrity shone for us like the good side of the German medal, approved shyly of my frankness, but Annie was horrified. To bolster her own insecurity, she usually invented some imaginary authority, often that rich German Consul, who could hardly have made all the pertinent remarks with which she credited him. For this occasion she quoted an important Herr Professor, who had stated emphatically and conveniently that Madame's little ones were far too young for such questionable knowledge. Anyway Annie found the general family enthusiasm rather indecent.

"Madame does not seem to realize," she sighed from the superior heights of her spinsterhood, "a baby makes much work."

"Not for you," I reassured her, for, despite the low pay, a cook's duties were rigidly circumscribed. "Anyway American mothers take care of their own babies."

She sighed again, her sallow face even more pained.

"Ah, when I cooked for the Consul they had a nurse *and* a governess. But *they* were rich, oh, how they were rich!"

I had checked up on Annie's books, after the broken leg, so

now she never missed a chance to rub it in that, not being millionaires, we were not proper Americans. To "have an uncle in America" was the German synonym for dazzling financial prospects.

(Later that summer, when we were rid of Annie and enjoying the quaint remoteness of the Brittany coast, Leni got up her courage to divulge that our ex-cook had not only lined her pockets but had foisted off her own work below stairs on our docile *femme de chambre*. From the moment of her discharge, Annie began hating Leni with a deadly hatred which erupted later in a drama almost as astonishing as Mariette's.)

In spite of Annie, the boys accepted Our Baby's prenatal domicile as amusing but no odder than the sun shining on China while night darkened Geneva and promised solemnly to keep the family secret. Ethan buttoned his lips but whenever callers came begged in a stage whisper: "Could we tell *him* about Our Baby?" while Curtis, in his first burst of enthusiasm, and with unusual practicality, had rushed out to forewarn the morning milkman.

Meantime Annie, unaware that Madame had already corrupted their innocent minds, was trying to exact soldier-like obedience by quoting an authoritative stork with whom she was personally acquainted and who promised, if they behaved, to bring a baby sister. For nearly a week my little Americans kept their mouths heroically shut, but one evening, supping in the kitchen while Daddy and Mummie dined out, they exploded in loud haw-haws. Pityingly, they enlightened Annie on the Facts of Life. It was at this juncture that she switched from the imaginary stork to the imaginary professor, and began trying severely to put Madame in her place.

We had not realized how real a member of the family "Our Baby" had become, however, until Christmas morning, when

Curtis made one of his best remarks. The veranda lay buried in ribbons and paper, and Pooh-bear's blue knitted outfit had been buttoned and rebuttoned several times. Curtis wandered in to the chaise longue, where I lay exhausted. With a mature twinkle in his round blue eyes, he laid a red celluloid rattle from his stocking in my lap.

"Mum-mie," he drawled solemnly, "I fink you ought to thwallow thith, tho Our Baby will have a Chrithmath prethent too!"

↣ 16 ↢

Having a Baby in French

THE little boys were still asleep that foggy winter morning when we taxied off to a silent hospital, where one dour scrub-woman on her knees in a wet front hall seemed the only sign of life. Presently, however, the two middle-aged nurse-directors, both powerful Katrinkas, appeared sleepily, showed us to my room, and vanished. It was pretty and homelike, with a small crib on wheels already waiting in one corner, buried under the midget eiderdown without which the Swiss believe no child can survive their climate. During the day the baby is left in the room with his mother.

The two Katrinkas attended me with quiet competence but no sympathy, either moral or medical, not even the early soothing hypodermic which is routine in America. Like most young men, apparently, our doctor did not relish being waked so early, and he would not have been there at all if Jerry had not hung insistently on the telephone for hours. Finally, he arrived about fifteen minutes before the event and began giving me a little chloroform on a handkerchief. It was very welcome.

Jerry, swallowed up in a big white robe, was allowed to stay throughout. Somewhat to my surprise, I found myself speaking to him in English and then easily in French to my special nurse. "Sister Lydia" was a dark-eyed woman in a Red Cross uniform who tended me and the baby throughout with a very personal and loving care. The Swiss training seems to turn out, not competent girls well paid for their trade, but spiritual women dedicated to a cause. Her smile was very comforting.

But Doctor Koenig's desertion must still have rankled. When at last enough chloroform soaked the handkerchief partially to detach mind from body, I heard my own voice, high-pitched as a little girl's, babbling over and over to an unheeding operating room: *"Mais ça ne me gêne pas du tout de parler le français!"* ("But it doesn't bother me a bit to speak French!")

The same plaintive voice kept begging the doctor for more chloroform. The handkerchief was no substitute for our merciful American methods, and I even felt the red-hot needle taking stitches after the finish. And yet—truth compels me to admit—there is much to be said for Nature's method. The European belief in letting a natural event take its due course has a good case.

For I had never felt so strong or made such a rapid recovery. While the important member of the family was being sterilized, weighed and bathed in the most approved modern manner, I lay in an adjoining room, wondering if I had really had a baby. I could almost understand the peasant women who retire behind a bush and then return to work in the field. Indeed, my sense of normality was so great that when a young probationer mistakenly brought me another patient's supper tray, with smiling orders to eat every bit, I had already begun docilely to sip the soup before Sister Lydia arrived to snatch it away. Despite the chloroform, there were no ill effects. I had hardly had enough anesthetic for that!

The baby's troubles and mine were over, but Jerry's had just begun. That affair of the marriage license was a mere rehearsal for further entanglements with Swiss red tape. After my New Year's "party," the chief directress handed Jerry a set of papers, certified by the doctor, upon which a father must swear several times and in various ways that this was indeed his legitimate offspring, then return the documents to the City Hall. Being nothing if not prompt, Jerry signed and mailed them that night. Then he went to that building on the rue du Mont Blanc where the good old Stars and Stripes hung night and day, looking far more beautiful than it ever does at home, and there obtained an American official record of birth with a red seal, stating once and for all, to save time and further trouble, that Malcolm Waters Davis was the father of Malcolm Eager Davis. Three days later, when he dropped in to visit his flourishing family, the directress took him sternly to task.

"Monsieur, you have not gone to the Hôtel de Ville to sign the register for the baby's birth certificate. The limit is three days."

"You mean I have to go in person?"

"Surely, Monsieur," she reproached, "since you and Madame Davis have had two other children, you knew the correct procedure?"

My husband explained facetiously that if every new father in New York tracked to the City Hall, traffic in the area would perpetually be blocked. But she did not smile. This was Geneva, Switzerland, not slipshod America. So he hurried off to the Hôtel de Ville to get under that three-day wire, and to confirm beyond doubt our son's nationality he showed the certification of the American Consulate. The Swiss official in charge stared astonished at the document, whose authenticity he could not question.

"But you did not yet have our official paper certifying the birth of the child," he exclaimed.

"No," said Jerry, "they took my word for it."

"You mean the Consulate of the United States made a sworn statement on nothing but your personal word?" The Swiss shook his head, completely baffled, then with a gesture he dismissed my husband and his entire continent.

"*Bien, bien, il est américain!*" he conceded, as though that covered all surprises, and proceeded to make the certificate official. He looked up once to inquire dubiously:

"Are you from North or South America?"

Either he confounded, as so many Europeans do, "the South" of the United States with South America, or else our Swiss official was remembering the famous Alabama Room in his own Town Hall. The old stone Hôtel de Ville on a cobbled street near the Cathedral was one of the sights of Geneva. Tourists never missed its outside "stairless stairs," up which medieval City Councilors used to ride comfortably, on horseback or in carriages, straight to the Council Chamber on the third floor. In the Alabama Room, Americans always visited the "Plough of Peace," made from swords voluntarily donated by Northern officers after the Civil War. Here the first international tribunal in history arbitrated a dispute between two great powers—the United States and Great Britain. The quarrel concerned, in 1872, a Southern ship, the *Alabama*, armed in English ports for the Confederacy to use against the North. The arbitrators—from the United States, Great Britain, Brazil, Switzerland and Italy—decided against Great Britain.

"From North America," my surprised husband replied, "the United States."

The Swiss nodded and dipped his pen in the ink, and so to this day the foreign birth certificate of our half-Rebel, half-Yankee son reads: *"Les Etats-Unis du Nord."* We have never located our marriage license, but the Geneva document we treasure carefully in our safety deposit box. Without it Malcolm could be drafted for Swiss military service. Even so, by the hospitable laws of the country which so reluctantly allowed him to be born, he may, when he reaches the age to vote and to fight, renounce "the United States of the North" and become a citizen of the Swiss Confederation.

But there was a still further postscript to our troubles. An international town is fertile soil for stamp collectors, and Ethan began that year a grimy and wobbly little album of what was to become a lifelong passion. Friends were generous, and even important men, with a reminiscent smile for their own boyhoods, went out of their way to augment his collection.

One day Ethan spied a fascinating new Swiss revenue stamp stuck to a paper on Daddy's desk. He tore the whole end off carefully and pasted it in his album. Several days elapsed before Jerry discovered that our hard-won birth certificate had been completely invalidated! Ethan, who adored the baby, wept copiously when he understood his crime, so Daddy reassured him with false cheeriness, and again wore a path to the door of the American Consulate. But again Uncle Sam's wit won out over foreign red tape.

The torn piece was pasted to the certificate against a backing paper, and the official seal of the United States was stamped directly over the joining place. Our Swiss-born son was again a legitimate American citizen. The final monkey wrench into what we thought was a settled issue was thrown, however, by young Malcolm himself.

By the time he had grown to a still beautiful but boyish

five, terrible waters had run under the bridge and the names of Mussolini and Hitler were on everyone's lips, even his little play-school friends'. One day he asked me, puzzled:

"Mummie, who rules America? Hitler rules Germany and Mussolini Italy, but who rules America? Is it Roosevelt?"

My Republican brothers back home could have answered him in the affirmative for one wrathful hour, for, unlike the Davis family, they did not love "that man." But I shook my head.

"No," I explained in the baby talk that had by now become second nature, "you see, in our country, every four years, all the grown-up Americans write on a piece of paper who they want for President, and then whoever gets the most papers runs the government for us."

The light of discovery broke on his face.

"Oh-h," he breathed, awestruck. "So the Americans rule THEIRSELVES!" After a sober moment he added excitedly: "You mean—*anybody* can be President? Daddy? Or Ethan and Curtis? Even"— he smiled deprecatingly—"even ME?"

I replied, thoughtlessly, that probably he could not be elected to a post for which only American-born citizens are eligible. My baby stared at me, his face suddenly pale, then he stamped his foot in a rage.

"Then why didn't you go home to have me then?" he cried, his voice breaking. "Now I can never be President!"

Daddy, who understood better than I the insult to the male ego, consulted a member of the State Department on the remote contingency. The solemn legal opinion was wholly reassuring for Malcolm. Probably the issue would never be raised, said our authority, since the Constitution reads "natural-born citizen" and this, in view of that battered but official birth document, could be construed as "born of native parents."

My son's indignation had already been echoed from a rather unexpected quarter. Jerry was by that time an American member of the Committee on Intellectual Co-operation, affiliated with the League. Its archives and assets, both tangible and intangible, have now been legally transferred to its modern descendant, UNESCO. At an Intellectual Co-operation luncheon I was placed next to Titulescu, Rumanian member. He was one of our most familiar Geneva figures, for besides being a delegate to the Assembly, he figured on innumerable international committees as his country's representative. Titulescu was a large, soft-fleshed Eurasian, rather like a worldly Buddha painted in shades of pastel browns, and he was famous for his apathy, especially on social occasions. Naturally, he did not know me from Adam—or Eve—and was not especially fond of Eves anyway. Soup and fish passed and I still could evoke no response. Now in Europe, and especially on these formal occasions, a woman who cannot get a man talking at least about himself has fallen down on her job. It was humiliating. Nothing stirred him from his bored lethargy.

Suddenly Malcolm's reproach popped into my mind—perhaps because European men always find a mother of sons interesting, if not for herself, at least as the medium through which the lords of creation reach the light of day. Without preliminary, I remarked desperately, in French:

"My five-year-old son is very angry with me because he has just discovered he can never be President of the United States."

Titulescu was a lawyer. For the first time he turned his heavy head and looked at me.

"How is that?"

I explained briefly. To my amused astonishment, his small sleepy brown eyes gleamed.

"*Mais il a raison, votre petit gosse!*" he exclaimed indignantly. "I wish I could talk with this child and tell him what I think of such a senseless law. Because his father patriotically leaves home to live here among strangers, your government rewards him by making his son ineligible to its highest honor! Hah!" And picking up his fork again gloomily, he added: "Madame, the greatest sacrifice I make for my country is coming to luncheons like these!"

It was hardly flattering. Nevertheless I felt triumphant as I caught amused glances, including my husband's, across the table. At least I had joggled the Sphinx into speech.

When Malcolm runs for office in the mysterious future of this Atomic Age, my lips and Titulescu's may be sealed forever. I hope American voters will remember the Rumanian lawyer's words. I never wanted to have a baby "in French" anyway.

✑✐ 17 ✑✐

Whooping-Cough, Swiss Style

Even to myself in maturer retrospect, it is understandable
that for the first few months a new mother's mind should remain completely blank on world affairs. My husband, living
conveniently in masculine compartments, could enjoy his
son with one self while carrying on his profession with another. But not I. That upsurge of primitive emotions which
accompanies childbirth like some deep racial memory goes
right on after labor. The single-track fierceness men give to,
say, their temporary love-making or their perpetual power
seeking, a woman pours into the protection of a new being
on earth. The League of Nations receded, and all life centered around one pink scrap in a blue bassinet. His enthusiastic brothers caught the mania, even Annie showed him off
proudly to her friends, and Leni, with the heart of a Madonna, did his dirty work adoringly. His American mother
was learning to pin those diapers Swiss-style, to weigh him in
kilograms instead of pounds and to warm him against damp-
ness and uncertain heating in knitted woolies from head to
foot. My French vocabulary of what Jerry called "funny

words" increased rapidly. Safety pins translated, logically enough, into *épingles de sûreté*, but a bottle was a *biberon*, a bib a *bavette*, a baby carriage a *poussette*, while the fond nursery term for that all-important bowel movement became *son petit cadeau*, or "his little gift."

Our dutiful early retreat from Geneva's evening parties always brought smiles, tinged either with contempt for my naïve desertion from sophisticated society or with mistaken admiration for my self-sacrifice. Not for all the stuffed shirts in the world would I have missed that magic circle of communion at home with my highly appreciative son. One evening I found a kinspirit in the wife of the American Minister to Switzerland. Mrs. Hugh Wilson was a pretty woman, who, despite her fluffy gray hair, looked more like a happy and impulsive girl than a correct diplomatic wife, and I always enjoyed her American talent for remaining on all occasions gloriously herself. When I rose to go she asked in immediate sympathy, "Oh, I hope you're not feeling ill?"

"No, no," I whispered back discreetly, "I've just got an important supper engagement with my new baby."

"Oh," sighed the American Minister's wife in a very loud and heartfelt voice, "I only wish *I* had as lovely an excuse as that for leaving!"

The first day our Swiss pediatrician paid us a visit to examine Curtis's chest cold, he had made me uneasy. Young, slim and quick-moving, with a long, brushed-back European haircut, exaggerated manners and a frank sentimentality towards children, Doctor Colomb acted like no medical man I had ever met. Curtis, on the contrary, nuzzled to him immediately like a wise puppy. After doubling over in such a paroxysm of giggles from the tickling stethoscope that both doctor and patient collapsed in a laughing hug, my son put his hand gravely in the pocket of his diminutive trousers and pulled

out a very world-weary bit of chocolate stuck to a frayed scrap
of silver paper. Breaking it carefully in two, he handed the
smaller piece to Doctor Colomb.

"*Tha,*" he said intimately, using the only grammatical form
he knew, "*th'est pour toi!*"

I record here, without embarrassment, Colomb's admiration
for a very common trait, for which I claim no credit. Europeans often apply to the American character the terms *débrouillard* and *énergique*. Both convey a sense of quick resource-
fulness in emergency. *Débrouillard* signifies literally able to
get oneself out of the fog, and *énergique*, far stronger than
"energetic," implies an intelligent "git up and go," with no
time wasted in achieving one's objective. *Energique*, I learned,
was what Doctor Colomb was calling me as he made his
rounds of small patients in the whooping-cough epidemic
which struck Geneva that winter. Children's diseases, like
dictators, are no respecters of neutralities or boundary lines.

Baby was six weeks old, fat and gurgling, gaining in kilograms what he was losing in hair, when early one foggy
morning, still in that drowsy state between dream and waking,
I heard Curtis cough, once. Instantaneously, like a moving
picture in which I too played a part, I stood on a Baltimore
sidewalk of red bricks flanking white marble steps, playing,
coughing and whooping with a group of neighbors' children
in the fresh spring air. Now and then one of us stopped our
game cheerfully to vomit into the gutter on a final whoop. I
awoke in my dark foreign bedroom, and my heart sank to
lead. I listened again in the early silence. No sound. Struggling up in the chill, I padded down the hall to look at Curtis.
He lay placidly asleep and did not even stir when I pulled
up the neat covers in a futile gesture of protection. Until
rising hour, I lay awake haunted by an unshakable convic-

tion, remembering terrible statistics about one out of every nine infants dying of whooping-cough pneumonia.

I kept Curtis home from school but out of the baby's room, but he would not oblige me with a single cough. Jovially, he trotted up and down the long corridor to the admired blue-flowered toilet, dragging a wagon piled with treasures—a ball, a wet washcloth, Pooh-bear and a collection of screws. That afternoon, feeling rather silly, I telephoned Doctor Colomb. He did not pooh-pooh my foolishness. He came, looked Curtis over, took his temperature, found nothing.

I described the split second of childhood memory. I could never have offered so nebulous a proof to my American doctor at home. But Colomb gave me an unhappy look.

"Ah, Madame, Madame!" he sighed, shaking his head. "You *mamans*! I have great respect for your intuitions. But even if it is whooping-cough, I shall not be able to diagnose it for at least a week or more."

"You'll think I'm crazy," I said, "but I'm going to move right out of the house with the baby today."

"But," cried Colomb in delight, "I approve with all my heart! How many times I have begged Geneva *mamans* to take such precautions. But you must remember—all your trouble may be for nothing."

But I already had all the proof I needed. By the next day my infant, his paraphernalia, a new *pouponière* and I had all moved into a small furnished flat in a near-by street. Colomb inoculated the boys and the baby and I waited, uncomfortable and forlorn, in my rented perch, while reports from avenue de Champel indicated both boys flourishing and Curtis appearing to have no more than a slight cold. Then one evening Jerry arrived to say that Curtis had begun to whoop, and Colomb had definitely diagnosed whooping-cough. Curtis was a husky little brigadier, with his feet already firmly planted in health, and I was confident he would come through easily, so my woman's ego could enjoy at last its belated triumph. For my husband and the doctor treated me like some sibyl of old. In a few days Ethan too was coughing companionably. Even here their brotherly rivalry found food for boasting: "I vomited twice in the night and you only whooped once!" Curtis choked indignantly over each insult to his dignity, but Ethan surveyed the results of one of his inevitable messy finishes very cheerfully and cried, "Oh, I'm glad it was the stewed fruit! I don't like stewed fruit!"

The baby did not catch it, and eventually we moved happily home. One cold March day before the milk business went bankrupt, Jerry came home to report enthusiastically that the League radio was preparing to receive our new President's inauguration speech, and many of the American colony were gathering there at six o'clock to listen. Didn't I want to skip the evening feeding, leave an extra bottle with Leni, and go along?

"Oh, no," I yawned. "Campaign speeches are all alike. Roosevelt won't say anything. It's not worth missing the baby for!" And I let my husband pull on his heaviest overcoat and tramp out rather wistfully into the bitter cold of a Geneva night. I became in later years one of Franklin Roosevelt's most ardent admirers, and I have often kicked myself for missing his brave phrase: "We have nothing to fear but fear itself." I take comfort, however, in remembering that when Abraham Lincoln was inaugurated a certain obscure government clerk named John Burroughs seized upon the welcome holiday to investigate a bird's nest in the woods around Washington. Somehow, I think both Lincoln and Roosevelt would have smiled tolerantly upon John Burroughs and me.

One day, that long-ago spring, I tried to justify my maternal preference for real babies instead of vague politics to Edgar

Mowrer, Paul's younger brother. Not long after he wrote
the courageous book, *Germany Sets the Clock Back,* which
caused his expulsion, under threat, from Nazi-land, Edgar
came to Geneva. I was helping him to find a gift at Kundig's,
our international bookstore near the Quai, for his beloved
daughter. Afterwards he invited me to lunch in one of the
many pleasant little restaurants overlooking the Lake, and in
the course of our conversation asked: "Suppose you had to
choose between killing your own baby and blowing up the
whole city of New York, what would you do?"

Wretchedly but honestly, I replied that though I should
doubtless spend the rest of my life in an insane asylum from
guilt, and so be of no further use to my baby, I believed I
would save my son. Edgar decided reproachfully that I had
a "weak moral sense" and never asked me to lunch again!

According to Paul's autobiography, *The House of Europe,*
Edgar himself was rather a delicate boy who without his
dauntless mother might never have lived to take his brave
moral stand against Hitler. Certainly there is nothing wrong
with our instinct. What could be more sane than a woman's
compulsion to keep her own bit of humanity alive? But instinct is not good enough. My third baby is now a youth of
fourteen, only four years removed from military service, with
a physique which would make him ideal cannon fodder for
another war. American "energy" saved him from whooping-
cough only to leave him exposed to the atomic bomb. Maternal
instinct, however sane, is not good enough. Man's instinct
to fight, also, has its good side—who of us has not waked her
husband in the night to investigate a funny noise? But if we
want protection, we must accept the danger that goes with action. If we want men to stop making war, we must also stop
exacting of them personal and national prestige and power,
luxury at home while the world starves. We must assume the

irksome burdens of citizenship, not as rivals or imitators of men, but as women, ready to learn facts and techniques, but very sure of the rightness of our instinct to save life. Hardest of all, we must face what it means to us personally that our country has at last joined an international organization. The United Nations Charter we signed places terrible authority in the hands of the Security Council. The League Council, more of an executive committee of the Assembly, held no such powers. Let's not fool ourselves. We had better see to it that our best men make up that Council. For if they believe that peace is threatened anywhere in the world, they need not wait for long legal arguments about "the aggressor nation." They may immediately summon your son or mine to go to the ends of the earth to be killed or wounded over a dispute which has not yet touched us directly. The Security Council cannot declare war, but it can call out the international police force of young men from all over the world. That is a bitter pill for Americans to swallow. But the alternative, global war and certain death for practically everyone, is worse. The third alternative—to take no national action at all, either early or late—would only leave power grabbers everywhere free to enslave the world.

So, Edgar, perhaps you were right and I was wrong. Perhaps it is better to lose one's baby bravely than to watch him tortured to death or shamed to a life of slavery. But perhaps, too, there is a fourth alternative. If we women could ever organize maternal love into a brake upon the hit-and-run mania of the power world, we might hope to bear our sons and have them too.

∽ 18 ∽

The Cottage in the Air

Bᴜᴛ that spring of 1933, I still basked in the maternal glow which I see now on the faces of younger women happily fulfilling their natural destiny. They seem as complacent about an instinct for which they deserve no credit as I was. Some now even eye me dubiously as a "career woman" who probably is always neglecting her family, since she prefers politics to preserving. That was the way I used to look at many of my own sex who came to Geneva actuated by a genuine social conscience. A woman an expert on armaments or on plebiscites?—she might just as well have been a hippopotamus in the zoo, for all I understood of her impulses. Babies were much more interesting. They are—but it is fortunate for me and my sons that so many intelligent women spent the years between the last war and this one preparing the American public to take its world responsibility.

So, with the whooping-cough danger circumvented, I began planning a healthy summer for us all. We longed for sunshine and the sea, and the Benjamin Gerigs had the same idea. Internationalists do not spend all their time sitting on the edge of their chairs biting their nails, and that March, Jerry joined the Gerigs for a jaunt in Ben's car to the Riviera, hunting vacation possibilities. Our friends, the Gerhardt Jentsches, who had no children, went along too, just for the ride.

Gerhardt was a slim, sensitive-faced and highly intelligent German from Northern Silesia, who had formerly taught at Harvard, where he met his blonde Kentucky wife. Mary Jentsch was anything but the dull *Hausfrau* Americans would expect a Prussian to pick. She combined irresponsible Southern charm with literary flavor, and while Gerhardt acted as Secretary for the International Students Hospitality Association, Mary ran an informal American library. It barely broke even but it gave her a pleasant pretext for ordering all the latest books from home. One had to tunnel pantingly up many dark stone stairs to their sunny top apartment, but it was worth it, to emerge from the medieval Promenade Saint-Antoine into a modern room, bright with familiar bindings and flourishing green plants, and see the *Atlantic Monthly* lying fresh and sedate on the table.

The five travelers came back, disheveled, sunburned and hilarious about a Pompeian villa they had discovered near Toulon. It was a magnificent replica, with painted friezes and mosaic floors, built by some rich and imaginative French family, who had then lost their fortune. Only a few sketchy bits of furniture remained and the water tank stood rusted from disuse, so there was no running water, but the agent promised repairs and a ridiculously low rental for the season. Our three families were to share this villa, sleeping on rented cots, sitting on soapboxes and disporting ourselves, in barefoot sandals and togas draped from old sheets, around the mosaic pool of the beautiful inner court. At least, such was the fantastic plan of the three husbands and the one childless wife.

Not so, Mary Gerig. Like most American professors' wives, Mary had learned thrift and common sense in a hard school. She was a wonderful housekeeper and a tireless mother and, like myself, had been cured for life of "co-operative housekeeping" with other women's children by one disastrous experience. Besides, she saw her toddler of two tumbling hourly into the shallow pool or down the steep, romantic gray stone steps leading to the private beach. There, if Johnny were not already dead, he could immediately drown in the sudden drop off the sand, where, the husbands manfully declared, the swimming was perfect. So Mary was immensely relieved when, with a sigh for the days of my carefree girlhood when Pompeian villas, rusty water tank and all, would have been my meat, I put my foot firmly down with hers.

Meantime, Doctor Colomb had forbidden the South of France in summer. "Why," he asked, "do you Americans always go to the Riviera in the hottest months? It is too enervating. North Brittany? M-mm, too cold and windy. Go to the West Coast," and he recommended as perfection Les Sables-d'Olonne: superb beach, simple cottages, quiet living, bracing sea air. Mary and I felt very triumphant. Pompeian villas—huh! We made plans for a common-sense tour of our own to Les Sables, where we would find exactly what we wanted: two small, neighboring houses, with gas, electricity and bathrooms, set amid shade trees but facing the water, isolated from neighbors for privacy but within easy reach of butcher, grocer, baker and milkman. We did not insist upon quaint checkered curtains, painted furniture and linoleum floors, but we could always hope.

Small babies make large holes in budgets and the dollar was depreciated by a third, so we bought third-class tickets. Armed with a toothbrush, a steamer rug and a pillow apiece, we traveled on wooden benches across Switzerland and France

from noon of one day until six A.M. the next morning, changing trains twice in the night. We arrived at Les Sables-
d'Olonne, making up in anticipation what we lacked in sleep.
We felt as adventurous as schoolgirls, as, still munching our
breakfast *croissants*, we made for the *Syndicat d'Initiative*,
the local Chamber of Commerce. The small city was rather
disappointing—paved streets, tramlines and narrow brick and
stone houses set close together, with stiff little gardens. But
once outside the town, those quaint shore cottages would
begin. Astonished pedestrians of whom we asked our way all
pointed in the same direction, and suddenly, as we turned a
city corner, we heard the ocean. There, across a wide motor
highway, where cars were already dashing at breakneck
speed, we saw the blue Atlantic. The famous beach was immense and beautiful; lovely ripples from spring tides lay
sculptured slantwise across the purified sand, but there the
dream ended. The enchanted cottages vanished into the thin
air from which Mary and I had fabricated them. Up and down
long avenues of high, narrow houses, each glued directly
against its neighbors, we trailed, hollow from hunger, sleep-
lessness and disappointment, seeing our disobedient little
darlings killing themselves daily in the summer traffic.

However, the prospectus promised us quiet seaside villages
near by, salubrious with *"vastes forêts de pins,"* so before the
day was up we had branched hopefully northward. Our dream
had already switched to a log cabin in the Maine woods,
primitive but sweet, a bit remote in its forest primeval but
still within handy range of the children's orange juice. With
luck, we would find electricity, but we were not proud.
Descendants of pioneers could accept oil lamps, provided
plumbing went with them.

We found electricity all right, and plumbing too. That was
why all the shacks huddled economically together on the

same sewage and cable system. Some *maisonettes* were possible; the *cabanes* were glorified bathhouses furnished in battered odds and ends, and all stood starkly along a glaring sandy shore, with no scrap of green even in sight. When we hunted for that "vast forest of pines" we were proudly directed to a dusty picnic grove of smallish pine trees, owned by the state and closed to real-estate construction.

The twin of that first sea village followed us like a bad dream. Mary and I telegraphed home about the delay and, grimly collecting prospectuses of new mirages, went racketing all up and down the West Coast of France. Descending from the dingy *omnibus*, as the local trains are called, we would ask some respectable-looking woman to indicate a decent hotel at no more than twenty-five francs (a dollar) a night. If we saw no signs of bedbugs on the mattresses of the double room, we parked steamer rugs, pillows and toothbrushes and looked for a restaurant. Hotel cooking is never the best in France. Guided by working people, we always found a delicious meal in some dingy, crowded but inexpensive spot, and thus fortified, we would start the hunt afresh.

The big problem of course during the day was where, euphemistically, to "wash our hands." Men's needs are only too openly recognized in the tiniest village, advertising convenience from afar to the delicate olfactory nerve, but ladies on the loose must synchronize their functions with mealtime. Restaurant facilities, such as they were, were put graciously at our disposal—sometimes, indeed, too graciously, and with such a public flourish that whatever one's original intentions, one felt compelled to accept. One might have to stand conspicuously waiting until the gentleman inside rattled the little lock from *"Occupé"* to *"Libre,"* then slid past with a bow of apology—not for the encounter but for the delay. Handwashing was usually not provided for, and we viewed master-pieces of medieval plumbing as remarkable as any Louis Fourteenth antiques. Mary Gerig was a neat, fresh-looking woman with a medical background and I could always tell by her face, when she returned to our table, just how bad this one was.

We were adding up our infinitesimal expenses one evening, but my head was such a hodge-podge of stopping places that I could not for the life of me remember the restaurant where Mary declared I had paid for our meal. She detailed the menu, but I shook my head. "Don't you remember," she reminded earnestly, "the place with the clean toilet?" I did remember —instantly.

However, neither of us caught typhoid or anything more horrible. In fact, what with the open-air life as healthy as any postman's, the sleep of dead fatigue and the wonderful food, we both flourished. I still possess the accurate record, sent to my family back home, of our most extraordinary meal: thick vegetable soup, tender little lobsters, tongue with tomato sauce, roast chicken with French fried potatoes, lettuce salad and French dressing, fruit, small sweet cakes, and red wine thrown in—for ten francs or forty cents apiece! Demitasses cost a few pennies extra. Thirty cents each once rented us a clean, whitewashed double room with two comfortable beds. But this was not until after we had made the discovery which changed our luck.

Disheartened and footsore, Mary and I sat in the soiled underwear in which we had now slept for several nights, on a pair of rickety beds in some Godforsaken little town whose name, even then, I scarcely remembered. Mary was leafing over again, hopelessly, our well-thumbed Bible, the *Syndicat d'Initiative* prospectus, reading to me sardonically about the vast forest of pines awaiting us at our next stop. She looked so gloomy and I felt so exhausted that suddenly I collapsed in a fit of hysterical giggles. There was something so ridiculously American about two women leaving comfortable homes in Geneva, with its cocktail parties and formal dinners, for a ninety-cents-a-night hotel in an obscure French maritime village. The more I laughed, the more American I felt. Mary, too, had to join in helplessly, and when we both lay back limply on the cheap blankets, suddenly I saw the light.

"Mary," I cried. "We're crazy. We've been looking for an American cottage. That's why we don't find anything. We're in France."

Mary agreed, reluctantly, for dreams die hard, and then she made her brilliant suggestion to desert the "vast pine forests" and the "splendid beaches" of the West Coast and strike up towards Southern Brittany where the pottery came from.

We both slept well that night. By devious trains and autobuses, we landed at Quimperlé. The West Coast had been flat and sandy as a flounder; Brittany was rolling and wooded, with rocky cliffs and unkempt fields of grass full of early flowers. We felt instantly at home and shortly came to rest in a remote coast village, Le Pouldu. Here, several rooms in a villa where I could cook for Baby, with three hotel meals a day, settled the summer for the Davises, and a small house still under construction suited the Gerigs. Even then we had not escaped that haunting "W.C." (The French abbreviate the British word, while we with equal delicacy borrow their *toilette*.) When the Gerig family arrived that June, the proprietor pointed happily to a small wooden cubbyhole to the left of the front door, where a brand-new *confort moderne* of porcelain stood proudly exposed to the road. Rain or shine, the neighbors' envious eyes could not miss one's comings and goings. He was rather hurt when the Gerigs criticized the omission of a door. He had not got around to that yet. After all, Madame could hang a simple curtain. It was not every home in Le Pouldu which boasted such up-to-date facilities. Our friends spent the summer with the curtain. The door, as I remember it, was not added until the following year, when they made it a stipulation before rental.

So we returned to our families in Geneva, greeted with wild enthusiasm by our children and the usual rather preoccupied affection of our husbands. Ben and Jerry both looked grave. For during those blank-minded months when the danger of whooping-cough loomed larger in my eyes than any war, history had moved on, irrevocably. The horror which was to condition my baby's most sensitive years was slowly gathering thunder. Our husbands were going to need that vacation—if they ever got to Le Pouldu at all. We still thought it rather perverse of them to care so much. As my mother had said, wasn't Europe always "situating" and everything went on just the same in America? Secretly I cherished the comfortable feeling that if things ever got too hot in Europe, we could always run safely home. I have heard American official policy criticized for that same irresponsible complacency, based on the illusion that two oceans spell safety.

Around Christmastime a special Assembly meeting was held to vote upon the League report according "the sovereignty of Manchuria" to China and calling upon Japan to withdraw all troops. Matsuoka claimed that Japan's reason for not submitting the dispute to League jurisdiction, but dealing instead directly with China, was "the delays inherent in League procedure"!

"No procedure," retorted Madariaga of Spain, "is too slow for good will. . . . The League will perish if the public is allowed to become convinced that the principles of the Covenant must be waived in exceptional cases—for, in future, all cases will be 'exceptional' ones."

To which Matsuoka declaimed passionately: "America, that great Power across the Pacific Ocean, is outside the League. Soviet Russia is outside the League. At our door we have China, that vast country in these fearful conditions. I ask you to use a little imagination. How would you have acted, had you been Japan?"

He voted Nay to overwhelming Ayes, then rose firmly, and the entire Japanese delegation filed slowly down the aisle and out the door, amid dead silence. Before he left Geneva next day he expressed his great sadness to the press—"not for Japan but for the League, for taking such precipitate action." He hoped "that some day Japan will be understood" and "that the members of the League will be enabled to see the light," and he departed "with ardent wishes for the success of the League."

A few weeks later Japan formally withdrew from the League. She remained, however, in the International Labor Office. Disarmament delegates, too, still lingered on, in a decidedly equivocal position.

The diplomatic record would be side-splittingly funny, with its perverse Gilbert and Sullivan logic, if one's heart had never ached over Okinawa and Bataan, if the boys who in those days were just slangy, hungry school-kids living safely between two oceans did not now lie helpless and dead very far from home.

Meantime the American public, like myself, was absorbed in its own immediate crisis. President Roosevelt, after the magnificent speech which I had refused to hear, closed the banks, startling the rest of the world into realizing that our golden-paved country was really in a bad jam. Big business was opposing Hull's policy of lowering tariffs and thereby reducing unemployment at home and abroad by stimulating world trade. The United States shook up the finances of the world by going off the gold standard, but refused to discuss the burning question of war debts at the London Economic Conference. The open break threatening between Germany and France in the Disarmament Conference was healed by Norman Davis, who saved the day with his plea for good will and mutual concessions. He was backed up by President Arthur Henderson. The Conference took a breathing space, so further private negotiations could continue behind the scenes. And then another crisis was precipitated by the United States. Norman Davis, with obvious reluctance, had to announce that although the new Administration had agreed to consult, in case some nation broke its disarmament agreements, our State Department was not ready to define the terms of that consultation. This practically nullified the American backing which had revived the Conference. That was what Mary and I found our husbands looking so grave about.

ᑯᔭ 19 ᑯᔭ

"Uncle Arthur's" Conference

THE Disarmament Conference began to seem interesting to me after I met its President one evening at Ethel Bullard's.

Ethel Bullard's apartment on the Quai Wilson was a second home to Jerry and me. It overlooked the Lake, with a tiny terrace garden pleasant for coffee in summer, and it breathed a soothing Old World luxury in which I relaxed happily from babies, housewifery and budgets. Mrs. Arthur Bullard and her sister, the Marchesa de Rosales, were both handsome women of cosmopolitan background, with a gift for leisure and for friendship, and together they carried on their mother's interesting traditions of international hospitality. Sooner or later one met everyone there, and so one evening that spring I had my first talk with Arthur Henderson, President of the Disarmament Conference.

He was a short Britisher, with a lined and humorous face already overcast by illness, and he bore the endearing earmarks of one not born with a silver spoon in his mouth. Once, confused by so many British titles—Viscount Cecil who was also Lord Cecil, Sir John Simon, Sir Eric Drummond—I inad-

vertently referred to him as "*Sir* Arthur Henderson." With
one accord, a whole group of English and Americans jumped
down my throat. "Sir Arthur" indeed! Why, Henderson was
the cornerstone of the British Labor party. He had started life
as an ironmonger. Had the King ever offered him a title, he
would surely have refused it. No, the President of the Disarmament Conference was plain Mister Henderson and proud
of it!

Geneva called him, affectionately, "Uncle Arthur." He
looked good and sad and tired that evening I sat beside him
on Ethel's French sofa, though he had a twinkle. He chuckled
over my account of the Joke Shop near Piccadilly where a
cheery salesgirl had reassured me: "You Americans have
rathah a good sense of humor, you know," because I was
buying bending spoons and dribbling glasses for my young
rowdies. This reminded the President of the Disarmament
Conference about Nancy Astor. Lord Astor's Virginia wife
cherished a set of fake teeth, he said, which completely
distorted her distinguished face when she whipped them out
of her bag and into her mouth at unexpected moments.

One evening at the Hendersons' a frumpy woman, whom
her host had never seen before, arrived late. Homely, with
buck teeth and a shapeless hat squashed over frowzy hair, she
seemed on good terms with his wife, so Henderson, though
bewildered, was polite. Presently, to his red-eared embarrassment, she began making love to him before the entire company. The more he edged away, the closer the creature
nestled. The labor leader had never found himself in a more
ticklish situation. Suddenly his guest pushed back her hat and
her hair, snapped out her teeth—and there was Nancy!

Henderson laughed with such reminiscent relish that I
decided the British rather expect the unexpected of Americans and love Lady Astor because she never lets them down.

One feels glad that even such absurd interludes colored Henderson's life. His was a hard-won and a noble career, and it ended in the collapse of his highest hopes—general world disarmament. As the Conference dragged on, for four years, from one deadlock to another, Henderson faded slowly with his dream. Towards the end, a sick and a broken-hearted man, unappreciated by his own government, he was fainting at committee meetings but clinging desperately to his purpose. When he died, in October 1935, the Disarmament Conference, though technically alive, was already morally dead. Six months earlier it had "adjourned" on final deadlock and failure. The office of President, left vacant by Henderson's death, was never filled.

Someday, under the United Nations, we shall have a new attempt to disarm within sensible limits and relieve ordinary citizens all over the world of their outrageous tax burdens. If only the new generation could learn from Father's mistakes! But children, faced by the same old human dilemmas on whose horns their ancestors struggled, usually consider their problems brand-new, to be solved by some magic new formula. Mrs. Roosevelt, returning last year from her first baptism as delegate to the Assembly of the United Nations in London, took a friendly dig at the young American newspaper crowd in London. Not one of them, she said, knew that Norman Davis had ever gone to Geneva as Chief Delegate to the Disarmament Conference, much less realized that he came as close as anyone to rescuing it from failure.

"I used to say to him at the time," said Mrs. Roosevelt, " 'Why do you bother to keep on going? Nobody here at home appreciates it.' "

(To which my husband commented dryly: "That's not why he went!")

We Geneva-ites, who saw the Disarmament Conference

dying with its President, the League succeeding when governments and people were back of it, and failing when they were not, smile a bit ruefully at America's first excitement over the United Nations and the present letdown to a dangerous indifference. What is the United Nations but the League of Nations in modern dress, with improvements? What is it but a new generation trying to steer its course around the same old rocks that shipwrecked Geneva? League members learned a dozen years ago that you cannot get disarmament without collective security and political agreement. As the second World War loomed closer and blacker, they saw helplessly that neither arming nor disarming saves the peace, but only speedy united action against the first aggressor. They discovered, too late, that strong arsenals never prevent war or save a country from attack. They found out that solemn promises to disarm never amount to a hill of beans unless governments have previously compromised together about their endless urge for power and prestige. Disarmament is not a cause but a result of peace.

The one genuine success of the Geneva Conference was the efficient technical organization, by which gradual disarmament could begin all over the world. Experts spent years of time, tons of paper, piles of cash to evolve the competent machinery of procedure. The disarmament engine stood oiled and waiting, but it never ran. No nation, including our own, would furnish the fuel—a will to peace stronger than a will to power. Nobody would give up pride today to avoid war tomorrow. Everybody sacrificed future security for immediate national advantage. But tomorrow, like old age, has an uncanny way of creeping up on us and being today. Then, as suddenly, it is the irrevocable past, a black memory of ruin, torture and death.

One would imagine that the atomic bomb would have

proved to the military-minded the futility of their weapons. But only recently Jerry heard an American general exclaim in exasperation: "These scientists! Why, they're spoiling warfare." Voltaire once said: *"La guerre est une chose trop sérieuse pour la laisser entre les mains des militaires."* If war is too serious to be entrusted to the military, what about peace? The bomb has not yet hammered into the thick blockhead of the world the old truth that only in union is there strength and security. It seems only to have split society into an even more schizophrenic personality—yearning passionately for peace but stubbornly arming to the teeth. That is exactly what was going on in Geneva, behind the scenes of the Disarmament Conference.

Japan was master in Manchuria, Germany was rumbling, Mussolini was orating, the United States had not yet got around to defining its terms of consultation in case of trouble. It was at this point that Madariaga made one of his most penetrating remarks.

He was chief Spanish delegate (B.F.—Before Franco) to the Disarmament Conference, an Oxford professor with a genius for brilliant speech. Our newspaper crowd revered no one, and something about Madariaga's small, upright figure, with its Punch-like nose and brilliant dark eyes behind horn-rimmed spectacles, had earned him the nickname of "Mickey Mouse." Since he neither loved animated cartoons nor understood Americans, he deeply resented what was in essence a tribute to a big spirit in a small body. In any event, it was Geneva's "Mickey Mouse" who summed up the lasting lesson of the Disarmament Conference.

"There are," said Madariaga, "no technical questions. There are only political questions in uniform."

Political ambitions in uniform masqueraded brazenly through the corridors of the disarmament building. They were called "technicalities." That hastily built structure on the rue des Pâquis had always looked temporary. Now it became more and more an empty shell, another League "failure." In the end, there was nothing left but for the Disarmament Conference and "Uncle Arthur" to die together.

∾ 20 ∾

The House with the Climbing Tree

WHEN it comes to vacationing, France and America are sisters under the sunburn. If anything, the French, who can be so formal on formal occasions, abandon civilized ways more gracefully than we. At Le Pouldu our children romped barefoot over sand mountains while we sun-bathed along the incredibly beautiful beach. People often dressed and undressed with miraculous dexterity under beach capes in a secluded corner, while small tots were disrobed in public with a refreshing naturalness, which I was charmed to imitate. Returning thus corrupted to my own country one summer, I was put in my place by a stern, gray-haired matron on a small Maine lake. She and I were the only people in sight, when I stripped my shivering baby to the skin, and then whisked him into a dry suit, while he turned his back modestly, chattering in French. The woman of wrath plowed over through the sand as though I were Gypsy Rose Lee herself.

"Back where *you* come from," she snapped, "they may do those indecent things. Over here, we don't allow it!"

Two American families on a remote French beach aroused great interest. *Mamans* of scrawny offspring asked Mary and me for advice on diet, or complimented us on our children's manners. They seemed slightly surprised—as were we. The American brat is as firm a myth abroad as the indecent foreigner is here. My pink-and-gold angel fascinated the peasant women—wrinkled, sturdy creatures who arrived every Sunday, in full black skirts, velvet-trimmed bodices and starched lace caps.

"How lucky you are, Madame, that he never cries! Especially since you leave him lying alone so much. Of course he is so healthy because he is so good."

Over and over I was urged to enter him in the contest for *"le plus beau bébé de France."* My objection that an American was hardly eligible for a government prize designed to stimulate the national birth rate of France they brushed aside generously. Such a beautiful child—he would surely win first prize. My baby, destined to become, like all small boys of his generation, an expert on flame-throwers, dive-bombers and every death-dealing weapon, came back, brown and cherubic, to the wrangling peace city.

That year twisted little Goebbels made his first appearance at the League's fall Assembly. He was so insignificant that I only vaguely recall everybody's contempt for his press speech justifying racial discrimination and the glories of war. Dollfuss, the Austrian Chancellor, was welcomed back to the Assembly with warm acclaim. He was resisting German annexation of his country and had just escaped a Nazi pistol-shot in Vienna. A year and a half later, when a second revolver reached its mark, the news hit me almost as a personal shock. It is one thing to read in a newspaper of some unknown's assassination, another to picture it happening to a real person one has seen. Dollfuss was such a ruddy, cheerful-looking, small man—it was unbearable to hear how he had been callously left alone to bleed slowly to death, while he begged more and more weakly for help.

It was at this 1933 Assembly that the Foreign Minister from Holland brought up the problem of refugees from Germany. Hitler had already kicked out some sixty thousand without funds. The Disarmament Conference opened late, deadlocked by political disagreements behind the scenes, although faithful Arthur Henderson had spent his summer touring the European capitals in the hope of removing a few stumbling blocks, by private talks with heads of governments. But that historic fall I wrote cheerfully home: "Thank heaven there is a lull in the Disarmament Conference, so Jerry can spend some quiet evenings with his family." Among my old letters I find no note of the mass meeting for Disarmament, organized by my husband's International Consultative Group. It was hugely attended, one October Sunday. Nearly five thousand letters had already poured in from organizations in thirty countries, speaking for millions of people. All urged the Disarmament Conference to complete its task. Messages came from Prime Minister MacDonald of Great Britain, from Premier Daladier of France, from Molotov, who was then Chairman of the Council of People's Commissars, from Secretary Hull in behalf of President Roosevelt. There was no doubt about the will of the peoples of the world.

The next evening the United States delegation issued a statement. We were in Geneva solely for disarmament. We could take no responsibility for the political conditions in Europe (diplomatic euphemism for Nazis and Fascists) which might help or hinder the objectives of the Conference.

Our American stand cast a new gloom over Geneva. Germany had just quit both the Disarmament Conference and the League. Hitler yelled the news proudly over his Berlin microphone and called for new Reichstag elections (with a single slate of Nazi candidates). He urged France to "banish once and for all force from our common life." Once the Saar was restored to Germany, "only a madman would consider the possibility of war between our two states!"

Meantime an important American arrived in Geneva. The League had created a special Commission on Refugees from Germany and appointed as High Commissioner James G. McDonald, formerly President of the Foreign Policy Association. But even when it came to the mess Germany had deliberately created, Germany must be appeased. The Powers still hoped that Hitler might find it in his heart to return to the League. So, to avoid hurting his feelings, the new Refugee Commission could not even be housed in Geneva. If they found a building, they could locate at Lausanne. No League funds were available, except a first loan, to be repaid in twelve months. All this was firmly explained to James McDonald by the new Secretary-General, who had taken over this key post in July.

There could hardly have been a more unfortunate choice for the crucial years to come than Joseph Avenol of France, a cautious, enigmatic bureaucrat whose chilly eyes always gave me the shivers. His relations to the attractive Englishwoman who accompanied him everywhere (there was a French wife in the offing, but he was Catholic) set more tongues wagging in Geneva than any mere international crisis. Would she receive for him? She did. Would he—when finally his wife died—reward her long years of devotion by marriage? He did not.

But it is not fair to blame Avenol for a political stand which was backed up by the acquiescence of governments all over the world. We had none of us learned the tragic lesson that dictators must be opposed, not appeased. Over the new

High Commissioner's objections, the Assembly decided that refugees were not an international responsibility. For two years James McDonald and that old soldier of peace, Lord Cecil, Chairman of the Governing Body, struggled to raise funds from private sources for a world tragedy growing daily more acute. Finally James McDonald voluntarily relinquished his post, urging in his letter of resignation that world opinion, acting through the League and its Member States and other countries (meaning chiefly his own), should move to avert "existing and impending tragedies."

"I feel bound," he wrote, "to conclude this letter on a personal note. Prior to my appointment as High Commissioner for Refugees Coming from Germany, and in particular during the fourteen years following the war, I gave in my former office frequent and tangible proof of my concern that justice be done to the German people. But convinced as I am that desperate suffering in the countries adjacent to Germany, and an even more terrible human calamity within the German frontiers, are inevitable unless present tendencies in the Reich are checked or reversed, I cannot remain silent. . . . When domestic policies threaten the demoralization and exile of hundreds of thousands of human beings, considerations of diplomatic correctness must yield to those of common humanity."

Of course, I met McDonald around at dinners and cocktail parties—a tall, gray-haired boyish figure with an engaging manner and an eye for the pretty girls, with whom one saw him dancing and lunching. But this American's brilliant devotion to his task I only appreciated long afterwards. Like my own country in those days, I was too near-sighted to put two and two together.

Besides, I was happily settling our new home on the route de Chêne, near the International School, where Ethan was now entering the first class. We were fed up with the blue satin salon and another woman's possessions. We were homesick for something American and our own. The departure of newspaper friends offered a chance to buy a mixed lot of furniture which even included cribs, a high chair, a sewing machine and a box of battered toys. Before we left for Le Pouldu we had found a simple house with a garden, and all summer my mind had been busy with plans. At Quimper I had completely lost my head over the pottery—not those obviously quaint figures so popular in America, but delicate flower designs painted on glaze as soft as velvet—and I bought lavishly of cups and plates. Having no intention of cheating the customs, I tied them up, for convenience, in two huge bundles and started the long trek back to Geneva with Leni and the three children. Jerry and the Gerigs had already left, to make preparations for the Consultative Group's demonstration meeting on disarmament.

So I arrived in the familiar Gare de Cornavin very late one evening with three sleepy boys, one trunk, four suitcases, one baby carriage, one folding bath-table, a pail of used bottles and soiled diapers—and the Quimper pottery. Our elderly Swiss official, evidently a family man himself, took one look at my burdens, opened a suitcase for a perfunctory poking, and then swiftly chalked everything, except the children, with his official pass-mark.

He put the usual question: "Have you anything to declare?" and I replied happily: "Only these two packages of china!—*de la faïence*." The man's jaw dropped as if I had admitted to a time bomb.

"Madame, Madame, de la faïence!" he cried, with a long, sad, exasperated sigh for my obvious honesty. *"De la faïence!"* he repeated with a tragic French wail. "Don't you know that the importation of china and pottery into Switzerland is

forbidden by law? We have our own manufactures to protect. My duty is to confiscate this property and impose a fine."

Already worn by a twenty-four-hour trip in second-class coach, I stood too aghast to answer. Leni and the children waited huddled together, dirty and tired, watching us with anxious eyes, while beyond the customs barrier outside Jerry peered in, wondering what was detaining his family. I waved to him reassuringly.

"May I just explain to my husband?" I asked the official, who stood deep in frowning thought. He brightened.

"Oh, is your husband there?" he said. "Ask him to step in."

Jerry came, and that perfect Swiss gentleman, with impeccable solemnity, began putting to him a series of leading questions. We were not really residents of Geneva, were we? Merely American tourists? Passing through Switzerland on our way home to our own country? Poker-faced, Jerry gave cagey New England answers and so, together, those two inheritors of Calvin and of Roger Williams wiggled an honest Southerner through the Swiss law with her contraband. How we enjoyed tea from those cups in our new home on the route de Chêne!

The boys still remember the "climbing tree" where Daddy astonished the neighbors by installing a huge packing box, high enough to be exciting and reached by a rope ladder, nailed steps and a monkey climb along a sturdy limb. Small Swiss from more conservative gardens soon came flocking to ours. Their afternoon roll and sweet chocolate tasted far more delicious, munched aloft in the climbing tree.

Our Geneva landlord, one of those upright, elderly men who form the mainstay of their community in any country, Mayor of his local commune, was a tall, white-haired giant with a paternal air. Jerry explained, apologetically, that the

depreciated dollar made us worry about future exchange un-
certainties, and he nodded genially.

"Oh, I have no fears about tenants who wonder beforehand
if they can pay their rent. It's the easy promisers who give me
trouble later," and he compromised on a reduction.

Monsieur Puthon thought it odd, but raised no objection,
when we asked permission to install gymnastic apparatus on
the top floor, but when I requested a linen shelf in the one
bare-walled bathroom, his Swiss blood rose.

"Who ever heard of shelves in a bathroom!" he cried. "Good
housekeepers keep their linens in a wardrobe."

The indoor swing and trapeze introduced us to our most
charming Swiss friend—the local carpenter and his wife and
son. The Martins lived in a tiny one-floor home back of his
shop, flanked by a scrap of garden, lovingly cultivated spring
and summer to a bower of leaves and color. Martin *père*, a
stout fellow with a great well-fed paunch which fascinated
Ethan and Curtis, accustomed to Daddy's leanness, had all
the philosophy and the patience of the contented craftsman.
He had scaled Mont Blanc in his younger days, but now, he
said resignedly, his wife made too much fuss.

"What sensible reason can you give," she cried, "for flaunt-
ing yourself in the face of danger—except your male desire
to dominate everything, even a mountain?"

Monsieur Martin sighed, took a nail out of his mouth and
poised it skilfully before tapping with his great, steady paw.

"She will not believe that it is not pride a man feels all
alone up there with infinity. I assure you, Madame, I am
never so humble as when I have just scaled a mountain."

But they were a happy couple, and their son, Pierrot, a
"big boy" of nine or ten, became a fast friend of *les petits
américains*. Madame Martin always put her ruddy face out
the window when I passed with Baby Malcolm. *"Oh, Ma-*

dame, qu'il est bijou!" she cried, and slipped him a chunk of sweet chocolate. One day, passing her closed window, my materialistic angel lisped one of his first consecutive sentences: *"Bithou,* that meanth *thocolat."*

For, despite my attempts to "have him" in English, my son's first baby talk smacked strongly of French. A bird was a "zahzo," from the elision of the "s" in *les oiseaux,* a fly a "moos" and his favorite exclamation: "Ooh la la!" The mixed phrases were so adorable that I fell into the lazy tolerance of most international mothers until one day Ethan shocked me into a sense of my linguistic duty. He had been happily cutting colored cars from a stray copy of the *Saturday Evening Post,* and brought me his fleet to admire. I asked if he had picked up the paper scraps from the floor.

"No Mummie," he replied cheerfully, "I didn't *ramasser* but I got a *balais* and I *balayed* them all into a *coin."*

I cried: "Ethan!" so intensely that he looked startled. "Say that in English." He obeyed, without difficulty. "Now, say it in French." He complied perfectly. "From now on," I said, "none of us will mix up French and English. If anybody uses a French word, we won't understand it."

The children caught me as often as I caught them. But the game was worth the candle; when we came home for good they had to learn slang and boy talk, but they spoke real American.

Petits camarades of varied nationalities soon began to congregate in the Davis "yarden." Besides the climbing tree, there was a sand pile, a seesaw made by Monsieur Martin and, most prized of all, an old wheel chair. I had bought it for two dollars from the local Salvation Army's second-hand store, where I often poked about for bargains. Scrubbed and disinfected, it became the jeep of the garden. I also bought an immense wicker Bath chair with a curved roof such as one sees sprouting like giant mushrooms along European beaches. It usually lay prostrate on its back, as a rocking boat, as a cradle, as a racing car, or as a bird's nest filled with pine needles for Curtis and his friend, Kika.

Kika belonged to Curtis and her sister to Ethan. This was firmly understood. Erica and Alison Pickard were the daughters of our English friends who ran the Quaker Center in Geneva. Both Bertram and Irene took active part in the meetings of the International Consultative Group. Every Thursday morning, rain or shine, my adopted daughters-in-law were at Villa les Charmilles to see the baby "bawthed," and when his golden curls were shorn each begged for a lock to "keep forever." They were unspoiled as only English children can be, fresh as primroses, and when I once gave them a little gold locket and a gold thimble, one might have thought I was handing them the Crown Jewels of England. Curtis and Kika, both chubby and blue-eyed, understood each other without words, but Ethan soon had an offer of marriage from romantic Alison, one of those long-legged children with intense eyes and a promise of future beauty. Ethan merely replied cagily that he didn't know about that but maybe she could marry Curtis. Our children found all their Anglo-American differences fascinating, but the Pickards complained humorously that their girls were saying "li'il" for little and "vurry" for "very."

Despite the Swiss-bought furniture, the slip covers of red sailcloth from Brittany, and the Quimper pottery, our house began to take on an unmistakably American air. We stopped trying to ape alien ways; we entertained simply in a pleasant living room, gave a few necessary formal dinners and frequent chafing-dish suppers, at which I served the famous Geneva cheese fondue, a sublimated Welsh rarebit concocted of Gruyère cheese, flour, milk, white wine and flavorings. Down the long table we set three lighted chafing dishes, each bearing a bubbling earthen pot, and guests spiked up broken bread on a fork and sloshed it chummily around in the same savory mixture. In restaurants the convention was that whoever lost his bread from his fork bought the next round of drinks. The dish is distinctly peasant. I telephoned my fastidious wine merchant to inquire what wine should accompany fondue, and when he had recovered from his surprise he replied disapprovingly that *l'estomac fort* could support white wine, which turned the cheese into indigestible lumps, but that *l'estomac délicat* (hallmark, he implied, of gentility) required cherry brandy of the purest vintage. It was also of the most expensive and strong as applejack. I suspect that the success of our fondue parties was due as much to kirsch as to informality. One of our Russian friends, Vladimir Romm, Tass correspondent, declared happily that it tasted almost like vodka, and he finished a bottle with no effects but a relaxed geniality.

It was Romm who exclaimed one evening, when a group of homesick Americans sat singing "Kentucky Home" and "In the Shade of the Old Apple Tree" together: "Agh, you Americans are sentimental, just like the Russians!" And he once remarked, with a grin, to my husband: "For a revolutionary, your country is what you call a headache. To make a revolution there, one would have to make forty-nine little revolutions!"

cۮ 21 cۮ

The Nazi Who Would Not
Play Murder

ENTERTAINING in our own way in our own home made us
feel like real Americans again. In the midst of one of the most
disastrous Assemblies of the League, the Davises gave an old-
fashioned Halloween party.

No American who has not lived abroad can understand the
emotional importance, for our foreigners here, of their national
holidays. The Genevese, too, probably thought our American
colony rather ridiculous. Every November we collected, a
heterogeneous lot, for turkey dinner with cranberry sauce,
served in a vast European hotel room by amused Swiss waiters.
Most public banquets soon bored us all—for peace, like an
army, seems to march on its stomach—but everybody flocked
to the Washington's Birthday dinner at the Hôtel les Bergues.
We groaned over the flag-waving platitudes, but I noticed we
all went back the next year. On the Fourth of July, Prentiss
and Charlotté Gilbert kept open house in their cool, mellow
apartment on the rue des Granges, with a charming terrace
overlooking the town. Miraculously, in a city where July the
fourth is just another hot day, Charlotte managed red-white-

and-blue flowers, cakes, ices, even napkins. At home we would have thought the touches too woman's-magaziny for words, but abroad it warmed the cockles of our hearts.

The rue des Granges, narrow and cobbled, is one of the most exclusive in Geneva, but one Middle Western matron who journeyed from Lausanne especially for Independence Day was scandalized to find herself in the slums.

"Well!" she sputtered. "I certainly never expected to see my Consul living in this narrow, dingy little street! Why, it isn't even paved!"

Even Halloween began to assume importance by its absence. There was something lonesome about an October with no jack-o'-lanterns in the shop windows, no yellow candies in the *Uni-Prix*, no glossy illustrations of apple-bobbing children and festive tables decorated with black cats.

Besides, the winter fogs were closing down on our Lake city, so that, whatever weather one might see by noon, all mornings broke equally gray and damp and depressing. At breakfast by electric light Jerry and I looked at each other and remembered:

> "Oh suns and skies and clouds of June,
> And flowers of June together,
> Ye cannot rival for one hour
> October's bright blue weather."

My husband was more preoccupied than I liked with his Consultative Group, his report of world affairs, and his committees, but he entered into my plans for a Halloween party with enthusiasm. The little boys welcomed any excuse for a party, especially one where they wore sheets and scared people. When I cut cats and witches from black paper and sculptured pumpkins (*des gourdes*) into grinning jack-o'-lanterns, they thought their remarkable mother had invented the whole festival.

Our English guests plunged into all the foolishness with abandon, but the Continentals, who arrived, despite my warnings, in formal clothes, remained politely bewildered all evening. For them, the two Anglo-Saxon nations had gone unaccountably crazy together. Their host, usually dignified, met them at the gate draped in a sheet, and waving his arms, and tagged by two smaller ghosts. Inside, two amused maidenly ghosts inquired in French if they could take Monsieur and Madame's coats. Russian Romm wasted fifteen minutes in the hall, flirting with our Swiss cook, before the pretty American for whom he mistook her walked in the front door. Even Baby, swathed in a pillowcase, with a hole framing his perplexed little pink face, joined us for a moment in Leni's sheeted arms.

We soaked our heads in the apple tub, rescued the ring from the flour cake in our teeth, munched doughnuts, drank cider and laughed ourselves sick. I managed to draw in most of our European friends, but when I asked the only German there to join us he shook his head. We knew him rather well; he represented the German society for the League of Nations in the Consultative Group, and wrote Geneva dispatches for Berlin newspapers. He was one of those big, soft, rather handsome men with a face bearing the perpetually sandbagged look of the boy too dominated in childhood to grow strong. Something lost about him appealed to a weak maternal streak in me—quite mistakenly. Despite his fuzzy German *Schwärmerei*, he was a shrewd opportunist. But he confided in me about his divorces and his love affairs, and I even invited to the house an enchantingly pretty Swiss girl at his request. He wanted me to find out what she really thought of him. Her matter-of-fact reply was very European. All very well for a passing physical attraction, but he was not a gentleman. She was marrying a young Frenchman whom she did not love at all.

"He turns pale when he looks at me," she said disdainfully. "I can't bear to have him touch me. The thought of getting into bed with him—" she shivered with delicate distaste. "But he has a solid situation and he will take care of me."

Her chilly realism gave me heartache, but I was up against a folkway more powerful than mere romance.

"Why marry either?" I asked. "Why not wait till you fall in love? You're so very pretty."

She shook her head. "Oh, I know I'm not bad to look at. But I am already twenty-five. Soon nobody will marry me."

After she left, Curtis declared stoutly: "Ooh, she's nice! I wish Daddy had picked her for a Mummie too." Then looking at me with alarmed affection, he added, "Oh, but you wouldn't have to go away! You'd stay too and be the first Mummie!"

Her German admirer prowled solemnly about studying our hilarious guests with Teutonic thoroughness. Around midnight Bob Pell, who despite his dignified post of press adviser to the American disarmament delegation had been the life of the party, cried: "Let's play Murder!" The procedure was explained to the baffled Continentals—how you drew lots, and if your paper said "Murder," you secretly felled a victim in the dark with a slap on the back. When the lights disclosed the corpse on the floor, the entire company tried to identify the killer with detective-story technique. We bumped around, giggling and shivering, through the shadowy first floor of Villa les Charmilles, murdering liberally, then turned on the lights to be judged by an Englishman in the best Gilbert-and-Sullivan manner. For an hour at least, everybody forgot the troubled world and the cold, foggy Allhallows

Eve outside our American living room. Jerry and I slept like tops that night.

A few days later our German friend invited me to lunch. He drove in an odd silence, to one of the pleasant lakeside restaurants, and then said solemnly:

"I was profoundly shocked at your home the other night."

"You mean our childishness?"

He shook his ponderous head. "No. That game of murder. Never, never, in a cultured German family would you find refined people *playing* at murder. For me, it was very instructive. Now I see what a primitive and barbaric people Americans really are."

Within the year he had joined the Nazi party. All during the war he occupied a Berlin post in Herr Goebbels' Ministry of Propaganda, perhaps—who knows?—as a qualified expert on the psychology of the barbaric enemy across the sea.

For six years we forgot him. A few months ago a letter came to Jerry's New York office, from Bavaria. He was safe, he assured us. He had spent the war cutting out pictures from *Life* and *Time* and other American magazines—which ones and to what purpose, one can easily guess. He enclosed a snapshot of his wife (the third) and his infant son. They would appreciate some food packages, as times were hard.

Jerry sent word that their only chance was through the International Red Cross, and then turned the letter over to the proper American authorities. I do not know how our Halloween guest explained our primitive coldness to his new wife.

∽ 22 ∽

Wanglings and Wranglings

Every Christmas we invited friends of every nationality to a hearty Christmas breakfast. We offered two attractions, "real" (i.e., American) coffee and three ecstatic little boys tearing open their presents around the tree, while we all sang Christmas carols. One Southern girl collapsed in tears on my shoulder under the scent of pine needles in a warm room and the familiar strains of "O Little Town of Bethlehem." Our foreign guests—German, Japanese, Swiss, Canadian, Austrian, British, French, Hungarian—all entered happily into a few hours of American family life. Our candid children heartily approved the hospitality because, despite my requests to the contrary, it swelled their pile of packages. By this time strange faces and odd accents in their home seemed as normal as the wallpaper.

That intoxicating shop on the rue du Rhône proved a gold mine for table "jokes." There was a chocolate pipe for Ken Harada, popular Japanese member of the Secretariat and a persistent bachelor. He brought me a pretty square of fine wool into which Japanese peasants knot up their sparse wardrobe and carry it on a stick. There was a chocolate man for Craig McGeachy, a blond, soft-spoken, keenly intelligent Canadian Secretariat member, who lived alone in a quaint apartment on the Bourg-de-Four. Geneva thought such an attractive woman just *ought* to be married to *somebody*! Craig became, after the war, the first woman to be a Secretary of the British Embassy and is now UNRRA's delegate to the United Nations, for Social Welfare.

There was an edible chocolate pencil for our dear Hungarian friend, Derso. He and his partner, Kelen, had been caricaturing the politics and the politicians of Europe for twenty years. Derso always arrived late and befogged, and needing quarts of coffee, because he had been drawing all night. I wish now I had kept that Christmas tablecloth upon which he illustrated the history of Mussolini's hats. For years he had watched the Duce trying to look impressive in a normal hat. But Benito's bald head was of such a peculiar egg shape that even a military visor either perched askew or fell down over his ears. Finally, said Derso, Benito personally designed the Fascist kepi—the only headgear that would stay put. Under the kepi he could stick out his jaw without appearing too ridiculous.

When the first photographs arrived in America of the captured Duce in civvies, sure enough, a commonplace man leered out from under a dark felt hat which sank around his ears like Daddy's on one of my boys.

Mussolini had long since forced Count Sforza, former Ambassador to the United States, into voluntary retirement from Italy. This great Italian liberal was on the European Committee of the Carnegie Endowment, and I had met him one summer at their simple Riviera home. He was a handsome man with a noble head and some inner calm which seemed to carry him through anything. I met Tarchiani, too, a liberal newspaper publisher who was expelled into years of pinched exile. He is now our Italian Ambassador in Washington.

Yet, in those days many Americans still admired il Duce. Some of us always respect power and success. "You've got to hand it to Mussolini," you heard people say. "He's taught those lazy Italians to work. He's got Italy in order, everything cleaned up, trains running on time. We could do with a little Fascism in this country."

About this time Mussolini proposed a "reform" of the League. He wanted "less voice for the smaller nations"; he thought the affairs of the world should be handled by the big powers, who would tell the rest what was good for them. Fortunately, where he succeeded at home, he failed in Geneva. Whatever the practice, the principles of the Covenant remained unchanged.

Three days after our first Christmas breakfast in the new home, President Roosevelt made a speech in Washington for Woodrow Wilson's birthday. The President of the United States had thrown a few kind words to the League of Nations. This was headline news for a continent watching each straw which showed how American foreign policy was blowing. The elected leader of the most powerful nation in the world had told his voters: "Through the League directly or through its guiding motives, indirectly, the states of the world have groped forward to find something better than the old way of composing their differences. . . . The League of Nations is a prop in the world peace structure."

After twenty years of isolationism, even to pat the League on the back was a courageous step. But he added, and the foreign papers translated, reluctantly: "We are not members and we do not contemplate membership. We are giving co-operation to the League in every matter which is not primarily political."

This sop to the voters who re-elected him three times reads oddly now, when we are all so intensely concerned with the same old political problems of which those League situations were the ancestors. One shivers, remembering that this speech was only six years before 1939 and that World War II already crouched in the shrouded horror chamber of the future. Those political questions in uniform were marching slowly but inevitably our way.

The Nazis, claiming, probably honestly, that they did not want war, only to get their own way, were wangling to secure the rich coal basin of the Saar from the French without a League plebiscite. (In this, at least, they did not succeed. An orderly regional vote was taken, a year and a half later, under a special League Commission. When a strong majority favored return to Germany, the people's wishes were followed.) I once caught a glimpse of the German belief in coal as a divine right, through Annie. Told that coal was cheaper in America than in Switzerland, because we do not have to import it, she exclaimed in disbelief: "*America* has coal? I thought you had to buy it all from Germany."

Hitler was also wangling to Nazify Austria. That revolver shot at Dollfuss had been one move. Five years later the Führer marched in and seized all the key industries. Not long ago our American papers headlined the Soviet Union's demand that all German assets in Austria belong to Russia as reparations. To the United States, a bit belatedly, Austria is now news.

In Washington, Swanson and Roosevelt began building the biggest navy in the history of the United States. Since we were doing nothing to stop the coming war, that was obviously our only alternative. "This," cried a Republican in the House of Representatives jubilantly, "is one of the greatest moves for world peace in ten years!" Within ten more, we had both Pearl Harbor and the Battle of the Bulge. Naturally, America's retreat into our own armed might had its repercussions abroad. Recently, in these postwar days, when everybody is wondering which way Russia is going to jump, I have remembered Europe's anxious eye turned on the aloof United States not many years ago. It feels so different when the shoe is on the other foot.

For months my husband's monthly *Geneva* had been running news of "The Anglo-Persian Oil Dispute." The paragraph dealt with some British company's quarrel with the Persian government over oil concessions; it was dull and I always skipped it. I remembered this, too, thirteen years later, when I saw New York subway riders eagerly scanning headlines about Russia's demands in Persia (now—just to make it harder—called Iran). We hailed the settlement of this Russian-Iran oil dispute as a first United Nations success. The League too had settled a similar situation long ago, only then England was playing Russia's role. The difference was that since Great Britain is a capitalist country, it was a private company which then sought the oil concessions. In the nineteen-forties it was the Russian government, with its state monopoly of business, which made the demands. But the Soviet Union based its modern claim on those oil concessions granted by the League to the British in earlier days.

President Roosevelt made another move that excited Geneva. Russia was not a member of the League of Nations and had never been diplomatically recognized by the United States. Officially, Norman Davis could not communicate with Litvinov in Geneva. Now Roosevelt invited the President of the Soviet Union to send a representative to Washington to discuss relations between our two countries. He recalled Ambassador Davis home at the same time. Geneva smiled wryly. At last Davis and Litvinov were going to meet.

It was a strange and jumbled year; a depressing one, too, which even the cosiness of our new home could not quite shut out. But I had not realized how gradually, despite myself, events outside my personal orbit had begun to seem significant, until Ethan and Curtis began objecting to my skimming the headlines of the Paris *Herald* to myself at the lunch table. "What is it, Mummie? What are you reading?" they demanded. When I explained, they gasped in delight. Did I mean that Big Letter came every day to tell us what was happening everywhere, all over the world? Even the weather in America? What does it say today, Mummie? What's the weather in New York?

That was their first question and the answer gravely compared with Geneva's climate, always to the latter's disadvantage. Even storm, hurricane and flood at home were somehow interpreted into a national superiority. The rest I became adept at clarifying in words of one syllable, so that even Daddy sometimes listened with astonished amusement to his complicated specialty boiled down to baby talk.

The little boys sat open-mouthed to hear that great big grown-up men who drove milk trucks in Chicago were fighting about money. Dreamy Curtis seemed more excited by one of Beebe's expeditions, but Ethan was immediately on the side of the strikers. Those drivers ought to get enough money to buy good dinners for their little children. When we heard that giant milk cans had been deliberately dumped into the dirty streets and all the Chicago babies' morning milk spilled, he modified his sympathy with labor.

"No, Mummie, that wasn't good. After the poor old cows had worked so hard!"

They cheered up when I explained about the International Labor Office. "You remember that big house where you went to tea with Janna Kapp and the lady gave you so many cakes? Well, her husband is Mr. Harold Butler, and he runs an office where people come from all over the world, to try to agree about how much pay men and women should get for how much work." Oh well, then, Ethan agreed, that was all right and they didn't have to spill the milk. The only trouble, I had to admit, was that our country had never joined that office. When the United States did enter the I.L.O. the following August, one small American on the route de Chêne was almost as delighted as Director Harold Butler.

Ethan had never heard of the Hoover proposals to scrap a third of the world's armaments, but when one Japanese torpedo boat accidentally rammed another, and both sank, his eyes lit up with an original discovery. "But that's good, isn't it? Because now it can't blow up any ships and kill people."

One morning the first page of the Paris *Herald* was plastered with photographs over which Mummie skipped hastily. Stavisky, who had been manipulating the public funds of the French town of Bayonne, involving a whole galaxy of famous political figures in the scandal, was pursued by the police to a mountain hiding place where he shot himself. My sons already knew that the really juicy bits came in the headlines, and they kept turning the page back.

"But what are all those pictures, Mummie? What are those gendarmes doing? Who's that man lying down?"

In desperation, I blurted out: "Oh, that's just a man who shot himself." The moment the words were out, I regretted my stupidity. Both boys stared at me, aghast, and then rolled in paroxysms of laughter on the floor. Haw haw haw haw— Curtis, did you hear what Mummie said? A man shot himself! Ho, ho, ho! Wasn't he a big dummy? He killed his own

self! Curtis chuckled for a long time, and could hardly wait
to tell Daddy the joke.

However, the "Blood Bath" in Germany that June shocked
them both profoundly. To kill yourself was stupid, but to kill
other people was bad. Life was wonderful and you didn't
take it away from anybody. Ethan sang his own version of a
French popular song we had learned on the beaches:

> *"Amusez-vous!*
> *Faites les fous!*
> *La vie est si courte et si belle!"*

"Mummie, I always sing it: *'La vie est si LONGUE et si
belle!'* " He wept with exasperation when Curtis, already
humorously mature, twinkled his round eyes and shouted
lustily: *"La vie est si COURTE et MÉCHANTE!"*

The "Blood Purge" in Germany occurred the week we were
planning Flag Day decorations for Curtis's birthday. Hitler,
Göring and Goebbels descended in the night upon Röhm,
General von Schleicher and other "conspirators" and killed
them off with cold-blooded efficiency. Our German Halloween
guest returned from Berlin in what can only be called "a state."
Until then he had talked admiringly of the Führer's appeal to
primitive truths—"thinking with the blood." Once he even
admitted to me that it coincided with his own rebellion
against an over-intellectual mother. But now he came back
from the nation's capital, pale, uneasy and unmistakably
frightened.

"To kill or to be killed," he argued with himself, under the
guise of convincing me. "That is every man's need." With
what tried to be pride, he told me how Hitler said sternly
that night: "This is man's work," and went forth alone—
and well armed—to murder Röhm with his own revolver.
Eventually, our German swallowed the whole horror. Why

not? He knew on which side his bread was buttered, and he had been raised, not on freedom or principle, but on blind authority.

It was a dreadful summer, and we could not escape its echoes, even down at Carqueiranne on the French Mediterranean. A thrifty French friend had sent us to a *pension* with a scrap of beach, incredibly cheap and patronized chiefly by tradespeople enjoying a carefully eked out holiday. Our proprietress served delicious meals on a flagged terrace under vines, leaning chummily against the doorway to chat with her guests. These amiable bourgeois liked Ethan, who was a sociable child and a great chatterer, and invited him to gather fresh almonds or to catch small fish, which Mademoiselle obligingly cooked. My oldest son, they told me approvingly, was *très fin*, and so good-hearted. Over Curtis, deeply sensitive but too absorbed in observing life and thinking it over to do much about it, they shook their practical heads. Baby Malcolm beamed hungrily upon every munching picnic group, but looked so pink and well fed he did not have much luck. One day he emerged stark naked from behind a rock which had been some Frenchman's secret *cache*, bearing in one hand a two-foot loaf of bread and in the other a wine bottle. He trotted over to me, begging sweetly: *"Manger? Manger?"* From that time on, the beach was his.

Back in Berlin that year Hitler was justifying his arrests and purges before a cheering Reichstag. Baldwin defended Britain's air-building program to the House of Commons. "Britain's frontier," he said, "is no longer at the chalk cliffs of Dover but along the Rhine." Between building houses of sand for his three little boys and swimming out to deep water with me, my husband was writing a paragraph for the August 1934 number of *Geneva*. Its modernity is startling, as one rereads it now. Nothing seems to have changed except the shuffling around of kings, men and pawns on the chessboard. The problems, the principles at stake, are exactly the same.

"Twenty years after the anniversary of the days when Europe plunged into the war that involved the whole world, Europeans are talking more of the prospect of another war than at any period since 1914. . . . The only certainty is the conflict of interest and will between the dynamic forces, seeking to remold the situation in Europe, and the static forces, tending to keep the situation as it stands. One side whispers, 'Resistance to change means war.' The other side shouts, 'Insistence on change means war.' Yet almost everyone will agree that none of the issues would be really worth a war, for either side. These issues engage, however, national prestige and pride. So almost everyone is beginning to talk of war as if it were unavoidable. The main question discussed is generally its imminence or its postponement. A chance remains to develop and extend the idea of the general interest in peaceful settlements. But it is only a chance, because the basic political questions remain unresolved."

ᙬ 23 ᙬ

Politics in the Nursery

Wherever one turned one bumped into these political questions. Back home, in a nation which was practically a continent, Europe could remain comfortably shadowy and remote, until danger suddenly leapt out like a nightmare from the air. But on a continent jammed with nations, many no larger than one of our states, the dividing line between domestic and foreign policies wore very thin. Whatever one country did at home immediately concerned everybody else "abroad." And "abroad" did not mean across an ocean but sometimes not a stone's throw away, where one frontier guard with a rifle faced another. To an American, it felt odd to drive from Switzerland into France for afternoon tea or to spend the Easter week end in the Italian Alps. Despite the current joke about the London *Times* headline: "STORM ON CHANNEL, CONTINENT ISOLATED," even England could not indulge in our pleasant illusion of protection by water. Nevertheless, "appeasement" by the democracies went on, under a paralyzed fear of war so great that it encouraged by inaction the very thing it dreaded most.

Everybody talked war; everybody, except the dictators, seemed to feel helpless; and try as I might to bury my head in the sand, I could hear the distant rumblings of approaching doom. By this time I had learned too much to be comfortable. I still resented the intrusion of the ugly world upon important private life, but I had begun to share Jerry's uneasiness and even some of his interests.

Anyway, I could no longer escape the facts. Echoes of politics drifted back to us, even from the baby classes of the International School. "L'Ecole Internationale" was housed on a lovely old estate of the route de Chêne with rambling grounds where Ethan's pioneer restlessness found room to roam. It was started by a group of Secretariat parents who wanted their children to learn something broader than Swiss history. Arthur and Ruth Sweetser were among its leading spirits. Our children's few years there as members of a cosmopolitan society in miniature we count as one of their most fortunate formations for the world to come. The International School, though attended by every nationality, was conducted, like the League, in two official languages, French and English. Its educational program successfully straddled the gap between the old and the new. Most Americans took their children home advanced beyond their age, but many Europeans, especially the academic French, sharply criticized its lack of "mental discipline." When it comes to intellectual cramming, the schools of France stand for no nonsense about outdoor play. If anything is to be sacrificed, it must be health. America is France's opposite number. When it comes to sports and practical skills, we stand for no nonsense about mere scholarship. If anything is to be sacrificed, it must be culture.

Living now so near the International School, the boys came home for lunch, and one day Peter Kapp's sister dropped in, as she often did. Helen Kapp was an attractive young Englishwoman, recently divorced from John Collier, the brilliant author of *His Monkey Wife*. She was a gifted artist, whose wood-block prints of flower-rimmed fountains and quaint corners were taken home from Geneva by many of our international crowd who still enjoy them with nostalgic eyes. That day Leni served Ethan's favorite *crêpes*—huge, crisp pancakes lined with oozing apricot jam. He surveyed his piled plate with satisfaction.

"Mummie," he said thoughtfully, "I'm glad I'm not *juif*, aren't you?"

With a Jewish friend at table, there was nothing to do but take the innocent bull by the horns.

"Why, Ethan!" I replied. "Helen is *juif*, you know."

"*Is* she?" My son stopped chewing to stare from her to me in astonishment. "Well, then, but—what does *juif* mean, anyway?"

We discovered that, from the chatter of his schoolmates, some of them German refugees, he had gathered that "Jew" was a synonym for anybody driven unfairly out of Germany by Hitler. Later I tried to explain the irrational prejudice by history, by old habits, by secret jealousies and superiorities on both sides, but he only looked blank. If Peter and Helen, and Peter's little girl, Janna, who had lived in our home for two weeks, were all *juifs*, then none of it made any sense.

However, any sentimental belief I may have entertained about the natural democracy of little children suffered a shock when it came to inviting Chang-chun to Ethan's birthday party. Most of his class were coming, and his teacher pointed out to me privately the omission of the one Chinese boy. The group held one other Oriental, little Japanese Shoshi, who looked so enchantingly like a slant-eyed doll I had once loved in Baltimore that I always longed to kidnap him. But Sho-shi was two years younger than Ethan, a mere baby, beneath the dignity of a seven-year-old's birthday party. I seldom interfered with their invitations, but this time I remonstrated about Chang-chun.

"Oh," remarked Ethan carelessly, "he's only a Chinese boy. He won't care!"

Apparently the superior young white men and women had concluded together that minorities, especially of another color, have no feelings. I was somewhat reassured about my son's judgment, however, when Chang-chun, a merry wild man, did come to the party after all.

Curtis seldom took sides, but everything that was psychological he saw shrewdly. Jerry had been deeply engaged for weeks in a long, objective treatise on "The Sino-Japanese Dispute," when Curtis came from L'Ecole Internationale and summed up the situation in a phrase.

"Daddy," he grinned, "at school, Chang-chun says to Sho-shi: '*Toi, bœuf!*' ("You—ox!") And Sho-shi says to Chang-chun: '*Toi, cozhon!*'" ("You—pig!")

The theme song of the New Deal echoed for months through our garden, in its French version:

> "*Qui craint le grand méchant loup,*
> *Méchant loup, grand loup noir?*"

Even Baby, sunning on the upper balcony outside my room, droned happily on one note: "*Mésant loup, mésant loup!*" Then Curtis came banging home from school, bursting with music which must be spilled even before he removed his coat. A "new boy" fresh from Madrid had taught him the Spanish words to the same tune. All I could make out was the ending, "*Del lopo, del lopo,*" but the world seemed suddenly very small and the influence of the United States very impressive.

Even in my son's new teacher at the International School, when I came to know her, I touched a political tragedy. About

Madame Gareis I could write a book, though this would horrify her, for she was the most modest of women. I shall always remember her as one of the truly great people I met in Europe. Although she was my first maternal rival, I loved her as much as my children did. We all called her intimately "Mawngair," from an old nickname some child had once evolved out of "Madame Gareis." One day I overheard Ethan asking Curtis in a baffled tone: "Curtis, which do you like best, Mummie or Mawngair?"

"Oh, Mummie," replied Curtis promptly.

"So do I," admitted his brother, still puzzled. "But why?"

As I waited, with bated breath, for the tender sentiment, Curtis cried staunchly: "Oh, because! Mummie gives us ice cream. Mawngair never gives us ice cream!"

Mawngair was far, far wiser than I, and her selflessness gave her an uncanny gift for stepping into a child's skin, but somehow our basic attitude towards children was the same. We both enjoyed them immensely as they are, and though we recognized a duty to train them, in social behavior, neither of us could project upon them moral condemnation or moral expectation. Naturally, she and I became friends.

She was in her forties, thin, plainly dressed, quick-moving, with short-cropped black hair and those great, dark, burning eyes which often hide tragedy behind a friendly glow. German-Swiss by birth, a doctor's daughter, she had for years directed a dormitory in a modern reform school in Germany, chiefly for children of criminals. All the housework—cooking, cleaning, laundry—was done under her direction by her charges, who lived together in one cottage. She sometimes talked to me about them with reminiscent love, and smiled wryly as she compared them with the well-to-do children she was now teaching.

"There is really very little difference," she told me humorously, "except that the children of the poor are more polite and more unselfish."

It is not often one meets what St. Paul called a "visible saint," but Mawngair was one. I never knew her to fail with a pupil. I did not bother to inquire into her scholastic standards, because at civilizing a child into a co-operative citizen she was a genius. Whatever his home background, whatever the emotional handicaps he brought with him to class, Madame Gareis never passed the buck to his parents. She did not look about, as over and over I have seen teachers in our American progressive schools look, for this easy "out" from her own dilemmas. The child, once inside the classroom, was her responsibility. If he misbehaved, if he did not learn to work, that was her failure. Humbly she studied him again to find the key to his interest. Somehow, she always found it.

Her effect on my two was magical. Even had they never learned to tell A from B, I should have sent them to Mawngair, just for the happy psychological atmosphere. Ethan's scattered and mischievous restlessness calmed down to sober concentration. Curtis fell into a tub of butter. Mawngair understood him. He learned, she explained, without appearing to learn, and absorbed knowledge in his own fashion. She had let him wander about watching the older children do their sums, and then took him in hand to teach him his first arithmetic. Curtis grinned at her. "*Je sais déjà,*" he said. Sure enough, without setting pencil to paper, he had already grasped the principles by observation. Once, to show him up, for he was paying no attention to rehearsal of a difficult song, she called upon Curtis to try it alone. Nonchalantly, he sang it through, words and music, without a hitch. Mawngair giggled appreciatively as she told me how my son had put her properly in her place.

A distracted Swiss mother once brought her a small boy

who had been expelled from six schools. "Oh, I know you won't keep him," she said, "but I heard about this International School, and I thought I'd try."

The child was accepted, and for the first few days pandemonium broke loose. He knocked over tables, jumped on the piano, smashed plants, and delighted in sneaking up behind a small person intent on a painting or a building job and sweeping it all to the floor. Naturally, tears and fights followed, the entire class was disrupted, and the new boy was openly and articulately hated. One afternoon, after he had gone, Mawngair held a class conference.

"We want to help this unhappy boy," she said, "but I cannot do it alone. I need your help. Now, all I ask of you is this: whatever he does, pay no attention. Just go right on with your work. Don't scold and don't complain to me. Pick up the pencils or the blocks, wipe up the spilled water, act as if he is not there."

Her shrewd technique appealed to the dramatic instinct of her small men and women. The class settled back to work, and the astonished disturber of the peace found himself politely ostracized. Within a month he was transformed into a good citizen, and he adored his teacher, like a stray dog who has at last found a home. In his family, where his parents lived at shrieking cross-purposes, he was still *un terrible*. But in school he became one of Madame Gareis's shining successes.

That big, glass-walled room full of plants and books and busy small people was like a glimpse of the paradise one had long since lost or had never had. Mawngair was always cheerful, and it was only after I knew her well that I learned her story.

The picture of her dead husband—a serious, mustached, intense German—looked out from a frame in her small apartment near the school. He had been an active Social Democrat, that liberal party which, with encouragement from outside, might have saved Germany and the world, and which he represented in the Reichstag. For six months, they were happy. Her husband's childhood, she said, had been wretched; he was hungry for love, and I can imagine how she poured it out to him, warmly and without stint. "Every evening I used to see him," she told me, with her radiant smile, "turn the corner to our house and start to run. He always arrived at our front door out of breath."

One night, some time before his home-coming hour, she heard pistol shots on the street below. She shivered, thinking, "Thank God, it is no one of mine." Then she reproached herself. "Some poor soul is in trouble. I must go down and see if I can help."

She opened the door on her husband, who had crawled that far and lay dying on his own doorstep. He never recovered consciousness. They had been expecting a baby; her grief brought on a miscarriage. Gareis had insisted upon telling the truth in the Reichstag about German secret rearmament. The day before he was to speak, the Nazis had killed him. Mawngair's husband was one of the first political victims in Hitler's Germany.

Like so many people who have surmounted tragedy, she was not an unhappy woman nor a frightened one.

"You see," she explained, with her strangely cheerful smile, "the worst has already happened to me. Whatever life holds, nothing could ever be so terrible again. So now I am no longer afraid. Except—" she admitted shyly, "sometimes when I must speak with parents about their children and say discouraging things. Then, just beforehand, I always talk to my husband. Oh, of course, I know, this is only in my own mind, but just the same, I say to him: 'You will help me, won't you?' And he always does."

❧ 24 ❧

The Poison Pen in the Kitchen

LENI had become by this time like an older daughter or a younger sister in the Davis family. Whatever she did, whether it was setting the baby on the potty-chair or serving a formal dinner to the Hugh Wilsons, she invested with a gentle grace of her own. As one of our British friends exclaimed: "She might be a little Duchess!" Leni looked more like a sad, dark-eyed girlish Madonna, and after her mother's death she clung to us, in her quiet way, as her only "home-folks."

The little boys took her for granted as an ever-flowing fountain of beneficence along with their parents, and Ethan firmly announced his future plans to marry her. *"Mais tu sais,"* he warned her, *"tu dois avoir des petits bébés pour moi!"* When she got back from her mother's funeral, restoring our whole home to normality once more, Curtis tagged her broom all over the house, squatting in the dustpan and gazing up with adoring eyes. *"Leni, j'aime toi."* Even Baby accepted her as the only satisfactory substitute for Mah-mie.

Leni never went anywhere evenings, and most afternoons

off she sat upstairs sewing and enjoying a sunny bedroom with the only comfortable bed she had known in her life. I had given her, also, her first comfortable shoes—American, of course—and a friend had bequeathed her a wardrobe of dresses which Leni's skillful needle soon transformed. With her unconscious distinction and her smart new clothes, she began to look indeed "like a little Duchess."

Presently I noticed that she always left early on her free Sunday afternoons, sometimes returning at the scandalous hour of eleven. One day she told me. Several years earlier, she boasted shyly—for women are humble in Europe—a young Swiss had considered her seriously for marriage. Or so, at least, she had believed. Then one night he demanded that, to prove her love, she offer him what he quaintly termed "a guarantee." Leni possessed all the stubborn chastity of the maternal woman who will protect her children from illegitimacy, even at the expense of the man she loves. Hurt and disillusioned, she sobbed: "I give no guarantees," and from then on never saw him again.

Now they had met by chance, he had begged forgiveness, and it was all on again. Every Sunday they spent her holiday and his together, making plans to win the approval of his parents for a girl without a dowry. He was the only son of comfortable grocers in German Switzerland and was learning his trade as a clerk in Burkhardt's.

Burkhardt was the canny Swiss who catered to the home-sick wants of an entire international community. All the familiar foods everyone takes for granted until stranded on foreign soil stood stacked on his neat shelves. There were those sweet oblong biscuits with scalloped edges, *"Petits Beurres,"* without which childhood is not childhood in France. There were English scones, Chinese preserved fruits, Scandinavian herring, German *Lebkuchen*, and the sturdy Quaker and the smiling Negro of Quaker Oats and Cream of Wheat. I wasted considerable money on these imports before I discovered that the Swiss equivalents, *flocons d'avoine* and *la semoule*, were just as good.

One morning the mail brought me a typewritten envelope which I opened unsuspectingly. A neatly typed page bore the signature of *"Annie Stärker."* Though it began and ended with all the correct salutations, it was a poison-pen letter. The phrasing and spelling were too perfect—Annie had paid someone to write it. In the most elegant French, she informed me that I was nursing a viper in my bosom. While in Madame's service, she had maintained discreet silence, but now she wished to inform me that Leni had always shirked her duties below stairs and often mocked at Annie for working so hard, since Madame was a lady who did not understand *le travail*. Moreover, she felt it her duty to inform Madame that Leni had been for months the mistress of a prominent lawyer in Geneva, with whom she had been seen in public places. It was he who had lavished upon her the many beautiful clothes she was now wearing. Realizing that Madame trusted this girl, she was, with the highest motives, informing Madame of the truth and she remained, with her most respectful salutations, Annie Stärker.

The thing made me slightly seasick, and I tore it into bits and threw it down the toilet, where it belonged. There seemed no point in distressing Leni, so we said nothing about it.

One morning I was awakened by Ethan calling shrilly through the keyhole of our bedroom, which we locked to prevent their jumping on our stomachs at early dawn. I told him sleepily to go away, but my son was insistent.

"Mummie, get up, quick! Leni is *crying*! She's been crying all night!"

This of course routed me out, and I found Leni with

swollen eyes trying to change Baby while she watered his yellow curls with fresh tears. After we got the boys break-fasted and to school, she told me the tragedy.

The day before, at her young man's lodgings, a strange young nurse in the blue costume of Geneva's highly re-spected *pouponières* came to tell him how wickedly he was being deceived. His fiancée had often been heard to say that she was merely working him for *une poire*. To be "a pear" in French is to be a soft and gullible damn fool. What was more, Leni had been for months the mistress of a prominent lawyer, with whom she was seen in public places. How could a mere *femme de chambre* afford her present elegance?

Being, though not a *poire*, a credulous boy aware of his own naïvetés, Leni's young man had swallowed the story, hook, line and sinker. Shocked, miserable, raging, lovesick, he had created such a scene that Leni finally threw back his ring and they parted forever.

She and I both knew, of course—Annie! I was so coldly angry that I could have moved mountains. My first step was to see Leni's young man. He was a ruddy youth with square shoulders and the unconscious egotism of the young European male, but he seemed sturdy and upstanding and Leni loved him. Once he began talking about Leni his bravado melted and he became a miserable boy. He had spent his night, not crying, but tearing up all her letters, and the poems he had written, smashing their favorite dance records. I let him get it off his chest and then remarked that I felt it was my place to defend Leni from slander, not to swallow a pack of lies. It seemed to me that this was also his role.

He flushed very red. "But why, why, Madame, would a respectable nurse come and tell me such things? There must be something behind it."

"There is," I told him and I explained about Annie. "If Leni is anybody's mistress," I added, "I hardly know when she has found the time. She is always at home. A man who was keeping her would demand more than that."

He smiled for the first time, then began pacing the room furiously in his heavy Swiss boots. Still, this prominent lawyer she had been seen with?

"The French lawyer downtown who handled Leni's affairs when her mother died," I told him. "I am going to get his legal advice."

He was an impressionable young man. He even offered to accompany me to the lawyer's, and he and Leni kissed and made up in our American living room. The next day I walked into the Frenchman's downtown office, having surreptitiously hunted up the word "libel" in my English-French dictionary. A tall, thin, black-bearded man with grave eyes heard my story with courteous attention.

"I know nothing of the Swiss law," I finished hotly, "but in America, Annie could be sued for—" I brought out the new word proudly, "*le libelle.*"

"Naturally," he agreed, with a smile. "Did you bring the letter this woman wrote you?"

Regretfully, I explained. Making the shrewd deduction that Annie would never know it had been destroyed, he took her address and promised to communicate with me shortly. About the nurse we could do nothing, since there was no witness to her visit.

When Leni and I dropped in at his office a few days later he presented each of us with a copy of Annie's signed retraction. Every word of her letter, she had confessed immediately and abjectly, was pure invention inspired by spite. We learned too that the nurse, hearing of Annie's summons, hurried to the lawyer in a panic, throwing herself on her knees and begging for mercy. She was so young; Annie had paid her well.

"I paid her nothing!" cried our former cook, ashy with fear, and when the two women left together, they were still quarreling violently. The lawyer laughed over the ease of the case, then he shook his head over Annie. A criminal type. She would be dangerous if she were not so cowardly.

Rather apprehensively I asked the French lawyer for my bill. The gentleman from France bowed.

"Madame," he said, "there is no bill. Like you, I was only too glad to act in the interests of justice."

Leni, in her gentle way, wished poor Annie no harm. She had her own vindication, a precious document, her young man and his ring. He soon left Geneva to start his own grocery business at a German-Swiss resort, financed by his father for the coming marriage.

Our little boys gathered garbled bits of the drama from the kitchen, and Ethan was very indignant.

"Annie said awful things about Leni, Mummie. Why, she said Leni was a *teacher*! Yes, she did, too! She said Leni was a *maîtresse*!"

Together, he and Curtis evolved their own version of a lawsuit. "Going to a lawyer" became their favorite yelling game.

"Curtis," Ethan would start suddenly, "I say you're too fat and your face is dirty and your nose is running."

"Stop saying lilebels about me!" grinned Curtis promptly. "I won't stop!"

"O.K. then, I'll get a lawyer to make you stop!"

And for five minutes each yelled: "Yah, yah, yah, yah!" at the top of his lungs, until they dropped, spent and hoarse, to the floor.

When it came time for the wedding, Leni cried bitterly at

leaving Our Baby, but within a few years she had two babies
of her own, the store flourished, and she helped her husband
while a hired girl did the housework. With the cash we gave
her for a wedding present, they bought a "superb bedroom
suite." It sounded, from her glowing description, like the most
revolting Grand Rapids imitation. All the rest of her life, she
wrote gratefully, it would remind her of Monsieur and
Madame.

Leni had seemed about as near perfect as a human being
can be—sweet, intelligent, modest, sincere, devoted. But alas!
Before she left we found that Achilles' heel which makes
even the "good" Germans such a puzzle and a problem. She
never tried, like Annie, to frighten the boys into good behavior, because as a child she herself had lived in nightly
terror of a black chimney-sweep who dropped down at night
and stole disobedient girls. Often, she said, she lay awake,
hearing the wind in the chimney and shaking with fear
under the bedclothes drawn over her head.

One week end Jerry and I escaped for a few glorious days
in the mountains, leaving only Leni happily in charge at
Villa les Charmilles, armed with telephone numbers of doctors, friends, teachers. But the weather turned rainy, so instead of Sunday afternoon, we got in rather late Saturday
night. We stole in for a fond look at the Baby and, when he
woke and cried, found a pretext for letting him nuzzle on our
shoulders until he fell asleep. There was no sound anywhere
in the house.

Several times, during the night, I dimly heard a woman's
thin wail from some neighboring house: *"Monsieur, Monsieur!"* or sometimes, *"Madame, s'il vous plaît!"* Once a pedes-
trian answered; there was a short colloquy, a curt remark,
and then the footsteps echoed on past the house through the
silent street. Next morning early I opened my shutters and

stepped out on the balcony to survey the weather. From Leni's window above mine I heard a faint cry:

"Oh-h-h-h! Mais c'est vous, Madame!"

Looking up, I saw a white, drawn little face, above a huddled figure in a nightgown, close to the window. It was Leni, a wreck from terror. She had waked at the baby's cry, and then heard the rumble of Jerry's voice. From that moment on she had been too paralyzed to stir. She locked her bedroom door in a panic and sat sobbing alone, hearing the bandits kidnap her beloved baby, seeing his little brothers murdered on their pillows. But she could not take one courageous step to protect her charges.

The revelation of her weakness was a lesson in the psychology of Schrecklichkeit which I have never forgotten. There must have been many Lenis in Nazi Germany. All during the war I remembered thankfully that she was a Swiss citizen selling groceries and raising children, safely behind neutral mountains. Perhaps for her own babies she might have braved even the black chimney-sweep in the night—who knows? I am glad she never had to be put to the test.

As for Annie, she returned to her native land, a "natural" for Hitler. For a time at least she must have found hysterical vent for all her miseries and her hatreds. I never knew what became of her, but her family's farm was on the line of the Russian march.

ᥰᥱ 25 ᥱᥰᥱ

Swiss Curtains at a Paris Window

For an entire year, while even small Switzerland was increasing our living costs by speeding up armaments, I had been engaged in a senseless struggle with my conscience and my budget. Should I splurge on curtains for our high Swiss veranda, or should I wait? In a household of mere males, there was no one to cast weight on either side. Finally, the winter little Malcolm turned two, I took myself severely in hand for missing out on today's fun by worrying over tomorrow and, much more reckless for the delay, bought meters and meters of handsome striped drapes from *Le Grand Passage*, our local Macy's.

The bulky package, wrapped in flimsy paper, arrived just as Jerry was leaving for a Carnegie Endowment conference in London. I was watching him pack with his usual lightning dexterity when the telephone rang. Paris calling. Our friend Doctor Babcock, Director of the Endowment's European Center, had just died at the American Hospital in Paris. I laid away my curtains spiritlessly and Jerry went on to London.

The Carnegie Endowment for International Peace, at Doctor Butler's suggestion, was calling a conference at Chatham House. Chatham House is headquarters of the Royal Society on Foreign Affairs and corresponds to our Council on Foreign Relations. Both groups started after the famous Paris Peace Conference in 1918, when some of the special advisers and experts decided that it was vital to continue objective study of international problems. Commercial, monetary and political-affairs specialists from six nations came to London to make a survey of the serious world situation and to decide, if they could, upon moves to recommend to governments. After only three days of discussion they reached agreement on principle. The contrast with our interminable disarmament and League deadlocks was striking. "The politics of power and profit," one speaker commented, "can usually reach no real understanding. So the politics of peace and prosperity remain the concern of educators and the independent leaders of public opinion. Public opinion is the force which can improve national policies."

The Chatham House Conference recommended to the governments of the world, if they wished to avoid a world war: Finding ways to help debtor nations to meet their obligations to creditor nations (this meant chiefly the much discussed war debts to Great Britain and the United States). Lowering tariffs to increase the natural flow of world trade. Stabilizing the gold standard as a money scale for the whole world. Strengthening the League and backing the World Court. Halting the armaments race. Applying "economic measures" against aggressive disturbers of the peace.

The latter was a polite reference to Germany and Italy. The previous October, Mussolini had refused to accept League arbitration on a rather nebulous dispute about a boundary line with Abyssinia, and invaded Ethiopia. (Just to make

things harder, "Abyssinia" and "Ethiopia" were two different names for the same country.) For months, there echoed
through Geneva one of our most misleading words, "sanctions." The English verb "to sanction" carries an aura of approval. In League parlance it meant that disapproving nations were refusing—up to a point—to sell Italy their goods.
The United States declared itself neutral and refused to ship
arms either to attacker or to attacked—an "embargo." (We
lifted it the following summer.) Meantime, however, Mussolini could trade freely in everything else with us as well as
with Germany and with some of the smaller neutrals.

Emperor Haile Selassie, an appealing and picturesque dark
figure in flowing robes, came personally to Geneva to plead
his case. He chose among his defenders before the League
Council our good American friend, Pittman Potter, professor
at the Graduate Institute of International Studies. ("Pitt's"
oldest boy used to ride Ethan to and from the International
School on the handlebars of his Swiss bicycle.) Time proved
only too clearly that those half-hearted "sanctions" against
Italy were a failure. Mussolini knew they were not backed
by the finality—international armed might, united to squash
an aggressor. The French were hanging back and accusing
England of Anglo-Saxon hypocrisy. The great British public,
genuinely concerned about League principles but also about
British business interests in Abyssinia, went all out for
"sanctions." They held indignant meetings and huge public
demonstrations.

"Yes," Jerry remarked to me, "watch out for the British
when their economic interests coincide with their moral principles." Remembering our righteous American concern with
China, I decided that the United States and Great Britain
were cousins under the skin.

After seven months of a "punitive" expedition, Mussolini

proclaimed that Abyssinia belonged to Italy. But il Duce drew a blank—the rich mineral resources proved grossly exaggerated and hardly worth all the dead Italian boys.

While Jerry was busy in London I managed to measure and cut my curtains for the seamstress. My husband returned to a town buzzing with the latest Anglo-German incident. Sir John Simon, British Foreign Minister, had been invited to Berlin for "conversations" with Hitler. Unfortunately a White Paper (meaning an official document) which told a few plain but tactless truths had just been issued by Premier MacDonald. Hitler sent regrets—a cold caught in the Saar at a celebration of its return to the Fatherland by the League plebiscite he had been opposing. Geneva knew that this was a "diplomatic sore throat" of deep significance, and the British government was hotly criticized on all sides for its awkwardness.

However, this was not all that was exciting my husband when he got home. From his careful casualness I sensed something personal. After all my bits of family news had been told, he remarked with his best poker face that Doctor Butler had asked him to take Doctor Babcock's post. We were to move to Paris.

"Oh, dear!" I wailed. "My curtains! They're already cut! I can't return them! Why couldn't he have appointed you a few days sooner?"

"Oh, hang the curtains!" cried Jerry. "I thought you'd be so pleased."

Of course I was, and of course we did not hang the curtains—not in Geneva. I packed the bulky yards in our trunks for France, hoping they might fit in the new home which I soon traveled up to Paris to find. When you have pulled up deep stakes in your own country, a mere switch from Switzerland to France is nothing. I had already grown familiar with

the dilemma of curtains bought for one house which never
fit in another. When Jerry and I were engaged we had
visited a Baltimore brother in his charming suburban home,
full of handsome children of all ages. Billie, their eldest, a
blond and humorous small boy, like a prophecy of our own
babies to come, had planted his own live Christmas tree every
year around the house. Proudly he showed us the graduated
line of evergreens, with space for many more to come.

"This makes sense, living this way!" cried my internationalist with enthusiasm, but in the first ten years of our marriage I settled seven places! I had dreamed my honeymoon
dreams of a lifelong home with roots, but there was also a
stimulating challenge in trying to make a home of wherever
we were. Our children missed out on planting the Christmas
trees, but perhaps they understood Christmas more deeply
for that. The same sweet old ceremonies repeated in different
settings take on a special poignancy. Creating together one
small American oasis in a foreign land intensified both our
national and our family loyalty. Daddy and Mummie symbolized fatherland and motherland, and one American brother
stood for hundreds of American playmates the boys never
had.

Experience had soon taught me to find our school first and
then a home within convenient walking distance. In Paris we
could have chosen from several conventionally American
schools, with American pupils and American textbooks. "It's
the only way to keep your boys sports-conscious," one enthusiastic mother boasted. But Jerry and I wanted to do better
than that by our sons. We both felt that there is nothing more
stultifying and artificial than a transplanted national institution. Why have the good fortune to be living abroad in a
rich old civilization like France and sacrifice culture for a
football and a Macmillan spelling book?

At the Bilingual School of Neuilly we found our answer.
Neuilly was a calm, dignified suburb of leafy avenues, where
a house and garden cost no more than a Paris apartment. It
lay within subway or bus ride of my husband's new office on
the boulevard Saint-Germain. The school directress, Madame
Jolas, an American married to a Frenchman, had found no
satisfactory school for her own two daughters, so she had
started one of her own.

My American acquaintance was horrified by our decision.
Eugène Jolas belonged to an advanced French literary group
who had published James Joyce's *Ulysses*, so she was sure
our children would learn indecent, garbled, stream-of-consciousness English and become contaminated with "Leftist"
ideas. Monsieur Jolas, a quiet gentleman busy with his own
affairs, I saw only once. His wife was a born executive,
like so many American women. Later during the war she ran
magnificently the *Cantine Marseillaise* in New York for
French sailors and soldiers.

The educational aim of L'Ecole Bi-Lingue de Neuilly in itself argued a woman of courage. She was trying to combine
French scholastic standards, their fine impatience with slop-
piness, whether of thought or of handwriting, with American
liberalism and a modern psychological approach. All her staff
were bilingual and all studies taught in both French and
English. The children were of almost as varied nationalities
as at the International School of Geneva. Fascinating pink
and yellow reading cards bore the French phrase on one
side and the English on the other: "*Le jeune homme—con-
duit—son auto,*" and "The young man—drives—his car."
There was ample attention to art, to music and to outdoor
play, and even a baby class for small Malcolm.

The new school had been easier to find than the new
home. I tramped the wide-paved Neuilly streets for hours,

wearing out shoe soles and patience but covering in a few days a lifetime of intimacy with French upper-class homes. I saw only those whose owners needed to rent, but those reminded me of the genteel poverty of the old South. In crumbling villas, stuffy with old brocades, faded velvets, gleaming parquet floors and incredibly antiquated plumbing, French families lived thriftily, correctly and exclusively behind high iron fences around exquisite gardens. Gardeners were cheap and so were maids. Most homes had two or three servants, who sometimes slept in quarters to which Geneva's basement rooms had been luxury by comparison. In one gloomy old three-story house where a polite but hostile lady showed off her decaying grandeur, I asked about maids' rooms. The little *femme de chambre* led me through the back door, across an unkempt half block of wild grass, to a two-storied wooden building. Above the family garage were two bare bedrooms in a state of wild disorder, one shared by the two maids, the other, by virtue of her superior rank and professional grumpiness, occupied by the cook. There was no heating, and through inch-wide cracks in the rough wooden walls I could see out into the cold, wet garden.

"But—don't you freeze?" I gasped to my sharp-eyed guide in her neat black dress and white apron. She gave me an odd look, as though she thought no better of me for my concern.

"Eh b'en, Madame," she shrugged. *"On s'y habitue."* ("Oh, well, Madame, one gets used to it.")

I do not say this was typical, but it happened. Marie Antoinette and her cake were, after all, less than one hundred and fifty years dead. Though France is a far more liberal country intellectually than the United States, the class distinctions of an aristocratic tradition still permeated her social life. The servants themselves seemed sometimes the most insistent upon snobbishness in their superiors, since it left them free to lie and cheat. I never got along with French maids. My democratic trustfulness and the two-faced correctness of their conditioning were poles apart, and it was only after much trial and error that we finally hit the domestic jack pot. At the Neuilly Scandinavian Y.W.C.A. I found Oddny, a small, perky, clever cook, and Hjordis, a beautiful, tall, gloomy *femme de chambre*, both blonde and both Norwegian. They became loyal members of our household. They had been as unhappy with French mistresses as I with French maids.

One year when the Davis family went home to America for Christmas I told the girls to invite their Scandinavian friends in for a party. When we returned at New Year's, they were mysteriously ready for us, with a real Norwegian supper served at our table spread with pine branches, lighted by their small tree, carefully preserved from Christmas. Next day two of my French neighbors hurried over to inform me of the scandalous goings on of *les domestiques* in our absence. To be sure, only young girls had been seen entering the garden, but no doubt men must have been sneaked in. Laughing and singing went on till after midnight, and wasteful lights were ablaze all over the first floor, even in *le grand salon*! When I explained that the orgy had our permission, the good ladies departed in horror.

But this was only one aspect of French life, which America with its share-croppers and its underprivileged Negroes can hardly criticize. Jerry and I had admired the sturdy Swiss; we were fascinated by the French. Politically, Switzerland, with its democratic confederation of cantons, was almost a United States in miniature. Yet personally we both felt instantly more at home in France. Nor can I say why. Our two cultures are vastly different, but individuals from the two nations often find immediate congeniality. The whole Davis family began that year a love affair with France which will never end. The

French are the most exasperating, the most interesting and the most likable people in the world.

Practically, of course, they drive an American crazy. I thought I should never disentangle myself from the red tape which chokes the simplest transaction, from paying a water bill to writing a reference for a cook. (The reference is useless to her unless you visit the *mairie* in person with your passport and pay for a red seal and a tax stamp!) But social contacts were charming and facile, and the humblest working people used their own language so beautifully that an argument with a plumber became a positive pleasure. My vocabulary of "funny words" swelled rapidly, and I was soon chatting glibly about drainpipes, buttonhole thread and bituminous coal, calling a wrinkle in a dress-fitting *une grimace* and finding "magicians" at five dollars an afternoon for a children's party in the telephone directory under *"Prestidigitateur."* Those who came to our parties, however, always referred to themselves as *artistes*.

We found a home on a broad, tree-lined street, boulevard du Château—impressive stucco, three narrow stories high, secluded behind a tall iron fence and a formal garden. The wide space at the rear was easily transformed into a boys' playground. I had turned my back reluctantly on an adorable small house on the rue Perronet, freshly papered, with modern kitchen, real bathroom, even a child's bedroom papered in animals, and a tiny garden with a vine-covered well as a tea table. Here, I felt, were French people who knew how to live. But it was too small for a growing family. Just as I took my regretful leave I spied something familiar in a corner. A dusty pile of old *Saturday Evening Posts*!

The French like renting to Americans. We spend so much on improvements that we usually leave a place in better condition than we find it. Owners in France never waste a franc except on the outside walls and roof repairs specifically mentioned in the lease. The tenant's game is to wangle as low a rent as possible and then pay for all decorating. In many ways the system is quite as satisfactory as ours.

So, having signed a lease and secured a painter, after many ludicrous stumbling blocks, we had said good-by to Geneva. It had been only four years since that first sleepy glimpse from the *wagon-lit* window, but they had been crowded and fruitful. We had both changed. Under the flowing stream of constant international encounters, my husband's sense of his own convictions and powers had deepened. My childish blinders had melted away and I lived in a wider consciousness of my world and my century, an easier poise for diverse social situations. This was good, because we found to our amusement that we had moved to a position of distinction. *Monsieur le Directeur* of an Endowment Center noted both for its sincere peace aims and for its American purse was treated with a European deference to which we could never grow accustomed. When my husband's face was grotesque with shaving lather or he had just turned a somersault with the boys, I used to protest: *"Mais, mon cher Directeur!"* The French never omit a title, even for an ex-minister whose party fell out of power years before. We both had constantly to prod ourselves to remember. "You Americans," a Latin once cleverly put it, "are personally humble and nationally proud. We smaller nations are personally proud but nationally humble."

The Geneva friends who entertained us at a farewell round of dinners and teas envied us our richer life in one of the world's most interesting capitals. Everybody in Geneva complained of its dullness, its fogs, its high living costs, and its provincial stodginess. We had begun to feel that our international small town was a backwater. The endless deadlocks among representatives of governments who must always look homeward for their cues gave Geneva a second-hand air, twice removed from reality. For a change, one would have enjoyed watching the process of any essential object being manufactured for, delivered to and then consumed by a human being, if only a Shredded Wheat biscuit.

But Paris, we soon realized, though cosmopolitan, was not international at all. The French, like Americans, were pre-occupied with carrying on their own traditions. They became far more excited over Premier Léon Blum and his Socialist Popular Front than over Hitler. One actually heard reaction-aries say: "Better Hitler than Blum!" ("*Mieux Hitler que Blum.*") Paris, like New York or London or Berlin, was only a nation's capital. In Geneva we had really lived in the inter-national hub of the world. We soon missed its smallness, the close if irritating congeniality of a common purpose, the easy friendships. From then on, whenever anything important happened at the League, Jerry was back on the old stamping ground, and I always went with him.

We plunged into new adjustments, Jerry to learn the ropes of the European Center, its students' international library, free lecture courses, its subsidies to independent enterprises in European countries. Their value to peace my husband must assess. Meantime, like a distracted ant trying to cope, one crumb at a time, with an anthill, I was quarreling with paint-ers, haunting employment agencies and adjusting a bewildered youngest boy to a strange new house and "yarden."

Remembering the weary state of our household stuff, in-cluding the old wheel chair, we had no worry about French customs fees. To the Swiss moving firm we entrusted three precious papers, one from the Geneva tax authorities, one from the Hôtel de Ville, and one from the American Con-sulate, all certifying that the Davises had paid their back bills and that no citizen of any Swiss canton had any complaint against us. When our van, like its brothers all over the world, chugged in several hours late, we were astonished to hear that the delay had occurred at the French frontier.

"It was all that dress goods," reproached our sweating driver. "Madame should have told me. After they found it, they pulled everything else to pieces, searching all the trunks."

"What dress goods?" I asked blankly.

He threw back his burly arms in a measuring gesture.

"Those meters and meters of cut cloth, Madame. French duties are high on materials not yet made up. They protect their own industries. Here is the bill, Monsieur."

So the Swiss tax I had evaded on Quimper pottery was collected by the French government for my Geneva curtains. This time Jerry did not tell me to hang the curtains. But I did, at the great tall French windows of our new dining room, where, with a false hem, they looked almost intentional.

❧ 26 ❧

Madrid on the Eve of War

Despite a Baptist upbringing, I offered up thanks every night to "Uncle Andy." Now that my husband was a full-fledged officer of the Carnegie Endowment I had the right to tag along with him on all his visits to other European countries. Andrew Carnegie had been a poor boy, so he not only endowed a ten-million-dollar fund for the cause of peace, but provided also that when its officers traveled, wife or daughter was to go also at the expense of the Endowment. I remembered the little Scotchman fondly on those vacations for two in exciting new cities. To one not born with a silver spoon in her mouth, the modest freedom from finance was the Great Refresher. I could breakfast in bed, idle mornings away along fascinating streets, lunch or dine with unusual people and attend the sessions of international conferences. The last seemed the least important of my privileges, yet gradually, without quite realizing it, upon the base already laid by Geneva I was beginning my postgraduate course in world affairs.

England, Germany, Hungary, Austria, Denmark, Czechoslovakia, Spain can never again be colored geographical shapes peopled with robots. I have sat in their railroad cars, slept in their hotels, eaten their food, heard their language, admired their shop windows, puzzled over their newspapers, and watched their people come and go about their daily concerns. The map of Europe began to come alive. The foreigners whose delegates I had seen at the League of Nations were no longer strangers. Here and there, over the face of that map, friendships began to form. If intellectual barriers break down with each new language, emotional fences melt away with every new friend in another nation.

The spring after we hung our Swiss curtains in a Paris dining room, "Uncle Andy" sent Jerry and me to Spain. The occasion, in Madrid, was discouragingly named "The Interim Conference of the International Studies Conference on Peaceful Change." During the forty-eight-hour journey southward from Paris, my husband had ample time to explain what it was all about this time. Like most of his interests, its purpose was simpler than its terrifying title.

Every two years distinguished scholars from thirty different countries and from half a dozen international institutions met together to confer, with scientific objectivity, upon some international problem. The Conference was not a political body. It studied its subjects seriously and agreed upon solutions, but it made no recommendations. This left its participants freer to join honestly in debate. Afterwards the full records were published, for governments and national publics to take or leave. The method has great advantages as source material for any honest seeker after political truth.

"State Intervention in Economic Life" and "Collective Security" had already been thrashed out. Now, opinions were to be exchanged upon a very pertinent topic—"Peaceful Change." How could an existing situation, justifiable on his-

toric grounds but no longer tenable internationally, be altered
without resorting to war?

Jerry explained all this as our *wagon-lit* carried us out of
a lovely Paris spring with chestnut blossoms into a still lovelier
May of palm trees and hot sunshine. But the Madrid meeting
was only an "Interim Conference," for preparing an agenda,
he said. The real Conference would take place in Paris next
year.

Long meetings to discuss what to discuss at other long
meetings a year hence sounded hideously dull. I was glad to
be a mere woman, with my mind free to wander from the
conference room to the bright blue sky outside and the foreign
noises drifting in from the pleasant avenues of a Latin city.
The wide sunshine, the dustiness, the ancient beauty elbowing
shabby modern neglect, reminded me of Southern France. I
was fascinated by the dark-eyed, vital-looking boys and girls
who crowded the streets every evening. The Spanish used
Madrid affectionately, like a personal possession. Long after
midnight, smiling crowds sauntered about, elegant youths,
girls with flowers in their hair, enjoying just being young and
alive under a southern sky.

The reality, of course, was not so rosy as the flowery surface. Jerry, who had been through the Russian Revolution,
wisely requested an inner room on a court, out of reach of
stray bullets in case of trouble. About two o'clock, we were
waked by a sharp explosion. Nothing further happened, so
we went back to sleep. Next morning we learned that hotel
workers on strike had planted a bomb in the entrance door,
exactly under the window of Professor James Shotwell,
Chairman of the Conference. This dauntless American peace
veteran had crossed the ocean and traveled steadily for two
days to reach Madrid in time for the opening sessions next

morning. He and Mrs. Shotwell, dead tired, had just fallen asleep when the bomb exploded.

Just six weeks after our scholars, following a long debate, decided exactly where "peaceful change" began and ended, Spain began fighting Spain. But, except for the bomb, no breath of Franco's war troubled the Studies Conference. Other international tensions, however, crackled ominously through all the sessions. Even the most dispassionate experts are only human men with deep patriotic ties. It took courage and an even deeper patriotism to keep recalling the debate back into the rarefied air of reason. I sat there, stifling my yawns and admiring our American chairman, with his kindly, keen and rather wistful face, keeping his mind on the ball, like a football referee on a confused and rainy field.

The Director of the Deutsches Institut für Aussenpolitische Forschung, though granted full courtesy inside the conference rooms, moved about outside, a lonely figure. He was an enigmatic man, with a round, pasty face, neatly plastered black hair and a careful yet simple manner. Like my Halloween guest, Dr. Fritz Berber seemed isolated in a chronic personal loneliness, as if he had been born solitary. Berber claimed not to be a Nazi party member, but it was evident that he loved his country with abiding passion. Germania, he told Jerry and me, he saw, like the sick boy of the erlking legend, as a precious image being carried in the arms of a man on a wild horse.

Beneath his Teutonic dignity the man was as nervous as a cat. When he rose to speak to the Conference he introduced himself, in his slow, rather awkward way, as a representative of "National Socialist Science." The term made no sense. Smiles were suppressed all over the room. Berber tightened, and then he launched into a passionate plea for the German case. For Germany, "peaceful change" meant getting back her colonies and the port of Danzig.

Under his square-cut German suit, the man was obviously in a dripping perspiration. "The Conference in Paris next year," he finished, with suppressed feeling, "may be our last opportunity to consider together the possibility of peaceful change."

Immediately, Eisenmann, a dark-eyed French historian with a jutting black beard—a Jew—leapt to his feet.

"May I inquire," he demanded, "just what my German colleague means by his statement that this may be our last opportunity to discuss change without war?"

The Chairman smoothed over the tense moment. That evening Doctor Berber went to bed with a violently upset stomach. Doctor Shotwell, Jerry and I found him propped neatly in striped pajamas against his hotel pillows, pastier-faced than ever. He was waiting for a German doctor, as he trusted no others. Berber was convinced he had been poisoned. To me, it was obvious that the Director of the Deutsches Institut für Aussenpolitische Forschung was the victim of emotional indigestion.

By the time the Conference held its Paris meeting the following summer of 1937, Germany had quit the League for good, openly increased its arms, remilitarized the Rhineland, secured control of Danzig and formed the Rome-Berlin Axis to fight Communism and regain her lost colonies.

Listening to the endless debates merely about which topics were to be discussed next year, I began to see that behind the agenda, too, lay all the old political questions. If you left out the adjustment of colony claims, you were skipping the big bone of contention between the Axis and the other nations. Unless you took up the economic quarrels between the five Danubian countries which had once been part of the old

Austro-Hungarian Empire, you were ignoring a hang-over from the first World War which might brew larger trouble. Finally the Conference drew up a prodigious agenda of "Difficulties and Suggested Solutions" for practically every issue upon which nations might go to war. My husband, being an impartial American, was handed a nice, fizzing little bomb. He was to chair a special group of Danubian economic experts from Hungary, Czechoslovakia, Rumania, Bulgaria and Yugoslavia. Though practically dependent upon one another, and with the Beautiful Blue Danube in common, these five smaller states seemed unable to live together or to live apart.

We had lost the Madrid address of our friend Alfonso Albeniz, and we found no word from him at our hotel. But one day, strolling through the Prado grounds, whom should we spy but Alfonso, sauntering towards us along a flower-bordered walk.

"Oh," he smiled, "I knew that sooner or later I should meet you in the street."

He took me to lunch, after carefully asking my husband's permission, and told me how deeply he was worried over Spain's international affairs. He was implacably opposed to the Popular Front government.

"You Americans," he said, shaking his head, "don't understand what's going on here, the lawless elements that are loose under the surface."

The moment General Franco began his opposition, Alfonso offered his services. He told us this, proudly, when he visited us once in our Neuilly salon, before returning to the struggle again.

"It's so calm here," he sighed, looking enviously around the big, quiet room. "You all speak so quietly. At home, we all yell at each other all the time. Ah, we Spanish are a bloody people! How quickly I have become accustomed to violence!"

It was the first time in my life that a friend of whom I was fond had joined an opposite moral camp. It bothered me, considerably. Most men do not mind disagreement, provided their own convictions win in the end. A woman is happiest when everybody she likes feels the same way. But Alfonso's going pro-Franco taught me what a civil war is. It is not a division of "good" against "bad" people, but a serious split in the country itself about a fundamental philosophy. Fighting wins an immediate victory, but it never solves the moral issue.

That May I met a new Spanish friend of my husband's who was as passionately Loyalist. Castillejo (I learned to pronounce him "Casti-lyay-ho") was a humorous professor with a bald head and a long, rather homely face. He taught law and philosophy in the University of Madrid and directed a preparatory school, where we saw some of his interesting educational theories in full swing. Modern education, he believed, in its effort to scrap the older theories, neglects the precious gift in the very young for imitation and memory. This is where the stress should be laid, in the early years. Small children should learn many languages by imitation, and then, as the instinctive fades and the logical grows, these should be clinched into permanent possession by grammar, reading, writing and literature. There must be no break as one study merges into the other. The mother tongue is vitally important, and the same adult must speak the same language to the child, else the result is mental confusion.

Following a group of his six-year-olds one morning from class to class, I took a lightning tour from France to Germany, to England, to Italy. These Spanish tots, undisturbed by visitors, chattered French with a vivacious *Mademoiselle*, answered the patient questions of a blonde *Fräulein*, joined hands with a pretty English girl for an old folk song, and laughed at the dark-eyed *Signorina*'s jokes. One small girl, when asked in the corridor what language she was singing, replied: "Oh, I don't know. It's about a rose—the blonde lady taught it to us today."

Castillejo had an interesting analysis of the strength of the Anglo-Saxon countries. As a young man, studying first in Berlin and then in Paris, he discovered to his surprise a strong intellectual similarity between France and Germany. Both lived by a "Procrustean philosophy," evolving a system first and then fitting life to it. English scholarship, when he first arrived at Oxford, seemed wildly confused. Then he came to see that the British, like the Americans, evolve a working plan to fit a reality. "That," he declared, "is the great strength of the democratic Anglo-Saxon nations."

America he had found a land of intense contrasts—heat and cold, riches and poverty, crime and idealism, bungalows and skyscrapers. Even in marriage he had seen the skyscraper marriage, fine and enduring, and the shoddy bungalow affair that soon fell to pieces.

Castillejo escaped, penniless, to London, with his wife and family, and died there during the war. We have heard nothing from Alfonso, but we know that Berber survived the war. His precious image of Germania could hardly have fared as well. If I remember "Der Erlkönig" correctly from high-school German, it ended:

> ". . . Erreicht den Hof mit Mühe und Not,
> In seinen Armen das Kind war tot."

> ". . . He reached the court with pain and dread,
> In his arms the child lay dead."

27

Three Musketeers in Munich

IT WAS thanks again to "Uncle Andy" that I met, ten years ago, one of the top German war criminals executed at Nuremberg. Hans Frank was already a high-ranking Storm Trooper and Hitler's Minister without Portfolio, but had anyone warned me that he was to become the notorious "Administrator" of Poland I think I should have laughed. It is so difficult for peaceful people to believe in violence until it occurs.

The occasion was the founding in Munich of the Academy of German Law, of which Hitler made Hans Frank President. At the time, Germany still desired outside approval, so my husband and Dr. James Shotwell were formally invited to the laying of the corner stone. Frank was to preside over the occasion. I started off for Munich as lightheartedly as one begins an exciting new detective story. I can easily credit the story I was told about an American girl who telephoned the *Braunhaus* and explained to an astonished Nazi officer that she was in town and would like to meet Hitler. There was flurry and questioning, but it never crossed a solemn German mind that this was just an airy young American out for a lark.

Next day she had tea with the Führer, talked to him in bad German, and went home in high spirits. The story did not tell of what secret mission his entourage assumed her to be the emissary.

So I hunted up a small red German dictionary, hugged my disapproving blond angel, promised his cheery brothers "something nice" from Germany, and, with Jerry and Dr. Shotwell, boarded the train for Munich. We named ourselves The Three Musketeers, and I amused my comrades at arms by picking out inappropriate phrases from my pocket dictionary: "Will you kindly assist me out of the bathtub?" and "At least, give a bed to the lady. As for me, I am content to sleep on the straw."

The two men were better prepared than I for the sudden shift of mood which closed in on us the moment we crossed the German frontier. There was stiffness in every encounter, harsh correctness from customs officials, wary silence among the German passengers broken by surreptitious curiosity when we turned our backs. Baggage and newspapers were inspected, uniforms swarmed through the train, and *Heil Hitlers* punctuated conversation like the perfunctory Amens of a Wednesday night prayer meeting. The Munich streets looked old-fashioned, shabby and silent. By the time we had reached our hotel, the Vierjahreszeiten, I had begun to feel uneasy. The mood was not new to Jerry, but to find myself actually wondering if the walls of our huge Germanic bedroom hid a dictaphone gave me a hysterical desire to giggle. Our suite— great gloomy wooden beds, heavy curtains, lavishly scrolled wallpaper and giant framed engravings—was styled to a Master Race. The bathtub looked indecently huge, and the hottest water could not warm those great unfriendly sides. I swathed myself gratefully in one of those sheets which save European bathers from pneumonia, and shouted to Jerry: "Will you kindly assist me out of the bathtub?"

Breakfast was a long time coming. The Vierjahreszeiten had not served foreigners in a long time, and Jerry made the mistake of ordering orange juice. Nearly an hour elapsed before our tray was brought by a waiter who eyed us as if we had escaped from the zoo. The next morning we were told that they were out of *Orangensaft*.

We had scarcely unpacked before a knock came on the door and a brown uniformed officer with a shorn head and a sulky profile clicked his heels at us. Peremptory, he presented a blond boy in a gray suit as our interpreter and guide. He was a charming lad, with a frightened smile, and the moment we were alone he asked eagerly if Frau Davis would come home to lunch with him and his wife. Oh, yes, there was an official luncheon today but he was sure this was only for men. Delighted, I went off with him to a tasteful apartment to meet his bride of six months. She was a vivid girl, outspoken and boyish, who had lived in England and spoke the language fluently. With a few changes of manner and dress, she might have been an upstanding young American. Here was no docile Gretchen. She dominated that marriage.

All during lunch, while we chatted of innocuous things, her husband cast uneasy glances over his shoulder at the maid. Once she had left, the tension relaxed. I had been racking my brains for a leading question, and over the coffee I found it.

"Are the young people of your generation in Germany," I inquired, stirring my sugar casually, "interested in what young people in other countries are doing?"

They both knew that the moment had come. There was a silence while the two blond heads exchanged glances.

"Well, you see," said the girl, "we don't really belong to this generation. I mean—our sympathies are all with our parents' generation, the old culture. We don't feel at home in this new Germany."

"But," added the young man, "we think maybe for Germany, this is good. Not for us, but for the common people."

"Since Hitler came," admitted his wife, "we have no more unemployed. A few years ago, you were hardly safe in the streets. Now there are no beggars."

(Hitler of course was solving unemployment by keeping everybody busy manufacturing armaments, with the devil to pay only after the output of labor had exploded into the waste of war.)

"But what can we do?" she said. "Even if we tried to start a revolution, we would just get killed."

"And so—" the blond boy gave his reserved smile, "we stay out of politics and live quietly, enjoying our personal life."

"But I assure you," cried his wife, intensely, "we hate these brutal faces in uniform as much as you must!"

It was a bold remark. Her husband changed the subject. Had I brought any newspapers or magazines? They both looked disappointed when I explained they would have been confiscated at the border. The girl sighed.

"We see only our own newspapers. Tell me, is it true that America is going Communist?"

I laughed.

"France is already Communist under Léon Blum," explained the young man earnestly. "President Roosevelt's New Deal means he's a Communist, doesn't it?"

"Hardly," said I. "Besides, Roosevelt was elected to office by an overwhelming majority. He expresses the will of the people."

"But the people," said the girl, "are so ignorant. What if they voted to make America Communist?"

"I should hate it," said I, "but I should still feel that a free majority has a right to choose its own destiny, provided the minorities are left free to become majorities in their turn."

"How strange!" murmured the girl. "Then you stand for no principle, just the decision of the masses?"

"That," I said, "is our principle."

They eyed me with a touch of suspicion. Controlled German newspapers had done their work well. Even these educated youngsters with no Hitler sympathies felt Germany as an oasis among nations slowly rotting into Communism. One chance American visitor from the outside could hardly compete with clever Doctor Goebbels. We parted cordially, my young friends and I. When I returned, brimming with news of my interesting encounter, Jerry met me with a chuckle. I had not only been expected at the luncheon but I had been seated at the place of honor to Frank's right. All during the food and the speeches my chair beside Hitler's Minister had stood conspicuously empty.

"You should have seen the commotion when they discovered where you had gone! I only hope it doesn't get that nice boy into trouble," Jerry said.

We never heard of him again, but whether he and his wife lived on in Munich "staying out of politics and enjoying their personal life," or whether the girl's outspokenness got them into trouble, their fate was doubtless the same. Their apartment, I know, now lies among the rubble of Munich.

At the next luncheon I met Hans Frank, but the post of honor was now occupied by the wife of an Italian officer. The President of the Academy of German Law had a heavy, blank face, narrow brown eyes under thick brows, a straight nose, and a full mouth set in a heavy jaw. He sat pouring liquid into his cup from a small china pot conspicuously labeled "Kaffee-Hag." I glanced around. While the rest of us drank real coffee, every uniformed Nazi, even Kaiser Wilhelm's younger son at our table, had the same little pot of caffeinless beverage. The Führer disapproved of alcohol and other stimulants. This adolescent idealism was especially ludicrous in contrast with August Wilhelm's degenerate profile, that Hohenzollern nose and weak chin and those weary, humorous eyes. The brown-uniformed prince drank his Kaffee-Hag instead of his champagne, and chatted easily with a buxom Spanish lady. Photographers darted about everywhere with blinding flashlights. When one burst near our table, with the cameras pointed on Frank, the Spanish lady shrank back.

"Oh," we heard the Hohenzollern reassure her drily, "they won't include me. They're only taking important people."

About Hitler's new German law we heard many passionate orations. One phrase ran like a theme song through everything: "The new German law is the will of the Führer." I wondered why these men bothered to call it law, and as I heard them so ardently attacking reason and learning I wondered if they had all once had considerable trouble with their homework.

Frank's voice corkscrewed up and up to a dramatic hush before he pronounced the holy name: "Der Führer!" Each time the hall burst into *Sieg Heils* and *Heil Hitlers*. Arms shot forward in that gesture which we now call sinister but which struck me then as ludicrous. At an evening reception, full of fat, bare arms and portly black "tails" already straining at the seams, it was side-splitting. I could not take such humorless people seriously. After one of Frank's most impassioned speeches I managed to convulse the other two Musketeers by whispering: "And now, boys, go out and fight for dear old Siwash!"

Frank was not a hypocrite; Hitler's Protector of Poland was what my boys used to call a "dumb pig." He must have ordered the torture of Polish thousands less from sadism than from bull-like stupidity. When forced to view the horror movies of Buchenwald in Nuremberg, Frank gagged on a handkerchief stuffed into his mouth. Captured by the American Seventh Army at Berchtesgaden, he tried to perform the heroic by slashing his throat and wrists—but not fatally. He was the only one of all the Nuremberg war criminals to plead guilty. In prison he turned Catholic. Before the Military Tribunal he poured out his soul anxiously, confessing all his crimes and the guilt of Germany, which will not be erased, he cried, in a thousand years. It is not strange that the President of the Academy of German Law went emotional and made no legal plea in his own defense. He had whipped others, and now they were whipping him. It must have been as simple as that.

The cornerstone of the new Academy was laid at a gigantic outdoor ceremony where we saw what was to me our most shocking sight. The entire Faculty of the University of Munich, gray-haired men in caps and gowns, stood at attention and lifted their flowing black sleeves in the Nazi salute.

The last evening a gala dinner was held in the vast Deutsches Museum. After we checked our coats, we walked a quarter of a mile to an immense stone hall, dank as a tomb. The German women, knowing what to expect, had kept their coats around their ample, bejeweled forms. In my naïve American way I kept hoping the heat would be turned on, and by the time soup arrived, tepid after its long journey from the hinterland, my teeth were audibly chattering.

So next morning, while the other Musketeers went on to Berlin, I lay for two days in my gloomy wooden bed, sneezing and coughing and cursing Hitler. If he had taken the Saar coal basin from the French, he might at least have been more generous to his foreign guests. The morning I dressed and descended wanly, I found a changed hotel. The radiators were cold, the menus down to war rations, the uniforms vanished. The Nazis had put on a wonderful three-day show. Now Germany had settled grimly down to business again.

Thankfully I boarded the train for Paris, and I was halfway home before I remembered my promise to my little boys. I had not brought them "something nice" from Germany, after all.

~~ 28 ~~

The Paris We Loved

By the summer of '37, when the Studies Conference held its Paris session on peaceful change, boulevard du Château had begun to feel like home. Though internationalists, we were true Americans, so our first concern was our plumbing, a mad twist of open pipes ingeniously designed to thwart drainage. In a clothes closet on the third floor we installed a unique invention known in our plumber's catalogue as a *baignoire-fauteuil* or bathtub-armchair. The bather sat on a porcelain hillock, with knees doubled up like mountain peaks, and buttocks, calves and feet submerged in warm water below the tide-line. It made adventure of the evening bath for the children, while the maids, even tall Hjordis, spoke gratefully of the privilege. I never discovered how housemaids are supposed to keep clean in France, though I was told that if they were really fussy they could patronize the public baths.

The Goldberg cartoon of unrelated pipes in our bathroom so annoyed my logical husband that one morning he burst all lathery out of the door, crying, "Good God! As if the affairs of the world weren't senseless enough at this moment, without my having to look at *that* every morning!" So I summoned my meek little seamstress, who devised flowery cretonne drapes to hide the worst of them and who always asked thereafter with a roguish giggle, "And does Monsieur feel himself more gay now in the mornings?"

Formal entertaining was in order by *Monsieur le Directeur* of the Endowment's European Center. Our lovely new salon of many high windows, with parquet floor and fine marble mantel, and our handsome dining room, must be furnished with dignity.

We relegated shabbier pieces to the upper family floors, and I embarked on a long treasure hunt for good antiques, simple enough to suit a future home in our own country. Poking around the Paris streets, so rich in history, I began to see why ancestor worship persists in any old civilization. I was glad not to be buying modern, so sleek, so shallow, so sure of itself. The tiniest antique shop on the Left Bank cried all the glories of old France. A battered Louis Seize mirror, a delicately inlaid table set one dreaming of those unknown hands, so patient and caressing, shaming our vulgar haste. France seemed like a lovely old belle who had seen her best days but still conserved a secret charm no younger rival could touch. There was something heart-breaking about it because she could not go on waltzing while all the rest of the world jitterbugged and jived. French factory production per capita ranked far below the industrious Germans', and "efficiency" was regarded by both management and labor with indifference. But when it comes to devoted personal work with the fingers and the heart, they beat the rest of us, hands down.

I struck up a friendship with a boyish Breton of sixty who earned his living by upholstery but sustained his soul on antiques. He was the old France, an artisan wounded by shoddiness who maintained his stubborn artistic integrity in the face of all modern slapdash.

"Just look at this, Madame," he would sigh, rubbing an antique brocade lovingly between thumb and forefinger," "and then that," and he slapped fretfully with the back of his hand at some modern imitation that would not last a year. Insides of chairs were for him an affair of honor. "Sometimes I only break even on a job and that angers my wife. But, it is stronger than I. I cannot sew up a chair, knowing the stuffing is inferior."

Monsieur Wytters used to walk the five or six miles from his home to ours. *Eh b'en*, it was just a good morning constitutional! At early dawn he donned his shouldered beret, a small table or knotted a heavy pack of upholstering samples into a black handkerchief slung across his back and was clanging the bell of our high iron gate just as the Davises sat down to breakfast. He once wrote me, on the cheap, blue-lined paper of which no tradesman was ashamed—he never telephoned, for it cost a few *sous* more—about a small Louis Seize sofa, and I ordered it, sight unseen. One morning, he came all the way to Neuilly to apologize. The piece was genuine, *bien sûr*, but its back had once been shortened by sawing out a section and gluing the two halves together. Madame must feel under no obligation. Of course I took it, and it filled just the right corner of our salon.

In Paris, unlike Geneva, we made mostly English and American friends. The French do not readily open either their homes or their hearts to foreigners, and though we had endless social contacts, my illuminating experiences were with the grocers, the carpenters, the seamstresses, and now and then a friendly Neuilly neighbor. I never laid eyes on the elderly lady who lived next door across a formidable brick

wall, but the day of Curtis's June birthday party she got wind
of the festivities, baked a beautiful cake, and left it at the
kitchen anonymously. Our children, she told the cook, were so
gay, and always polite if a ball happened to land in her
garden.

Through our friends the John Coxes—John was a gifted
artist, Liggy did literary work, in an Old World studio many
flights up—we did get glimpses of a serious Latin Quarter
life among men passionately concerned with creative theory.
We often saw Picasso, a thoughtful, dark-haired man with a
preoccupied air and no touch of the Greenwich Village
poseur, at the Deux Magots—a café near the Endowment's
building.

We met, but never cultivated nor were cultivated by, the
conventionally unconventional Americans. Their women
made of clothes a fetish more snobbish than any French co-
cotte's—for she at least has a practical objective. They haunted
the openings, envied or scorned a new acquaintance according to whether or not she was wearing Suzy's latest black
model and were as bourgeois as any small-town matron, com-
peting over pink mints and bridge prizes.

Clothes are, of course, more fun in Paris than anywhere in
the world, for small dressmakers and milliners with a touch
of genius sprout like mushrooms. Even without benefit of
Piquet and Molyneux, I did not do so badly. At a reception
one afternoon a gallant Frenchman with a flirtatious eye said
I looked like a charming American friend of his and did I
know her? Her name was unfamiliar to me, though later I
kept seeing it over and over, being voted, along with the
Duchess of Windsor, among the ten best-dressed women in
Paris! I apologize to Mrs. Harrison Williams for the gentleman's unwarranted comparison, for I was wearing a Swiss
wool suit and cape made by Leni two years earlier from a

Butterick pattern and a two-dollar hat concocted from the scraps.

My husband had good friends among American business-men there, but some regarded any peace worker with sus-picion. The American Club of Paris decided not to increase its ten-per-cent French membership to fifteen because "We've got enough foreigners around here already."

While Vice-President of the American Club, Jerry gave a talk on "Recovery and Rearmament." The speech was made the January after our jaunt to Munich, and while the Rome-Berlin Axis was in process of formation. Jerry compared an Endowment for International Peace to a thoughtful man in an irresponsible neighborhood, where it was customary to leave straw, old packing boxes, and other inflammable material lying about, to store fireworks in the cellars, and then to stroll around throwing lighted matches over the fences. If this modest fellow suggested clean-ing up or founding a fire department he was called crazy. If he asked, "But what if you have another fire like the last one?" he was told, "Oh, things have always gone this way. If there's a fire, we throw the children out of the window and carry the mattresses downstairs." Asked "Why?" the neigh-bors replied indignantly, "Because the mattresses are valu-able." He asked his audience to look around and speculate how many European countries and even our own could take another general war without an inevitable aftermath of social upheaval and revolution. If war and ruin should come, however, that man who wanted the fire hazards cleaned up might well ask his indignant neighbors, "Who's loony now?"

There were men in the Club who saw the point and com-modity-swappers who were irritated by unpleasant truths. My husband was elected President of the American Club the following season, but when he resigned, owing to pressure of international duties, some members told the Nominating Committee they wanted "somebody more regular." "Davis speaks French too well," they complained. "He sounds almost like a Frenchman."

Barely fourteen months from the American Club meeting, Hitler started the conflagration by marching into Austria. But there was no world fire department, and everybody went on stacking their cellars with fireworks. The flames had already reached Poland before Great Britain and then France had to begin throwing their children out of the windows. And none of us saved any mattresses after all.

⚙ 29 ⚙

Quisling and Patriot in Budapest

THE following October the Society of the *Hungarian Quarterly* invited my husband to speak on Danubian economic problems before the members of the Society in Budapest. Naturally, I tagged along. Never having heard of this distinguished group, I boned up ahead of time on their *Quarterly*, "a periodical designed to spread knowledge of Danubian and Central European affairs and to foster political and cultural relations between Hungary and the Anglo-Saxon world." Columbia University handled the English edition. There seemed to have been quite a lot of Hungarian-American interchange going on while I looked the other way.

Budapest had always blurred in my mind with Bucharest in Rumania, and both capitals, like Vienna, I had imagined as gay and unreal backgrounds for musical comedy. I was totally unprepared for the beauty and dignity of Budapest. One felt instantly here in the real heart of Europe, a historical center of which the more familiar places were only the outskirts. Here the old and the new met before one's eyes at the Danube, fascinating medieval Buda on one bank, Pest, with its baroque Austrian buildings, on the other. The Danube, neither beautiful nor blue, was a narrow, muddy stream, but sunset across it from our hotel windows overlooking the old town is still an exciting memory. We read sadly of those necessary Allied bombings which left half the lovely old city in ruins.

Jerry delivered his address on Danubian economic problems in an impressive room of the Hungarian House of Parliament. A distinguished audience had gathered to listen to him. It is always salutary for a wife to watch her familiar spouse take the post of honor and suddenly become an honored public figure. As he talked, I learned again that there was no escaping those political problems of prestige and power. The Danubian states, united by sharing the same river, could not solve their pressing economic interdependence because they had not settled their political disputes. Tactfully, my husband pointed to the advantages of federation and our own colonial history of friction and rivalry, and let it go at that.

Béla Imrédy, Director of the Bank of Hungary, introduced the American speaker. Afterwards, he said to me, thoughtfully: "This problem is a familiar story to me, yet today I learned things I never knew before." His wife said: "We all found your husband so charming. He has such a nice smile." Mrs. Imrédy was a refreshingly natural woman, and before the three days were over I was wishing that Paris and Budapest were closer, so that our sympathetic encounter might become a friendship. The Imrédys gave us a dream of a dinner at the Gellert, Budapest's most famous restaurant. Every day there was more lavish hospitality to make two modest Americans feel like visiting royalty. My two Paris evening gowns were studied with friendly curiosity by all the ladies, and a gold circlet on my head, bought only because it was becoming, they took for the latest Paris rage. Whether it is politics or clothes, these countries of Central Europe feel out of the current, anxious to keep in touch with the main stream.

I sat at Imrédy's right at the Gellert dinner. He was a tall, courteous gentleman with a long, thin nose in a long, keen face—rather like Voltaire's without the humor or the greatness. It was not surprising, I suppose, that the Director of the Bank of Hungary and I should talk about money. I tried to explain the difference I felt between the French and the American attitude towards it.

"To the French, money is something static, property to be stowed away in a sock. To us, money is a force, a kind of energy, always in movement. Easy come, easy go!"

Imrédy sighed.

"In my country," he commented dryly, "I'm afraid it's hard come, easy go. We are not a thrifty people. In spite of invasion, poverty and depression, memories of glory under the Austro-Hungarian Empire still linger in our consciousness."

I judged that being Director of the Bank of Hungary was no enviable task.

Next day his wife drove me past the quaint houses of old Buda, and to tea at Pest's most elegant pastry shop. She talked of her husband with that glow of the contentedly married woman. Important men—didn't I think so?—who must ponder heavy problems all day, needed an understanding wife.

"Not that they admit it," she laughed gaily. "My husband does not say: 'Darling, I need you. I could not live without you.' Oh"— she cocked her head saucily— "sometimes. But usually he just calls me, the moment he steps inside the door: 'Irma?' " She smiled to herself. "I hear his key in the latch and then that little 'Irma?' "

Mrs. Imrédy asked eagerly about America, and especially

how its women lived. Like most Europeans, she imagined us all lolling idly in nests of luxury, with men waiting on us hand and foot. She listened incredulously to my explanation that aside from everything else, the servant problem alone made this vision absurd. No nursemaid had ever cared for my children, except once, when my unborn second put me on crutches from sciatic pressure, and we hired a girl to take care of my first. This cost twenty-five dollars a week, which I earned myself with odd jobs of writing.

My hostess made a rapid calculation into pengös and looked startled.

"Twenty-five dollars! But that's more than I pay all three of my servants together."

She sat frowning over her steering wheel, trying to fit this into the slick Hollywood fantasies which Europe mistakes for a reflection of American life.

"Oh, well," she decided finally, "but you all have such wonderful machines to do your work for you."

"The machines are not robots," I retorted. "Somebody has to run them. Besides, they cost money."

"Still," she persisted, "we have so little modern comfort here. We simply must have servants."

I was contrasting my luxurious Geneva breakfasts in bed with those early winter dawns in New Haven, when I struggled awake, shivering and nauseated, to heat a bottle for one-year-old Ethan, while Curtis pressed his embryo head on my sciatic nerve.

"Nobody," I retorted irritably, "has yet invented a machine that will change a baby's diaper!"

We both laughed, but I caught her glancing at me surreptitiously, as though she still could not reconcile my Paris wardrobe, my husband's position, and our social breeding with that diaper-changing.

"This is the penalty," I explained, "that we white-collar people pay for living in a democracy. Americans just don't like to serve other people."

"I see," she said with an air of wisdom. "I see—you suffer from an excess of democracy!"

During the war Imrédy became Premier of Hungary under the Germans, resigned because he had a Jewish grandmother, and then returned to his post. Seven years after our Budapest visit, Jerry passed over the morning paper to me silently. It was folded back to a news photograph. Under an old felt hat, a familiar lean profile with a long nose was smiling sardonically down at military handcuffs being fastened on his wrists by stern young Russian soldiers. Imrédy, fugitive from Allied justice, had been captured. A month later another picture was printed casually among the mopping-up news after V-E Day. The tall figure which had looked so distinguished in evening clothes stood blindfolded and alone against a wall before a firing squad. Béla Imrédy, former Premier of Hungary, had been executed as a German collaborationist.

I know his guilt was clear and that indirectly he helped to kill thousands of American boys. But those pictures haunted me. I wondered if he cried that little "Irma?" just before the shot. Who knew how much his policy of expediency before the German battering-ram had been dictated by his family's welfare? War, I reflected unhappily, is the real Criminal, the great Quisling, the Traitor to the Right Side. A dictator's Blitzkrieg, mowing down everything in its path, even everyday honor, puts too harsh a strain on us frail human beings. Even Laval might have ended his days only another self-seeking politician like plenty in our own country, had war not resolved all issues into stern, falsifying black-and-white. Who of us knows, in safety, how well his principles would stand up under bloody threat?

A conqueror on the march puts a strain on small countries incomprehensible to a citizen of an unbeaten continent. Count Teleki, one of Hungary's great patriots, was a member of the Endowment's European Committee. He, too, gave a luncheon for us in Budapest. Teleki was a frail scholar of tremendous psychological strength, a geographer, who came from an old noble family of Transylvania. He had never approved its slicing off from Hungary, to become a part of Rumania, though he believed the issue could be adjusted. Teleki was an idealist with a deep vein of pessimism, and even in 1937, when we were in Budapest, he was not sanguine about the fate of his small and impoverished country before Hitler's power drive.

"I have never asked a rabbit," he remarked ironically to my husband, "whether it prefers to be eaten by an animal of a higher or a lower culture."

The war winter of 1940 Jerry went to Hungary on a Red Cross mission. Teleki was Prime Minister. He caused considerable flurry in Budapest by leaving a Parliament session, locking the door of his private office, and talking for an hour and a half with an American. He divulged then an incident which he had never made public. That fall of '39, when everyone knew Hitler was going to strike, but not where and how, a request amounting to an order came to Budapest from Berlin. German troops demanded the right of way through Hungary in a march upon Poland. Teleki summoned his Cabinet, and, he told Jerry proudly, their resistance was unanimous. The Hungarian government refused, gave orders for general mobilization at home, and waited. Hitler decided to invade Poland instead by way of the long-disputed Polish Corridor, and World War II began.

"Of course," said Count Teleki, with the humble realism of the small nation, "we could not save Poland. But the delay, while the German armies marched by the longer route, allowed thousands of Poles to escape."

That October day, as we lunched with the elite of Budapest in his apartment, his wife lay incurably ill in an adjoining room. Countess Teleki insisted upon greeting me. She rested against lacy pillows, her finely modeled face very pale under abundant white hair, her dark eyes smiling graciously on an American intruder, as she apologized for not being at table. She was still bedridden when Teleki shot himself in 1943. Rather than be personally eaten by the animal of lower culture, he had, after calmly talking it over with his wife and son, taken what he believed to be the only honorable way out.

Teleki's suicide haunted me less than Imrédy's execution. His was the resolved and noble end of a weary patriot, but Imrédy, with his handcuffs and his blindfold handkerchief, leaves a bad taste in the memory, the degradation of an unfinished life. We all wonder how we would stand up to these trials, but we know what we admire.

ᴖᴖᴖ 30 ᴖᴖᴖ

Geneva Begins to Split

Before we left Geneva I had conscientiously devoted a Thursday school holiday to showing the boys through the International Labor Office and, near by, the magnificent but still empty Palais des Nations. The "permanent" Peace Palace, as it was called, had been under construction for years. Lack of funds, violent disagreement among its international board of architects, and workmen's strikes had halted the work, but now, though not quite ready for occupation, it was open to visitors. Neither Ethan nor Curtis, who recall vividly less educational afternoons, retains the slightest memory of the expedition. That day, however, they trotted, awestruck, along the great, gleaming corridors, and Ethan sighed rapturously: "Oh, Mummie, I wish me and Curtis could roller-skate here!"

The boys were disappointed that Daddy would not be moving into this new magnificence, but they learned with pride that an American of whom they had never heard, one John D. Rockefeller, Jr., had built a two-million-dollar library, and that Mr. Sweetser, anyway, would share the glory by working in the new League buildings. Thereafter they referred to the entire billion-dollar edifice as "Alan's Daddy's office."

The Peace Palace was still incomplete in February of 1936, but the Secretariat of the League moved in, just a few weeks before Hitler, repudiating the Rhine Pact, marched into the Rhineland, without opposition from anyone. A German told my husband, with honesty, that he and his compatriots did not understand why they had been allowed to "get away with it" so easily. He seemed to be pumping Jerry for inside information on some subtle policy of the other powers, waiting to deal Germany a sudden blow from an unexpected quarter.

It was now that Geneva friends began to complain to us that the old team spirit of the community was gone. Intense nationalism, they said, had taken its place. Peace workers lived in psychologically armed camps of conflicting "ideologies." Discussion became strained and everyone wondered what everyone else was "really thinking." Some, unwilling to admit the truth, tried to blame this new strangeness upon the cool, untried immensity of the Peace Palace.

"Geneva's not what it was in the old days, when you were here. It was friendlier in the old quarters. Now you walk half a mile to somebody's office; there's no more visiting back and forth informally. People get into hot arguments or keep quiet. Everything you say is construed with a political meaning."

Coming back, with the fresh perspective of absence, we felt the change sharply. We practically commuted to Geneva, for despite our fondness for our lovely Paris home, the international town still drew us like a magnet. Jerry went for the League meetings, each more crucial and ineffectual than the last, I to wander affectionately through old haunts and to see my friends. I spent, I admit, scant time in Council or

Assembly, yet in my own way I gathered vivid impressions. Politics, seeping down from the top, permeated Geneva's social life more intensely than ever. Wherever one turned among old friends, one caught the echo of an international crisis.

Fritz Schnabel, a genial German in charge of League publications, "Onkel Fritz" to our rollicking boys, had visited often in our home, with his gentle wife. Now they were leaving for Argentina. We never guessed why, at the time, but we have often wondered since. Clarence Streit, with the aid of his French wife, who gave him much secretarial as well as domestic support, had finished a book called *Union Now*. It advocated a federation of the democracies before Fascism went any further. Prentiss Gilbert, Counselor of Embassy in Berlin, had died so suddenly in the German capital that Charlotte, skiing in the Swiss Alps, had not had time to reach his side. Absurd rumors were still afloat in Geneva that Prentiss had probably "known too much." The Herbert Mays, devoted Geneva residents, were still mothering and fathering the younger American community and giving their marvelous parties. Herbert was Vice-Chairman of the Permanent Opium Board. Politics may come and go, but the problem of controlling traffic in dangerous drugs goes on.

Our friends the Gerhardt Jentsches, comrades on that Pompeian villa expedition, were being ostracized by the international community. Despite his American wife, his former Harvard instructorship, his Swiss residence and his international beliefs, Gerhardt had always remained, as was his right, a German citizen. He was, at the beginning, anything but pro-Hitler. He refused, however, as some of his excited friends demanded, immediately to repudiate his entire country wholesale. Too young to fight in World War I until he was drafted at the very end for a few months, his boyhood had been left singularly free, for a Prussian-born, because of his elders' preoccupation with life-and-death issues. This had left his mind untamed and his spirit boyish. He and Mary had always managed charmingly on a shoestring. Now, however, there were two babies. Gerhardt was teaching history at the Girls' College of Céligny, and the family had moved from the Promenade Saint-Antoine to a rural cottage, where Mary kept house cheerfully, casually but effectively. She was raising a trilingual family. The baby still spoke every baby's international language, but blonde Erika talked Kentucky American with her mother, North German with her father, and Swiss French with the *femme de ménage*.

We had heard of the ostracism, but I was not prepared, when I bumped out on the trolley for outdoor lunch at their new home, for the change in Gerhardt. His thin, high-bred face looked pinched and older. With a catch of compassion which he would have bitterly resented, I saw pride, shabby, down-at-heel but defiant, looking warily out upon a hostile world. His wife never bothered her literary blond head with politics. She stood staunchly by her husband and talked with wry humor of their new social isolation.

"I feel like Typhoid Mary," she laughed with deliberate frankness, pouring a glass of milk for her daughter. She laughed again, defensively, as she told how a former friend, author of dispassionate treatises on international problems, had stalked up to Gerhardt at a social tea and demanded loudly: "Gerhardt, are you a Nazi spy? We all want to know." The question was stupid and the insult only too intentional.

I happened to bring Erika that day a child's cup from the *Uni-Prix*, of a jovial pattern which had become tradition at our family table—a round, rosy china face with twinkling blue eyes and a wide grin, making milk-drinking ecstasy.

Next day Gerhardt told me, with a touch of his old charm: "Harriet, that wonderful cup! It was the first thing my eyes fell on when I woke this morning, and I felt cheered for the day."

It was a mood that could hardly last in the new Geneva harshness. Mary fared rather better than Gerhardt, partly because she was American, but chiefly, I suppose, because she was a woman and so could not, potentially, carry a gun. The women in Geneva all seemed more reluctant to enroll in the stern camps of "ideologies," clinging instead, in their misguided fashion, to warm, personal loyalties. I was one of them. I still boil to remember the brutality of an international community towards a German in the throes of making up his mind. Perhaps I am only naïve. Perhaps the swelling tide would have backwashed him into Nazidom, anyway. When war comes, where can a man go except to his own country? But I still wonder whether intelligent patience from his former associates might not have kept Gerhardt Jentsch an internationalist. Driven further and further against the wall, he finally vanished, in a last desperate patriotism, into Germany.

But it was not without great travail of soul. That summer of '36 he sat a long time in our Neuilly garden, freed by the intimate and concealing dusk, and talked to us in troubled tones about his recent visit to Germany. His younger brother had turned ardent Hitler Youth.

"To me," he said, "these ideas are strange. They go against my training, my personal philosophy up to now. Yet my brother and his friends sincerely believe in them. Perhaps, for him and his generation, they are right. Perhaps they are best for Germany. But I don't know, I don't know."

Hitler's claim to a reunited Germany he accepted sincerely if misguidedly. He believed that to consolidate the German peoples—Czechoslovakia's Sudetenland, German Poland,

Austria, all the scattered German territories—would be best both for Germany and for the harmony of Europe. He believed that with a strong home government this could be achieved without bloodshed. That government, Hitler, with all his drawbacks, seemed to provide.

Gerhardt was still in Geneva the hideous March day of 1939 when Nazi uniforms and tanks stole overnight into Prague, and the dismayed Czechs, looking down from their morning windows upon the swastikas camped below, woke up to find themselves German again. A few days later Gerhardt Jentsch went to Geneva Hospital with a high fever. He lay delirious for several days, under observation by baffled doctors who found nothing systemically wrong. After he recovered, some "friend," with no more proof than suspicion of any German, got him ousted from the College of Céligny as a spy. There was no living to be earned in Geneva. Before he took his German-American family to Berlin, Gerhardt sought out my husband to bid him good-by.

"I am breaking," he said, "with the philosophy of the Western world."

He joined Professor Berber's Institute of Foreign Policy Research and all through the war helped to furnish the Nazi government with information about other countries. Gerhardt is being held now in Germany. Mary, caught in Upper Silesia with his parents, managed to keep fleeing just ahead of the Russian advance. She had always kept her American passport, and she has recently arrived, after painful experiences, safely back in America with her children.

Those two years before the war, while Germany tightened her belt, we found on every visit a Geneva more and more uneasy, and underrun with suspicion and despair. How dramatically it proved that any international organization, whether League or United Nations, only reflects the wider world it represents! The peace city was torn by the same dissensions which were surging up all over the face of the globe.

Chamberlain with his appeasement umbrella in Munich became everybody's ghastly joke. We called him, punningly, "*J'aime Berlin.*" We were deeply ashamed when Hitler, Mussolini, Chamberlain and Daladier sold the Czechs down the river, and yet war had edged so close that, despite all our principles, we all breathed easier at the shameful and short-lived success. At home Chamberlain was defending Czechoslovakia's loss by England's gain—time to prepare for war! By this time I had well lost my awe for important men in important posts. I did not need Jerry to tell me that while serious compromise by mutual agreement of all parties may endure, dishonorable appeasement at the expense of small friends is a shaky prop even for great nations.

ᦞᦞ 31 ᦞᦞ

One Last Golden Summer

ALL that last year in Paris I was hounded by uneasiness, like the oppression of a sultry day before the thunderstorm breaks. I tried to cling to my old confidence in peace as normality for citizens of a war-hating democracy. If trouble started in Europe we could go home. Something would surely happen, some last-minute miracle, before tragedy touched ME or MY family or MY country. So easy is it for an American to preserve his dangerous illusion of special protection by God and by geography.

But the truth, like an annoying mouse, kept gnawing and nibbling at my mind. Jerry was rather silent these days and very gentle with his boys. He had talked more freely about the danger while he still believed it could be averted. My own patchwork of knowledge by now was sewed together into an uncomfortable personal possession. I could no longer ignore it. I never folded those high foreign shutters over our ground-floor windows at dusk without a sense of hurry. "It" might grab at us from the dark garden outside. Even with our gracious lamps lit and a wood fire crackling under the marble mantel, "It" still prowled in the night, biding its time, because it would get us in the end.

Sometimes I mentioned these thoughts to Jerry, with the protecting lightness we use to those nearest to us. Mostly, I pretended, even to myself, that everything was all right. All around us the disunified French were clashing in national politics—forecast of a speedy collapse under a blindly unified Germany. I hardly ever passed the Place de l'Etoile without seeing street fights. They raged all around the undying flame on the tomb of the Unknown Soldier, blowing steadily and beautifully under Napoleon's Arc of Triumph. Always a silent Frenchman stood staring down, with his hat off.

That summer we sent Ethan and Curtis across the Atlantic again to Camp Kawanhee, and for the three Davises left in France we rented a small cottage at La Baule, near Saint-Nazaire, on the West Atlantic coast. It was too civilized for our tastes, with its Casino and its restaurants, but the beach stretched long and beautiful, the ocean smelled as tangy as ever, and in the quiet pine groves back from the sea one could sit and dream. I was determined to have a happy summer.

Strangely enough, I did. It floated by like a fluff of thistle-down on the edge of an abyss. The long, leisurely days were an idyl, timeless and ephemeral. Now they feel a hundred years ago. I lay idly watching little bodies in scraps of bathing suits building huge sand forts and stacking them high with cannon balls. Small Malcolm always stood in the middle, a martial baby in a yellow sun-suit, leading the attack on the enemy with shouted commands in perfect Parisian.

On the wide beach between the sea wall and the sea we found a gymnastics class, so Malcolm joined one for *les petits* and I another for *les grands*. Our teacher was a young man of thirty, with a broad, muscled physique, intense blue eyes and a flashing smile in a sunburned face. Health was his mysticism. Pierre Ledoux used to stand piously facing the sun, throwing back his head and breathing deep, like some pagan worshiper of old. After class was over he sometimes lay in the sand, talking to me about his visions.

"I am a bastard, Madame," he confided with pride, and a trace of wistfulness. "Ah, how much finer to be born of an *élan* between two beings than in a dull married bed! I say this in my book. Let me read you that page." And he would get out a thumbed manuscript and read aloud his poetic version of a harsh life. No publisher had yet accepted his autobiography, but he showed me several dog-eared letters praising the manuscript. One day he pulled out a photograph from a worn wallet.

"This is my son, Madame. Oh, no," he added with dignity, "I am not married. Here is his mother. We met while I was studying in Denmark. We hope to be married soon."

With endless patience, he taught Malcolm to swim and to hang head-down from the highest trapeze. All over France, he said proudly, these health classes were starting. The next generation would be stronger than the last. Ledoux was an out-and-out pacifist, the first and only one I ever met in France. Murder, whether legalized as patriotism or not, he said, ran contrary to his faith in the brotherhood of man. I asked what he would do if France were attacked, and he glared at me.

"You, the mother of this beautiful child, defend war? What are women thinking about? You are the great spiritual force in the world. Not while you are young and arouse only physical desire. It is after that, Madame, that the real sphere of woman begins."

While the French children molded their cannon balls of sand, their elders sat about in bright-garbed groups, talking of war. Was it coming or not? I met a French consul, of such a conventional type that he looked correct even in shorts. He was full of cocksureness about his own country and of disparaging generalities about all the others. The Germans would never get very far because their only allies, the Italians, were such cowards. Italy was a people that could be bought.

Meantime, getting our identity cards officially stamped at the *mairie* one day, we ran into Count Sforza, as calm and handsome as ever. He and his family had been summering in their villa near Toulon when a member of the French police came to call. A plane had been circling their villa almost daily but they had paid no attention. The authorities now warned them, on reliable information, of a Fascist plot to kidnap the Count. They advised the Sforzas to leave immediately. So here they were at La Baule, guests of their old friends, the Tarchianis.

Young Malcolm and I were invited there for tea, so I explained to him in words of one syllable the importance of our hosts and extracted a solemn promise about table manners— no spilling, no finger-licking. Soberly, in his best suit, with feet circumspect in freshly shined shoes, my youngest walked primly along the pleasant lanes to the Tarchiani villa. The Sforza's terrier, Jimmy, greeted him in an enthusiastic language they both understood, and we went in to sit down around the dining-room table in comfortable European fashion. It was piled with fresh bread, sweet butter, cakes and jars of jam. Malcolm's eyes glistened but he kept heroically still. Then Count Sforza turned to my child and asked: "Malcolm, how do you like your jam? This is how I like my jam!" And he ran his forefinger swiftly around the jam jar and popped it into his mouth with a loud smack.

Not long ago I sat in the Italian Embassy in Washington, talking to Ambassador Tarchiani. He inquired warmly about

Malcolm. His wife and daughter, he said, still talked about his beautiful manners at their tea party.

So our summy summer drifted by. The International Studies Conference was holding a meeting in Bergen, Norway that August, and despite all the rumors I was determined not to let Hitler cheat me of a glimpse of the fjords. When we reached Paris, however, the men at the American Embassy looked grave. Our Embassy in Berlin had warned that trouble might start at any moment. This was no moment to separate a child from both his parents.

Suddenly I woke up. I could hardly wait to get back to little Malcolm. We cabled our families in New York to hold the other boys there; Jerry left for Norway and I boarded the familiar train for La Baule. It was at the height of its holiday season. People clustered like bees around every newsstand, grabbing papers with ink scarcely dry. On September 1 the headlines shrieked the news. German armies had invaded the Polish Corridor. World War Two had begun.

No word from Jerry, cloistered in 'Bergen with the international experts. Bearded Frenchmen in bathing trunks lay on the beach, talking gravely to chic little wives in slacks, who wiped tears and mascara from their eyes. Pierre Ledoux no longer breathed deep under the beneficent sun but argued hotly with his friends. Let them go out and murder if they must. He would never agree.

Then at last one afternoon, strolling along the beach with Malcolm, I heard a shout and a large car stopped in the road. Jerry, reaching England to find regular Channel service cut, had caught the last steamer from Southampton to Saint-Malo, and made the rest of the way by hired car. The very next morning, a lovely Indian Summer Sabbath of bright sun and mild breezes, the news ran over the town like wildfire. Everybody knew simultaneously. England had de-

clared war on Germany. That same afternoon, posters everywhere called the French nation to arms.

Sober groups stood reading every word carefully to the end
then turned away without a sound. The Frenchman fitted the
familiar burden to his back and went off. All day long our
small railroad station was jammed with family groups. The
fathers and husbands joked loudly, the women tried to laugh
between tears, while the children scrambled excitedly between their legs or begged centimes for lemon-drops.

"Give me a round-trip ticket!" cried one burly chap with
a weeping wife on his arm. "Because I'm coming back!"

Overnight, the men vanished from La Baule. Next morning the beach, washed clean by the tide, looked immense. It
was empty of all but women, knitting and talking, youths
with sober faces, and the children, fetching water and building forts as seriously as ever. Pierre Ledoux had vanished too.
He had gone with his friends to report for duty at Saint-
Nazaire.

My husband seemed suddenly relieved from a long tension.
"I've been feeling," he said, "like a man watching people
playing on a beach, with a tidal wave coming. You shout
to them to watch out, but they say: 'Oh, it's so pleasant here
in the sun,' and don't even look up. Now it's here, and at
least I can do something active to help."

Norman Davis had cabled asking Jerry to go immediately
to Geneva for the International Red Cross. Paris was already
under martial law. My husband must get back and on to
Switzerland before the borders closed. He would send me
what trunks he could from Neuilly, and a Rockefeller Foundation friend would arrange our passage and motor Malcolm and
me to Bordeaux.

We said good-by in a strange mood of unreality, like the
emotionless wanderings of a dream. Together, little Malcolm

and I waited for news of our departure. One day, wandering along the beach road, I saw a man sitting alone on the ocean wall. His sunburned back looked so slumped I thought I must be mistaken, then he turned his head and I saw Pierre Ledoux. I had never seen eyes so desolate, a spirit so changed. He murmured dully, as if from a distance, "Madame!" and I walked on.

The next time he came back from Saint-Nazaire to his beloved beach, without permission, he talked volubly.

"They show me how to work a machine gun and I cannot even hear the words. My mind stops. Do you know what they taught me yesterday, Madame? If your bayonet sticks in the man you have just killed, hold the corpse with your foot while you pull it out." Ledoux turned on me his haunted and bitter face. "All my life I have been building my personal faith, alone. How can I repudiate it in a day?"

There was nothing for me to say. Every instinct of my heart told me he was right. I promised to take his book back to America and told him good-by.

Finally the sailing date was set, and we rolled off smoothly in our friend's car for Bordeaux. Saint-Nazaire looked placid in the cool, September air. The whole countryside lay bathed in peace. Bordeaux was jammed with clamoring Americans, and Malcolm and I were lucky to have a dubious room in a small, dingy hotel. That night I got my first inkling of danger from the skies. So tired I thought my head would crack open, I lay propped against a straw-like pillow, trying to numb myself into sleep with a book. The room telephone jingled. Very sharply, a man told me it was already ten o'clock and to put out my light immediately.

∾ 32 ∾

Safe in America

The sea was also a menace. The *Manhattan,* jammed beyond capacity, stole out into a pitch-black night with every light shrouded. Decks were piled to the very top with jumbled luggage over which harassed stewards labored perspiringly. The main lounge was a man's dormitory, and the gaily decorated Play Room was full of French priests. Standing in line for five hours for passport inspection, I saw a tired face whose features looked familiar. It was Stravinsky. Toscanini, too, paced our decks alone, his dark, uncanny eyes staring through us all. Young Mrs. William Randolph Hearst shared a room with nine other women. We were all just Americans, running home to hide under the skirts of the Goddess of Liberty.

Malcolm and I shared a tiny cabin with a young woman and her baby, with damp diapers on strings always flapping in our faces. Once, bringing an evening bowl of puffed rice, the baby's mother walked under a ventilator. The light grains flew everywhere, landing in our shoes, our hairbrushes, our water glasses. All the rest of the trip we were stepping on rice. One grew sick to death of people. The lounges, the decks, the writing rooms, the toilets were thick with humanity. Everyone clamored incessantly for baggage. My bedroom steward, a stocky German, grew so excited by my innocent words of sympathy for his superhuman tasks that he tiptoed over to the cabin door, locked it and, with that male light in his blue eyes, almost broke my ribs in an immense bear hug. I pushed him off, trying not to laugh, and demanded what had got into him.

"Lady," he replied with watery eyes, "I'm lonesome!"

I promised not to tell, if he'd behave and also find me the suitcase of clean clothes marked for the stateroom. He departed, a docile hulk, while I sank on my bunk, doubled over with laughter at such loneliness in the midst of human plenty. Hours later he returned, sweating and triumphant, with one bag. Unlocked, it contained the family silver and some linens. He tried again and fished up a suitcase full of shoes, mostly Ethan's and Curtis's. So I gave up, and Malcolm and I stayed dirty for the week.

The nearer we drew to home, the stranger I began to feel. As we docked at the familiar pier, I knew that America was a dream still to be faced. The North River tugs, the skyline of skyscrapers, street signs in English, the gaudy taxis, everybody speaking American—it was all only a remembered past, not a present reality. The immense streams of silent traffic seemed like a symbol of American power, unconscious and untried. It all felt worlds and centuries apart from the sharp, darting Paris confusion I knew so well.

Fifth Avenue shop windows gleamed exotic and luxurious after the sober elegance of the rue de la Paix. People seemed more alike, healthier, friendlier, less aware of each other. Their eyes were unreflective, their bearing confident, their faces haggard from activity. All women, both young and old, looked slim and nicely dressed; almost none elegant or seductive. Where were the shabby working people in thrifty black? What frightful hats—heavy sophistication for girlish eyes, gaudy flower gardens for wrinkled housewifely faces! How pleasant to see frank gray hair after the henna and purple and yellow horrors of the Paris boulevards! I remembered a Paris Professor lugubriously stroking his grizzled mustache. "I have such a horror of old age that I nearly dyed my mustaches. You Americans know how to grow old gracefully. Why, in your country I met white-haired ladies so utterly charming they actually aroused my sentimental emotions!"

I basked in the kindness that shone everywhere, like the honest sunlight we had missed so long, and recoiled, shocked, from our bad manners. Salesgirls either snapped, "Can't you see I'm busy?" or smiled: "That's a cute blouse you got on, dearie." Pimply soda clerks with red hands working slapdash miracles of speed at fizzing taps thrust out a thirty-cent check with an impudent grin. "That'll be thirty dollars, Miss!" After years of the respectful third person—"Is Madame served?" "Madame desires?"—such intimacy became an affront. Noisy boys and girls in flapping clothes invaded the subways, shrieking jokes and bumping their elders as if they owned the world. I realized with a start that I had grown snobbish about public encounters. To newly arrived foreign visitors our democracy must look sloppy and cheap. For the first time I was seeing America through European eyes.

Most alien of all was the psychological mood. Spiritual cellophane seemed to separate me from everybody except my children and the friends who knew Europe. Whenever I met another Geneva peace veteran, the old tie was instantly there, binding us in experiences unshared by peace civilians at home. I moved through old haunts like a friendly but baffled ghost. Or rather, I moved, alive and visible, in one rhythm among compatriots keeping time to another. It was not a matter of slower or faster tempo but of beat. I could hear theirs, from memory, but they could not hear mine. In America I was only half a person. Great chunks of my personality seemed left behind in Europe, never to be retrieved until I returned there. Warm old friends here had never heard of my closest friends over there. My heart was heavy with the weight of their burdens, but all around me, in America the war was still theoretical.

After the gossip, the arguments about Roosevelt, the long-winded funny stories, people sat back in their chairs digesting a good meal, and argued. Should America "go in"? Should America "stay out"? The tidal wave had not yet reached our own beach. They sounded like schoolboys taking issues about a dead war learned from textbooks. Interventionists who argued "Better early than late—it's our war, and inevitable anyway," were smiled at or bitterly attacked as dreamers with neither patriotism nor common sense. The great American people, the Middle West, were not "for" war, I was told. Even Roosevelt would not dare defy public opinion. Better stay neutral and continue to sell arms to all belligerents. Indirectly this favored England and France, who controlled the high seas. Commentators were in their heyday, radio fans hung breathless on the news, while Denmark and Norway, the Netherlands, Belgium, all were swallowed up. This was more exciting than the comics or the movies.

Meantime, while Europe crumbled under the Blitz and most Americans still played busily at "normality," the peace veterans were picking themselves up, dusting off their clothes and starting the good fight afresh. Already, in 1939, Doctor Shotwell, whose dogged ideals had survived the outbreak of two world wars, was creating his Commission to Study the Organization of Peace, a group of experienced specialists from all over the United States who would outline together the fundamentals of the new peace that must follow this war. Here was Arthur Sweetser, veteran of the first World War. With Ruth, he had pulled up stakes from their beloved Geneva, where their oldest boy lay buried, and came home to do what an American could. Here was Ben Gerig, called to Washington for "special research on international plans," and later appointed head of a new section of Colonies and Dependent Peoples in the State Department. He served in a series of "inside" official roles, from Dumbarton Oaks to the first United Nations Conference in London. Doctor Boudreau took time off from directing the Milbank Memorial Fund to join the Commission. Here was Clark Eichelberger, indefatigable Director of the League of Nations Association— which, six years later, significantly changed its name to the American Association for the United Nations. Here was Sarah Wambaugh, American authority on plebiscites, whom I had met at Ethel's in 1934, when she was appointed by the League as technical adviser and deputy member of the Saar Plebiscite Commission. I used to look at her at cocktail parties and wonder why on earth any woman should be so interested in plebiscites as to become an expert, actually consulted by heads of governments. Now I felt proud that it was a woman and an American who brought her ideals and her experience to Doctor Shotwell's Commission. Seeing the old crowd begin to gather, I remembered Kipling, who had grown "dated" since my girlhood but now seemed to be popular again among Ethan's friends:

"If you can bear to hear the words you've spoken
  Twisted by knaves to make a trap for fools,
  And see the things you gave your life for broken
  And stoop and build them up with worn-out tools . . ."

Suddenly that 1940 summer came the first great sobering shock for America. One month of fighting and France was gone. Only England now stood between us and Hitler. Even the armchair strategists grew worried. One felt an air of panic everywhere. This was real, this was coming close to home. I heard a conservative banker propose a fantastic plan to turn private cars all over our unprepared country into tanks, armed with civilian sharpshooters—"in case any of these parachuters begin to drop down on us."

Then England took the Blitz and the buzz-bombs and the blood, sweat and tears, and took it and took it again, while Churchill roared his challenges. We all breathed easier. The conflagration had reached John Bull's house across the pond, but maybe the wind would veer the other way. Maybe we could still "keep out." I even heard a dinner-party lady remark, with a smirk which betrayed previous success with the same bon mot, "Oh dear, I wish the war would get over, so I can be anti-British again!"

The boys and I had found a place to live, without "Daddy." He was flying all over Europe on refugee relief for the Red Cross—Belgrade, Bucharest, Budapest; Stockholm, Oslo, Copenhagen; The Hague, Brussels, Milan; unpronounceable cities of Latvia and Lithuania; even Berlin. Every place was still accessible to a representative of the only international organization left functioning in the world. (That is the answer to those who would disregard the Geneva Convention about prisoner-of-war treatment.) In his father's absence Ethan grew up suddenly into a tall, blond fourteen and began to look after me, touchingly; also to order his brothers about with an adolescent rigidity which raised ructions. If they did not hop to obey my words immediately, he would saunter over and drawl, with an amusing new Americanism which did my heart good: "You heard what the lady said!" Thanks to Camp

Kawanhee, both he and Curtis went native quickly. They were drunk with delight over American radio, American comics, American jokes, American milk, American desserts. But our youngest used to rush home from school as if the devil were after him, ecstatic to find me again, his only link with a mysteriously vanished life.

"At Paris," he said, with his wistful precision, "we had a big garden, but here"—he threw out his palms in a tragic French gesture—"our garden is just New York!"

One evening I found him sitting soberly on his bed in his pajamas, listening to the roar of the traffic below his window.

"Mummie," he mused, with a faint catch in his voice, "I think it would be better if there wasn't any world."

"Oh, no! Why?" He stared at the scrap of sky beyond the roofs as Pierre Ledoux had stared at the sea.

"Because there are so many people being tortured and killed everywhere, I just think it would be better if there wasn't any world."

I offered banal and artificial consolation. We'd have to do all we could to make things better, to keep another war from coming. But he shook his head.

"Oh, no, we can't do anything! It's all on account of those old spooky Germans."

It was not long after Malcolm blew out eight candles on his New Year's birthday cake that President Roosevelt told Congress—and the world: "We look forward to a world founded upon four essential human freedoms . . . freedom of speech and expression . . . freedom of every person to worship God in his own way . . . freedom from want . . . freedom from fear."

Meantime, one day a prisoner-of-war post card reached me from Germany. The sparse blanks on cheap paper were filled in the handwriting I had seen on Pierre Ledoux's manuscript, as he lay happily reading it aloud on the hot sands of La Baule.

"From the other doorsill of happiness," he wrote—and the Nazi censor, being no poet, never guessed his meaning— "I send you this word. Remembering the eyes of your little son I take courage."

When at last Jerry came home, after a year and a half of Red Cross missions, he confirmed the card. Ledoux was breaking stones somewhere in Germany. When he had refused, in France, to learn the trade of murder, his commanding officer had neither slapped his face nor called him names. With remarkable gentleness and that personal French touch, he granted the rebel a week's leave to think it over. Ledoux returned soberly to report that his sentiments had not changed. He could not kill but he would perform any service of mercy, however dangerous. Several times he was sent off again to reflect. Always he came faithfully back to his post with the same convictions. So, with his garrison chief's consent, he wrote to my husband offering to join the Red Cross and, with Jerry's help, became a *brancardier*—a stretcher-bearer. He was rescuing the wounded of both sides with the coolest courage when the Germans captured him. After that one post card I never heard of him again.

Jerry brought home such stories of civilian suffering that Americans preferred not to hear them. For me he had news of friends—one dead, another broken and ill, this one mourning his only son. We scarcely had time to catch up before he left again for South America, with a group of journalists and university specialists sent by the Endowment to make a survey of economic and political relations. He was away when Congress, with a bitterness akin to the old League of Nations fight in Wilson's day, fought through the last stages of the debate over Lend-Lease. The group were in Brazil when the news came that the United States had taken a positive position in the war. The effect upon all South America, he told me, was tremendous. Here, as in Europe, our decisions started international repercussions.

That June, Jerry and I actually spent our wedding anniversary together and began looking around for a salty American beach for the swimming Davises. We needed that vacation. Hitler had already captured Bulgaria and Greece and then, swollen with victory, brashly attacked Russia. Back in La Baule the summer of '39 we had been stunned by the Hitler-Stalin pact. Along with the rest of the democratic world, we wondered anxiously "what it meant." Now I realized, with ironic relief, that it had meant nothing at all! With no international referee to arbitrate, no police to enforce the signatures on a scrap of paper, one high-pressure power boy can double-cross the other whenever he chooses. It was always easy enough to wiggle out of the mere technicalities of a "treaty." I had to laugh, remembering my innocent awe, back in grammar-school history class, of this august word. I had believed any "treaty" was binding, something above the tug and pull of everyday human conflict.

On Cape Cod we found a funny little cottage, plastered with pictures and draped in fish nets by its native Wellfleet owner. "The John Alden" stood, with nice sentimentality, beside its twin, "The Priscilla." With a start, I discovered that neither Ethan, Curtis nor Malcolm had ever heard of the famous lovers of my school-day memories. Cape Cod was jammed with tourists and cars that August, Americans enjoying one last holiday fling before the tidal wave hit us. To be sure, Germany had begun to attack our ships; wrecked crews drifted ashore with tales of submarines. But such episodes still seemed slightly unreal; roadside inns advertised "Forty-Seven Varieties of Ice Cream"; the evening sand dunes and the sea looked lovelier in the black-out. We were swimming off the shores of Wellfleet when Roosevelt and Churchill met "somewhere" in mid-Atlantic and drew up the Atlantic Charter, declaring the peace aims of the democratic nations.

Back in New York, we found an apartment to house a reunited five, and little Malcolm, who with that odd philosophy of young children had taken the disrupted family for granted as permanent, stared incredulously at his father's bed in our new home. "You mean Daddy is going to live with *us*?" he cried rapturously.

Jerry, of course, joined the Commission to Study the Organization of Peace. Trailing through Central Park alone with the boys on Sunday, I began to feel like a Geneva wife again. So did Carrie May, whose husband, handling his Opium Board affairs from this side, now added his wisdom to the group. So did many other wives, but most of us had learned our lesson now.

The day after the Dumbarton Oaks proposals appeared in fine print in the newspapers, I saw Doctor Shotwell. He was quietly jubilant. No public announcement could be made, but the official document coincided at points remarkably with drafts which the Commission had placed in government hands.

One Sunday afternoon in December, while Ethan and Curtis were out with new American friends and Jerry had taken Malcolm to a Disney movie, I sat in our apartment near Columbia University, enjoying the blissful quiet of home all to myself. There persists in most married women an incorrigible old maid who savors tidiness for its own sake. In this mood the still curtains, the steady furniture, feel like mute old friends trying to break through their long, captive silence from another dimension. Peace, because it will so soon be filled again with warm voices, drifts like cool balm through the rooms, and home feels infinite and secure. I was not even reading the Sunday paper; it lay neatly stacked on the table while I mused dreamily over a cigarette. The telephone rang. Cursing its interruption to nothingness, so rare in a busy life, I went to answer. It was Doctor Shotwell, for my husband. Well, when he came in, tell him, in case he had not heard, that the Japs had attacked Pearl Harbor. Yes, this was It, of course. This would change everything.

I had never heard of Pearl Harbor. Ignoring the hollow emptiness in my stomach, I found one of the boys' geographies. Well, Hawaii still looked very far from New York. Like so many mothers all over the United States that day, I was already counting up Ethan's chances. He would be fifteen on Valentine's Day. In the other World War which had drafted all my brothers, the fighting age was twenty-one. That gave us six years. World War II could never last that long.

Soon I heard a key click in the lock and then Jerry's voice unusually talkative and jolly, with little Malcolm laughing in reply. I knew, before they entered into the broken peace of our living room, that he knew.

33

War

Overnight, a new mood swept our country. We grabbed the morning papers and hung on the radio, to follow the bloody push back through the snows of Russia. Sons of friends were shipped off for America's agonizing death grip in the Pacific. My brother's oldest boy, the merry child who had showed us his Christmas trees in Baltimore so proudly, enlisted in the United States Infantry.

Ethan turned sixteen, a whistling and cheerful youth, deep in American school life—the swimming team, the glee club, the "formals" with their problem of stretching an allowance to cover gardenias and a taxi. The calendar crept towards his seventeenth birthday as we took the acid taste of American defeats. Washington drafted teen-agers. My nephew was already overseas, an infantry lieutenant, among the forces preparing for D Day.

The Navy moved into the Columbia University buildings near our apartment, and all day long, before we rose in the morning and after Malcolm went reluctantly to bed at night, we heard young feet marching and running to the brisk "Hup, two, three, four" of their officers. Babies sat in strollers, mimicking the sounds as their first spoken words, and old ladies on the sidewalks fell helplessly into step. Malcolm asked me, puzzled, "Why is it the men are always changing but the commanding voice is always the same?" Curtis, whose in-turned dreams now flowed outwards into a passion for music, began to take note of the real world. One day he inquired, "Mom, what *is* propaganda?" Thinking quickly to find his own terms, I replied, "Well, I'll tell you. You and Ethan have a dispute and you come to me with it. Everything you say is true in a way. But you know very well that you lay it on pretty thick, to convince me that you're right and Ethan is wrong. Well, when countries do that, it's propaganda."

For some time now my husband, though happy to be at home again with his family, had felt restless and depressed. It was not just the war—this he had accepted as inevitable even before it broke. But with so much Endowment work halted abroad, he itched for a man's job in his country's cause. My futile suggestions to write or lecture or talk on the radio fell on deaf ears. He had long since reached his own cool estimate of what makes a nation change its mind. Back in the Geneva days of peace, he had written me from a trip home to America: "I am convinced that only actual events are ever going to smash home the truth to people's minds." If he had been a younger man, I am sure he would have enlisted. Finally, a service was requested by our government which satisfied him, and the Endowment loaned him for half-time. In the Office of Strategic Services, making confidential re-ports for our military heads, he concerned himself with for-eign political refugees in the United States, and their influ-ence upon groups of the same national origin among our own people. It was a fascinating and astonishingly logical sequence to his European experience. All those tangled political threads

he had followed over the Continent had for years been throwing out their tentacles to our own land. Among millions of
foreign-born and second-generation Americans, the internal
politics of other nations were profoundly influencing our
domestic elections, even our civic affairs. Wherever you
turned there was simply no dodging those international
politics.

My own discarded trade of magazine writing kept nagging
at me, but the old fields no longer looked attractive. I hunted
about for a way to pass on the richness of my European experience to other Americans. But the modest professional successes of my youth were forgotten and editors were not interested in my maturity. The war correspondents and the radio
know-it-alls were covering the war. Over and over I was
advised to "forget Europe and write about America. Adver-
tisers don't like controversial subjects." I tried a radio script
making Geneva come alive through the drama of an old Swiss
watchmaker who would not cater to the Germans. "We can't
touch politics. We'd get into trouble with the Swiss and some
of our listeners might object."

Yet the public, as I encountered it, seemed miles ahead of
its self-appointed mentors. Even back in 1942, waiting for a
package of glass to be wrapped in the ten-cent store, I heard
two gum-chewing salesgirls talking earnestly.

"You know what I'm scared of," said one.

"What?" asked the other, winding the flimsy string around
cheap paper. I waited, amused, for some "crack" about the
boy friend.

"Russia!" declared the girl, shifting her gum. "When this
is all over, Russia's going to say, '*We* won the war. *We* did
it. Now the rest of you can do what *we* say.' "

"M-m, maybe," drawled her friend. "But I dunno—I don't
believe Russia is going to be a dope about it."

My artificial Europeanism melted rapidly in the warm sun of America, and a hundred daily encounters were making friends for me among my own people. I loved them as I had never loved them before. After the suspicions, the chilly correctness of Europe, Americans felt so natural, so good, so friendly-hearted. On my way home from visiting Curtis in a farm work-camp one summer, I talked to another mother, supporting her daughter with office work. She knew nothing of my background as she told me earnestly:

"All those important men who understand about peace and politics ought to explain them to the rest of us. Most Americans want to do what's right, but we just don't know which is right and which is wrong in those sort of things." In her spare time she had gathered a group of women to try to find out for themselves. But so little, she said, was spoken or written for their use.

"Dorothy Thompson, Anne McCormick—" she shook her head. "They're 'way above my head. I just don't understand all those things they take it for granted I already know."

One day Doctor Shotwell asked me to talk to a lady from Washington who was hoping for Endowment support for a personal peace work of her own. She was a gentle woman with a soft voice, who envied me, she said, my years of being close to international work. A few months ago she had lost her "beautiful blond boy over Germany." The guilt of his death haunted her heart. All those years when she might have been doing something to prevent the war, while he grew up to die in it, she had pursued her personal life. Now there was little reason to go on unless she could help to convince ordinary people of their responsibility in a united world. A widow supporting herself in a Civil Service job, she was spending her time and her own money organizing women for lectures, advising smaller clubs throughout the country on programs, speakers, window displays, to explain the principles of the United Nations.

It looked as if my own hit-and-miss growth abroad had marched hand in hand with the growth at home of my own country. Those peace believers who had shuttled patiently back and forth across the ocean to Geneva had gradually sown their fertile seeds. A Gallup Poll even disclosed the astonishing fact that a fourth of the Americans interrogated believed we were members of the League of Nations. When the Wilson film came out, an elderly colored woman remarked to me in astonishment, "You mean to say we never joined that thing? Why, we started it, didn't we?" The Allied declaration of the United Nations, signed in Washington the month after Pearl Harbor, stirred surprisingly little opposition. Isolationists were loud but scattered; even Senator Lodge's son wrote an apologia for his famously stubborn father. What had been in President Wilson's day a sharp party issue now merged into a national sentiment.

My husband, already splitting his personality quite logically between an Endowment to promote peace and a government service to win the war, now added another week-end task to his crowded week. In the winter of '43, when a new international organization seemed certain, our friend Manley Hudson, Judge on the World Court, collected a group to draft a design for a United Nations Charter. Here they all were again, the old faithfuls. Doctor Shotwell, of course, Herbert May, Frank Boudreau, Benjamin Gerig, Arthur Sweetser, now a Deputy Director for the Office of War Information, and many others. Though overburdened with work in Cambridge, Manley came to New York for these discussions. Their plan was published a few weeks before the Dumbarton Oaks proposals were made public. Again one found many a significant identity between the newly proposed United Nations

Charter and that draft by what the State Department called "the New York Group." Official folders with documents thus marked traveled to San Francisco in the brief-cases of our United States delegates. Jerry told me about it when he returned from his grueling job on the Coast as Executive Officer of the First Commission of the Conference.

But there was still the war, the costly creeping advance in the Pacific towards Japan, the vast silent preparations for the invasion. Like all former passport holders, we received the government request to send our snapshots and post cards of Europe, for possible military use. We turned in a huge bunch eagerly. An air view of the coast of Southern Brittany, photographs of Le Lavandou on the Riviera, of La Baule, so close to strategic Saint-Nazaire, were carefully copied. The official who looked through the batch with me even retained a card of the pines of La Baule where small Malcolm and I had strolled that last summer. "Just to give our fellows an idea of the kind of terrain they'll find when they go ashore," he explained. It was a thrill to think that our holidays were proving of patriotic use. It sent shivers down my spine to read, months later, that Americans had made a landing at Le Lavandou, that Le Pouldu of Brittany was now in Allied hands, that the Nazis were cleared at last from La Baule and Saint-Nazaire.

After D Day and the costly miracle of the invasion, we knew only that my brother's Billie was fighting "somewhere in France." His letters home told without complaint of cold and hunger, crouching in foxholes for weeks without a change of clothes. It was worth it, if he could save his younger brother from the same horrors. When the sobering news came of the German comeback, the retreating Battle of the Bulge, Ethan was seventeen. By accelerating, he already had two years of college to his credit, for his European education had advanced him beyond his years. Some form of international work was to be his field. He was too young as yet to define its terms. Besides, now there was the war.

Like all Americans, we had raised our boys for peace. We had taught them that fighting, except in self-defense, was stupid. Ethan did not want to kill or to be killed—he was openly honest about that. But the Christmas before his eighteenth birthday, when America was still shadowed by the uncertain fate of her sons in Belgium and France, he decided to enlist in the Navy. He hoped to be sent to France, where his fluent speech and his instinctive understanding of the French people might be most useful.

In February came the Yalta announcement that a United Nations Conference would be held in San Francisco that June. Out of the ashes of "Wilson's League," a fresh hope had sprung. Peace was on everybody's tongue and desperate optimism in everybody's heart. But the war, as well as the peace, was still to be won.

We talked over Ethan's enlistment with a calm none of us felt. The day was set when Jerry would accompany our tall son, who looked so grown-up but needed his parents' consent, to the recruiting center. At home we were all very gay and talkative. Ethan cheerfully stored away his precious stamp albums, gave books and tennis balls and sweaters to his brothers. Curtis and Malcolm hung on his words and waited on him with unusual alacrity. Nobody could bear to be serious.

Ethan was out saying good-by to fraternity mates when my brother telephoned. Billie had been killed somewhere in France. No word of how or where, just the belated telegram from the War Department. He had died soon after Christmas. The stair-step row of planted evergreens in the Baltimore garden had stopped abruptly.

For me, screwing up my courage for the enlistment tomorrow, it was Ethan who died. How could I guess then that truth is sometimes kinder than fiction? If this were a novel, it would be Ethan who fell, somewhere in the Pacific, to save his younger brothers from another war. But by a strange twist of poetic justice, it was his father's lifelong concern with peace which decided his fate. The Navy was not interested in his French, but out of the helter-skelter thousands of young Americans at boot camp, our son, because of "unusual proficiency in a foreign language," was selected for officer training in the Navy Language School. Ethan, incredulous over his good luck, left Sampson for Oklahoma, to put in a grinding year learning Japanese. Of course, he and his fellow students were slated, as rapidly as possible, for the Pacific. But for a while at least I could sleep easier. Ethan was slaving diligently over Kanji symbols, out in a Middle West college, when we blew Hiroshima to dust with the atomic bomb.

But all this still lay in the closed hand of the future, that January day, only two years ago, when the tragic telephone message suddenly merged my nephew and my son into one. Somehow, I got through the days without his knowing, and then, having been a healthy woman all my life, I went down with pneumonia. High fever and danger and languid convalescence always blow a breath from infinity, a reminder that just to be alive is a rare gift. It is not only in the moment before drowning that all one's life passes before one's eyes. The years touched upon these pages floated through my thoughts in a fresh light, and so it was that I began this book.

ᑙᐦ 34 ᑙᐦ

What Can We Do Now?

WHEN you first wake up to the fact that you are, willy-nilly, a citizen of one world, you get very excited. Then your ego deflates until it becomes an insignificant speck in a harsh and illogical universe not of your own choosing. Since you cannot personally control the use of the atomic bomb or feed a million starving people, you wonder if anything you do will matter in the long run. That is a mood I know only too well. But for anyone claiming intelligence or maturity, it is a childish view. After all, what is any town or state or nation or United Nations but a collection of individuals trying to live together? Alone you can do next to nothing, but together with like-minded people you can do a great deal. A united world can be won only by united groups, and there are many of these already off to a good start. A tremendous yeast is stirring in Americans today—a longing to do away with war, to understand peace and to make some sense out of this business of being human beings. Somewhere in this new urgency, there is a place for you. It is not too hard to find. The choice depends upon your temperament, your talents and your situation in life.

I, for instance, am no good at running committees, organizing campaigns or making formal speeches full of expert political detail. Besides, I still have family responsibilities. So I write articles and radio scripts, contribute ideas to organizations and sometimes give informal talks about my international experience. That is my mite. Other people have other gifts and live in other situations.

Maybe you are a business man or woman with little time to spare, or a loyal and doubtless underpaid teacher. Maybe your occupation is Housewife and your professional title "Mom." You may be an artist with little head for politics or a professional already devoting all your energies to work of social value. You may be an older person with somewhat limited strength or a college student full of vitality and impatience. That's fine! Peace has for too long been the whole-time preoccupation of specialists and sentimentalists or the football of diplomats. More people, just normally absorbed in the important business of living, need to spend a fraction of their energy upon deciding their own and their children's destiny. Over and over, every day in every way, I hear the specialists themselves declaring desperately that unless the public becomes better informed and more responsible in international questions, the battle for peace is already lost. They know our importance in making our own fate, even if we do not.

So—what can you do? Endless things. Interesting, important and valuable things. There are three aspects to this One World idea. Educational—we have to understand the United Nations, our world and America's part in it. Political—we should act on what we understand. Practical—we must, if only in our own interest, help other nations back to normal. These United States are simply chockablock with splendid, nonprofit organizations working in one or all of these fields. If you do nothing else, send five dollars to support one of them —or five thousand, if you have it. But if you want to learn and then act, first look around in your own community. What is the church, the school, your society or club doing for peace, educationally, politically or practically? If nothing, start something, affiliated with a going movement. If something, join it, get your friends to join, and give all the time and thought you can spare.

Almost any national group of which you are already a member—veterans' organizations, library groups, the Federal Council of Churches, the Federation of Women's Clubs, the League of Women Voters, the Y.M. and Y.W.C.A., labor and farm associations—has an international program and will send suggestions and literature to members. Besides that, many organizations, old and new, work specifically for international understanding. There is endless information to be had and agencies providing speakers. Our own State Department furnishes excellent material upon request.

To read intelligently, to listen honestly, is already a constructive peace act. Democratic peoples should not leave all their international thinking to politicians, statesmen and State Departments. They need to have opinions and to express them. Every time you join with a social-minded group to urge upon your Congressmen an important bill about—let us say, lowered tariffs or a foreign loan—you are swaying your own and your children's destiny. Every time you send food, clothes or books to needy foreign countries, you are promoting American and world prosperity. In fact, you could hardly do anything more vital at this moment to prevent another war than to send aid abroad. Sentiment and generosity aside, this is indeed bread cast upon the waters which will return after not so many days. Our most cool-headed economists warn that a starved Europe and Asia will breed another war under other dictators. Our most hard-headed businessmen say that until we get the rest of the world going again, American goods cannot find enough consumers, nor can American industries buy their needs abroad. The United States today is like a prosperous manufacturer whose factory is left intact in a community ravaged by fire, hurricane and disease. His own family can use a certain amount of his cars or his shoes or his radios or what-have-you, but after that, what use is money or goods without customers? And how can he buy for his own needs if all his neighbors are too ill, starving and penniless to work? So, paradoxically enough, he must feed them from his own surplus and lend them some of his cash, in order to get them both buying and selling again. Trade, as the economists say, is a two-way street.

So, whatever your political interests, foreign food packages are your best insurance for the future. Yes, I know about that argument that the Communists will get all the benefit. This is by no means certain. But what is certain, beyond argument, is that hungry people will follow where food is promised. Wouldn't you?

Then, of course, there comes the problem of whom to believe and which men and ideas to follow. That is something each of us can only decide for himself—this is a democracy. America swings a great weight in the world today. If she is thinking honestly and acting intelligently, if she pulls together for peace as she did for war, then we are all that much safer from the atomic bomb, the unknown enemy and the war that must never happen.

I have not tried to list the excellent relief agencies and the national associations with an international program. There are too many of them. I offer here only a few of the organizations specializing in international work, which I know to be active and worth while. Most of them are open to membership; all furnish information. There are many others, and I am sorry not to list more.

American Association for the United Nations, 45 East 65th Street, New York, N.Y.
> Devoted to strengthening American public opinion in support of the United Nations. Has many branches and local groups. Distributes popular literature and supplies speakers. Open to contribution and to membership.

Carnegie Endowment for International Peace, 405 West 117th Street, New York, N.Y.
> Publishes international studies by experts, of interest to serious students. Sponsors International Relations Clubs in high schools and colleges, furnishing books and other material.

Catholic Association for International Peace, 1312 Massachusetts Avenue, Washington, D.C.
> Sends out material to help spread an understanding of the United Nations and of other international work. Open to contribution and membership.

Church Peace Union, 70 Fifth Avenue, New York, N.Y.
> Monthly news letter and other publications about world affairs, for members. Open to membership and contribution.

Department of State, Division of Publications, Washington, D.C.
> Distributes free such pamphlets as "What Are We Doing in Germany and Why?," "Understanding among Peoples—How Can We Increase It?," "New Horizons for World Trade."

East and West Association, 40 East 49th Street, New York, N.Y.

Provides interesting material about the peoples of the world, through films, books and pamphlets. Open to membership.

Foreign Policy Association, 22 East 38th Street, New York, N.Y.

Holds meetings with qualified speakers in many branches throughout the country. Publishes excellent popular reading matter for adults and older children. Open to membership.

National Council of Jewish Women

Though concerned with other subjects, has had an international relations program for about fifty years. Educational material, speakers, advice on action furnished to its two hundred sections throughout United States. Open to membership.

National Educational Association, Washington, D.C.

Discussion meetings for educators. Sends recordings and special "kits" of world-affairs reading to teachers. Open to membership.

Our World United Through Books, 551 Fifth Avenue, New York City.

Ships "Treasure Chests" made by American children and stocked with selected books in English, to children in the war-torn countries. Cooperates with American and foreign organizations. Shipping done through the Library of Congress and the Smithsonian Institute.

Program Information Exchange, 41 Maiden Lane, New York, N.Y.

Representatives from other organizations meet to compare notes on world-affairs education. Write for a list of useful periodicals and a practical booklet: "Here's How It's Done."

Women's Action Committee for Lasting Peace, 1 East 57th Street, New York, N.Y.

Membership is inexpensive and members are advised by mail how to take political action on questions concerning peace. Open to membership.

ABOUT THE AUTHOR

Harriet Eager Davis *grew up in Baltimore as the third-from-the-bottom in a minister's family of eight children. As a young woman she came to New York where she became managing editor of one of the Butterick magazines. She also wrote several children's books, and numerous stories and articles. After she married Malcolm Davis, an international specialist, she gave up professional work to raise her own family. Eventually her husband's work took the family to Geneva, which supplies the background for this present book.*

Since her return to this country Mrs. Davis has turned again to writing with emphasis on popular interpretive articles on international questions. She also edited Pioneers in World Order: "An American Appraisal of the League of Nations."